Punk Productions

SUNY series, Interruptions:
Border Testimony(ies) and Critical Discourse/s

Henry A. Giroux, editor

PUNK PRODUCTIONS

Unfinished Business

Stacy Thompson

STATE UNIVERSITY OF NEW YORK PRESS

Published by

STATE UNIVERSITY OF NEW YORK PRESS, ALBANY

© 2004 State University of New York

For information, address
State University of New York Press,
90 State Street, Suite 700, Albany, NY 12207

Production by Kelli Williams
Marketing by Michael Campochiaro

Library of Congress Cataloging-in-Publication Data

Thompson, Stacy.
  Punk productions : unfinished business / by Stacy Thompson.
    p. cm. — (SUNY series, interruptions—border testimony(ies) and critical discourse/s)
  Includes bibliographical references and index.
  ISBN 0-7914-6187-4 — ISBN 0-7914-6188-2 (pbk.)
  1. Punk culture. 2. Punk rock music. I. Title. II. Series.

HM646.T46 2004
306'.1—dc22
                                                          2003190074

          10   9   8   7   6   5   4   3   2   1

This book is dedicated to my parents,
Stacy W. and Sandra R. Thompson

Contents

Acknowledgments

I AM INDEBTED to many people for their contributions to this project and especially to Richard Dienst. This text would have been impossible without his help. He convinced me that my initial idea warranted a book-length investigation and suggested ways for me to think and rethink many of its aspects over the course of its development. I am also deeply grateful to Siobhan Somerville, Jeffrey J. Williams, Vince Leitch, Patricia Harkin, and Arkady Plotnitsky for their close readings of early drafts. John Goshert, Leila Rauf, Isaac Gottesman, and Ailecia Ruscin, all punk insiders, have generously shared their expertise with me. Daniel Jernigan, Joy Wheeler, Aaron Jaffe, and Tatjana Soldat-Jaffe have been wonderful and supportive friends.

An earlier version of chapter 4 was originally published in *College Literature* 28.2 (Spring 2001): 48–64 as "Market Failure: Punk Economics, Early and Late." An earlier version of the epilogue appeared in *the minnesota review* 52–54 (Fall 2001): 299–307 as "Punk's Not Dead." An earlier version of chapter 5 was published as "Punk Cinema" in *Cinema Journal* 43.2 (Winter 2004): 47–66. Copyright © 2004 by the University of Texas Press. All rights reserved.

My best reader and editor is always Kate Hinnant. My love for her is immense and without end.

Abbreviations and Acronyms

7"	45 or 33 rpm record, 7 inches in diameter
A.C.	Anal Cunt
AEC	Alliance Entertainment Corporation
AIDS	Acquired immunodeficiency syndrome
AOL	American Online
APF	Anarcho-Punk Federation
AT	Alternative Tentacles
BBC	British Broadcasting Corporation
Bee Gees	Brothers Gibb
BGK	Balthasar Gerards Kommando
BMG	Bertelsmann Music Group
BYOFL	*Book Your Own Fuckin' Life*
C-M-C'	Commodity—money—commodity prime
CBGBs	Country Bluegrass, Blues
CD	Compact Disk
C.O.B.W.	Children of Barren Wasteland
DIY	Do-it-yourself
DJ	Disk jockey
DKs	Dead Kennedys
DVD	Digital versatile disk
ECT	Electroconvulsive therapy
EMP	Experience Music Project
EP	Extended play
GI	Government Issue
H2B	Heavens to Betsy
HIV	Human immunodeficiency virus
IPU	International Pop Underground
ISA	Ideological State Apparatus
ITV	Independent Television (U.K.)
KRS	Kill Rock Stars

LAPD	Los Angeles Police Department
LI	Lettrist International
LP	Long playing
M-C-M'	Money—commodity—money prime
MC5	Motor City 5
MDC	varies, for example: Millions of Dead Cops, Millions of Dead Capitalists
MRR	*MaximumRockNRoll*
MTV	Music Television
NIDA	National Institute of Drug Abuse
NOFX	No Fucking Straight Edge
NYHC	New York Hardcore
NYSE	New York Straight Edge
OMFUG	Other Music for Uplifting Gormandizers
PD	Police Department
PE	Profane Existence
R&B	Rhythm & Blues
RAR	Rock Against Racism
RGNY	Riot Grrrl New York City
RIAA	Recording Industry Association of America
RSA	Repressive State Apparatus
SDS	Students for a Democratic Society
SI	Situationist International
S.O.A.	State of Alert
SST	Solid State Transformers
TRL	Total Request Live
T.S.O.L.	True Sounds of Liberty
VHS	Video Home System
WTO	World Trade Organization
YOT	Youth of Today

You Are Not What You Own

Jesus was a communist.
—Reagan Youth

ANTI-CAPITALISM

ON JUNE 4, 2000, in Dolores Park in San Francisco, a crowd gathered for Soupstock 2000, a celebration marking the twentieth anniversary of the anarchist collective, Food Not Bombs. The event included a performance by Sleater-Kinney, a punk rock band comprised of three women, which originated in Olympia, Washington, in 1995. Greil Marcus, a longtime commentator on punk, wrote an account of the band's appearance for the first page of the *New York Times*'s Arts and Leisure section for Sunday, June 18, 2000. According to Marcus, in "Raising the Stakes in Punk Rock," when Sleater-Kinney plays, "everything is in jeopardy and no destiny is fixed" (29). The lead singer, Corin Tucker's, voice "can be thrilling, confusing, scary, but it's no effect: it's a voice that was discovered, and passed on" (29) by earlier punks, including the Riot Grrrl movement of the early 1990s and the Sex Pistols, a band to which Marcus compares Sleater-Kinney (he notes that Sleater-Kinney "is almost never played on commercial radio, and for good reason—like Sex Pistols music, it is so strong, so quick and far-reaching, it makes everything that today might surround it on the radio feel cowardly" [29]). He concludes by describing what he considers one of the best moments of the San Francisco show: when the band played "Dig Me Out," from their 1997 album of the same name, he notes that "you could in the instant feel buried by . . . whatever you feared was set against you in the world at large" (29). For him, the lyric "Dig me out" transcended its context and was "no longer a line in a song by a punk band but something in the air, a warning, or a promise, or an event taking place as you listened" (29).

Marcus attends primarily to the aesthetics of Sleater-Kinney, although he also notes that the band releases its albums on Kill Rock Stars, an independent punk label that not only "functions very well as the center of its own universe" (1) but strengthens the band's "ability to treat a musical career as at once a form of free speech and real work" (29). He adds that the band sells about one hundred thousand copies of each of its albums. What strikes me as problematic about Marcus's article is that it exemplifies a tendency in much of the commentary on punk, both academic and non. Marcus describes punk and its effects using aesthetic and often idealist categories: punk is a transhistorical and transcendent force that destabilizes everything in "the world at large." It has something to do with "destiny," "strength," "warnings," "promises," and "events," and all of these categories are linked to "independence" and "free speech."

I do not mean to suggest that the aesthetics of punk should not be investigated, and Marcus's *Lipstick Traces: A Secret History of the Twentieth Century* (1989) contributes significantly to that ongoing project of cultural studies. However, the aesthetic exploration launched by Dick Hebdige as well as Julie Burchill and Tony Parsons and continued in the works of Marcus and Neil Nehring, among others, must take place alongside considerations of economics, because, in punk, questions of aesthetics and economics are intertwined: economic concerns will necessarily lead to and find expression in aesthetic forms, and aesthetic forms will both reflect and inflect economics. For this reason, I will not examine the triangulation of semiotics, punk, and identity in this text. Lawrence Grossberg's essays and Dick Hebdige's *Subculture: The Meaning of Style* (1979) are valuable forays in this direction, but I am less concerned with what occurs—it seems to me—in the brains of punks as they construct and are constructed as subjects and subjectivities than with punk as a set of material practices that produce certain effects, including subjectivity. As Raymond Williams writes, a materialist critique concerns itself with people "working on physical things and the ways they do this, and the relations they enter into to do it, working also on 'human nature,' which they make in the process of making what they need to subsist" (*Keywords*, 200). With this definition in mind, I advance a materialist investigation of punk economics and punk aesthetics in this book, in order to formulate some of the ways in which punk both resists and is resisted by capitalism, a term that is largely absent from the work of most critics of punk.

The entire field of punk can be understood as a set of problems that unfold from a single contradiction between aesthetics and economics, between punk, understood as a set of cultural productions and practices that comprise an aesthetic field, and capitalism and the commodity, an economic field and an economic form in which punks discover that they must operate. Throughout punk's various moments and textualities, this central contradiction spins out a variety of interrelated problems that punk mediates, demonstrating, as it does so, the utility and inutility of certain approaches to the task that Marx lays out in the Eleventh Thesis on Feuerbach: "The philosophers have only interpreted the world, in various ways; the point is to change it" (Marx and Engels, *German Ideology*, 123). Punks want to change the world, and many believe that what most needs to be changed is capitalism. Consequently, punk both raises and attempts to work through two related problematics, one economic and one aesthetic: Can the commodity form be taken up and used against capitalism? Can all aesthetics be commodified?

PUNK: A PROVISIONAL DEFINITION

punk . . . [a] molded stick . . . used to ignite fuses esp. of fireworks
—*Webster's Third New International Dictionary*

One of the most difficult tasks that writing on punk demands is that of formulating a working definition of the term from which to strike out. To begin, I will advance four propositions in order to broaden and narrow the field that I will be investigating in the following chapters. First, there are several major genres of punk textuality: music (recorded and performed), style (especially clothing), the printed word (including fanzines, or "zines"), cinema, and events (punk happenings aside from shows); together, these texts make up the "punk project." Over the course of the history of punk, music has not always served as the textual form that best embodies the opposition at punk's core, and, for this reason, I will concentrate on different textual forms at different historical moments.

Second, the building block of the field of punk is the "scene," and punk is made up of a series of major scenes, beginning with the New York Scene of 1974–76 and continuing through the California Pop-Punk Scene of the early and mid-90s. Although hundreds of small punk scenes, containing a few hundred members each, have sprung up across the United States and around the world since 1974, I have chosen to schematize punk history in terms of the seven largest scenes, each of whose participants number in the thousands. While numerous texts, both academic and non, document the New York and English scenes, only a few predominantly nonscholarly books touch upon the later scenes. It is in zines, though, that punks produce and articulate their own histories in the most detail. It would be difficult to overemphasize the importance of the internationally distributed punk zine *MaximumRockNRoll (MRR)* to any accounting of punk history. *MRR* has appeared monthly since its inception in 1982 and has traced or generated most of the major and minor debates in and around punk during that period. Other zines proffering histories of punk and informing my work include the widely distributed *Punk Planet, Flip-side* (Al Flipside began publishing it in 1977, and it is the longest-running zine to date), *Search and Destroy, Punk, Sniffin' Glue,* as well as numerous zines that are distributed locally or regionally.

Third, two vectors shoot through and condition all of the various textualities of punk. From punk's birth in 1974 in CBGBs (a small nightclub in New York City's East Village) to its present multiplicity of scenes, which spans the globe, punks have always mounted economic and aesthetic forms of resistance to capitalism and the commodity as its most ubiquitous form. Because punk's oppositional practices have mutated radically over the past thirty years, it is impossible to establish a transhistorical definition of "punk aesthetics"; therefore, the best attempts to describe punk in aesthetic terms have focused not on punk as a whole but on one of its seven major scenes. On the other hand, punk's economic modes of oppositionality have never been well documented, and it is to this task that I turn in this work.

Last, it is worth noting that, for many (but not all) punks, the corporate music industry stands in for the whole of capitalism, for it is when they confront the major labels' business practices, music, and bands that punks best understand themselves as opposed to capitalism. What I find most hopeful about the punk project is its underlying refusal to give up on imagining something other than the world as it is. In his introduction to *Postmodernism, Or, The Cultural Logic of Late Capitalism* (1991), Fredric Jameson describes the present as "an age that has forgotten how to think historically" (ix). In Marxian terms, his claim suggests that the present does not realize that the current mode of production and the modes of being that it produces are historical and, consequently, changeable. In truth, capitalism is neither natural nor necessary, and punks have not forgotten this fact. They cannot fully imagine what the better world would look like, but they refuse to accept the one that they know as final.

A DESIRING PUNK/PUNK DESIRE

In 1999, GTE conducted a direct mail advertising campaign for its "Caller ID" service that allows customers to learn who is calling them (or at least who is being billed for the call) before they pick up their phones. The envelope containing this offer is a concisely worded ad, whose copy appears in the upper left quarter of the envelope. It reads, "Before You Talk To Strangers . . . Ask for ID. Caller ID. From GTE." A black and white photo of a punk occupies the right third of the envelope. His black hair has been molded into spikes, one multiply pierced ear is visible, and he wears a black jacket, black metal-studded boots, and a white T-shirt with black stenciling. Numerous decorative pins adorn his jacket, and he wears a necklace fashioned from paperclips. With a stereotypically punk sneer—between a smile and smirk—he scowls up at the camera, whose positioning above him combines with the ad's use of black-and-white film to suggest a still shot taken from a surveillance camera's tape. The ad implies that Caller ID works like such a camera: it allows its customers to deny entrance into their homes to undesirables. For the ad's purposes, the punk is an undesirable. But what makes the punk a threat? My aim in the first chapter is to argue that the ad's punk—and punk in general—represents threat and, obversely, liberation, because they represent repressed cultural impulses or desires. Why does the punk want in? According to the logic of the ad, he is what has been barred from the posh home whose grounds the security camera surveils. Who knows what he would do if he gained entrance? Perhaps he is the return of the repressed, in which case the real threat is that at some level we want—or should want—to let the punk in.

Central to my reasoning regarding punk in general—and this ad in particular—is Raymond Williams's assertion that "no mode of production and therefore no dominant social order and therefore no dominant culture ever in reality includes or exhausts all human practice, human energy, and human intention" (*Marxism* 125). For Williams, human practices, energies, and intentions that fail to find expression within the "dominant culture" come in the back door as "residual" or "emergent" social phenomena, because, one way or another, they must be expressed. This idea closely parallels Jameson's concept of a "political unconscious": Jameson theorizes capitalism as a system that promulgates "impulses" that are propitious to its growth and represses those that would oppose it. Like Williams, he assumes that the dominant mode of production cannot express the full range of impulses or desires that emerge within its purview and represses those that threaten to destabilize it. Those repressed impulses and desires return, however, in sublimated forms in all the various registers of production: economic, social, political, etc. For Jameson, the cultural productions of mass culture are specifically designed to redirect these impulses:

> [I]f the ideological function of mass culture is understood as a process whereby otherwise dangerous and protopolitical impulses are "managed" and defused, rechanneled and offered spurious objects, then some preliminary step must also be theorized in which these same impulses—the raw material upon which the process works—are initially awakened within the very text that seeks to still them. (*Political* 287)

Mass culture must summon precisely the desires that oppose the dominant culture before it can exorcise those impulses. Presumably, the prohibited desires serve as the bait that lures consumers and encourages their consumption, but, having enticed consumers to part from their money, cultural productions must subsequently redirect the desires that have been awakened away from their initial targets, in a perfect example of bait-and-switch. Examples might include the films *American Beauty* (1999) and *Fight Club* (1999), both of which begin by critiquing consumerism in contemporary U.S. culture but detour unexpectedly toward a saving mysticism *(American Beauty)* and a heterosexual relationship *(Fight Club)*.

With the above repression model in mind, the project of naming and mapping punk's desires becomes possible. Although, at first, desire would seem to exist only in the brains of punks, it has a materialist shape: the commodity. The commodity marks the place in the process of production where desires become material and is therefore the fundamental form of the punk artifact. Punk commodities are the products of the work that a set of knowable collective impulses perform or demand. In other words, punk commodities figure as crystallized forms of collective desires: they are produced and thrown off as constellations of related commodities where desire and repression collide. Because commodities are the bearers of desire, they can be read as expressions of the forces that shaped and became embodied in them. Punk in general can be grasped as a material exploration of how a specific set of illicit desires repressed within a dominant social order return to haunt it and, in the best cases, blast cracks in its surface. The first chapter of this text is, then, a hauntology.

Where Jameson assumes an a priori pair of qualities for the desires that he anticipates finding in mass culture texts—ideological (in concert with capitalism) and utopian (opposed to capitalism)—and finds the ideological impulses always and ultimately foreclosing on the utopian impulses, my own findings correlate less precisely with this incorporatist model of an all-consuming capitalism. While I agree with Walter Benjamin's assertion that "the bourgeois apparatus of production and publication can assimilate astonishing quantities of revolutionary themes, indeed, can propagate them without calling its own existence, and the existence of the class that owns it, seriously into question" ("Author," 229), I find it worth noting that Benjamin refrains from claiming that all revolutionary themes are therefore assimilated. Some of them escape, and it is to a narrative of those that escape that I will turn below.

For Jameson, capitalism functions as a repressive set of containment strategies that code desires or impulses into forms useful to capitalists, but desires constantly break free from these codings and threaten to escape or return in sublimated forms. I, too, will derive desires from punk's artifacts that I read as material attempts to explore the limits of commodification in order either to mediate between desire and commodification or gesture beyond it. However, I do not aim to cleave too closely to Jameson's argument that no mass culture form ever wholly escapes capitalism's limits. Maybe he is correct, but I am uncertain that this problem is not a false one. Slavoj Žižek reads Hegel in order to argue that demanding purity—for example, cultural productions or expressions totally free from commodification—is akin to "positing the presuppositions" (*Sublime Object* 215) that will prevent one from having to act. If I posit the presupposition that no such purity exists, then I find myself justified in my inactivity, in quitting before I have begun. Perhaps punk's attacks upon and mediations of capitalism's limits only serve to inscribe the limits' contours more clearly and render them more legible. But my sense is that punk achieves something more than this modest aim.

chapter one

Let's Make a Scene

THE MULTIPLICITY OF CONJUNCTIONS and disjunctions among punk's desires do not separate out readily into discrete fields, but, for the purposes of this chapter, I will group them into seven major scenes, major because the participants in each scene number in the thousands rather than in the hundreds. Each of the major scenes emerges in a specific geographic site as a determinate constellation of commodities/desires. The seven scenes are: the New York Scene, the English Scene, the California Hardcore Scene, the Washington, D.C., First Wave Straight Edge Scene, the New York Second Wave Straight Edge Scene, the Riot Grrrl Scene, and the Berkeley/Lookout! Pop-Punk Scene. I have chosen to concentrate upon these specific scenes, because punks describe them as the largest and most influential in the history of punk.[1]

If punk artifacts/commodities are understood as the effects and accretions of the emergence of repressed desires, then these artifacts can be interpreted for clues to the desires that formed them. One difficulty with approaching punk scenes, however, is that each one amasses myriad artifacts within the social field that it establishes. Even creating a taxonomy of only the most significant artifacts for any scene would prove an exhaustive and possibly useless endeavor. For these reasons, I have chosen to focus upon certain artifacts, sifted out of each scene, that, while by no means defining the scene, serve as nodes at which either new (to a particular scene) or recurring (from scene to scene) desires intersect. I will draw these examples from the major social groupings and genres of punk textuality: bands, music (recorded and performed), style (especially clothing), the printed word (including zines), cinema, and events (punk happenings apart from shows).

THE NEW YORK SCENE

The New York Scene emerged in 1974, lasted through 1976, and was centered around two small nightclubs, CBGB and OMFUG (the name of *one* of the clubs; the initials stand for Country Bluegrass, Blues and Other Music for Uplifting Gormandizers) on Bowery Street in lower Manhattan and Max's Kansas City in Greenwich Village (also in Manhattan).[2] The bands most integral to establishing the scene included the Ramones, Television, Patti Smith, and Blondie; later, Suicide, the Dictators, the Heartbreakers, Richard Hell and the Voidoids, Talking Heads, and the Dead Boys, all attracted to the hype around the clubs, bands, and New York, joined the scene. The epicenter for the scene, however, was CBGBs and the Ramones that, together, serve as a locus where several of punks' early desires intersect.

Hilly Kristal opened CBGBs in March 1974, when very few venues in New York City booked underground rock bands. Clinton Heylin defines "underground" in the context of the New York Scene as a term referring to "bands self-consciously aligned with noncommercial popular music trends. More specifically, it refers to New York City bands supported by cult followings developed through live performances at local nightclubs rather than recording contracts and mass media hype" (135). Writing for *The Nation*, Mark Crispin Miller notes that, in 1974, the "Big Six" major record companies—Warner, CBS, PolyGram, RCA, MCA, and Capitol-EMI—controlled 81 percent of the U.S. market share (11). In short, when Kristal opened CBGBs, commercial music could be equated with the Big Six; all other record labels and unsigned bands were considered "underground" or noncommercial, provided that they did not appear to be aping the aesthetic choices of commercial acts in the hope of obtaining recording contracts.

In 1974, CBGBs became the only club in New York dedicated exclusively to underground music,[3] and Kristal charged patrons one dollar to see unsigned bands play there. Read as an artifact, CBGBs attests to one of the most fundamental desires that constitutes not only punk's first scene but all of punk: the desire to resist the commercial realm, and especially commercial music— the Big Six in 1974. This desire is synonymous with punks' felt need to escape from the realm of the economic. In 1964, Herbert Marcuse defined "economic freedom" as "freedom from the economy—from being controlled by economic forces and relationships; freedom from the daily struggle for existence, from earning a living" (4). Although I do not read CBGBs as expressive of a desire for anything as profound or sweeping as Marcuse's "economic freedom," the club does represent early punks' desire to establish a realm not wholly conditioned by economics, a realm in which music and entertainment could concern themselves with something other than making money. Under capitalism, the club could not wholly succeed in this endeavor; Kristal did charge a dollar, but this token charge downplayed the role of economics in the realm of punk, as did the underground aspect of the bands. The fact that the bands and Kristal were not making much money, while the audience was not parting with much of its money, allowed for the possibility that both audiences and bands gathered at CBGBs for predominantly noneconomic reasons. The audience did not come solely to purchase entertainment, and the musicians did not come solely to earn a living.

However, CBGBs was a bar, and although Kristal did not charge customers much to see bands they still had to purchase their alcohol. Participants in the first three punk scenes—New York, London, and California—were famous for their excessive drug and alcohol use, which contributed to the deaths of many band and scene members. These well-publicized deaths, and especially the drug-related deaths of Sid Vicious and his girlfriend, Nancy Spungen, forged associations, for punks and non-punks, between punks and drugs that continue to linger, even where they no longer actually exist (such as in the Straight Edge Scenes).[4]

CBGBs was (and still is) a small nightclub. Tricia Henry notes that its size "allowed freedom of movement of the audience [and] close proximity to and interaction with the performers. . . . This was a far cry from what was by then a traditionally distant physical relationship maintained between performers and their audiences at rock concerts" (53). She adds that "band members mingled with the audience before and after a set, and watched other groups" (53). The club's layout materially renders another of the desires that constituted the New York Scene: the desire to erode the difference between performer and audience member, to allow these roles to become interchangeable so that any audience member could also be a performer and vice versa. This desire finds its expression in the literal proximity between band member and audience member in CBGBs: it is a small step from the floor to the stage.

Simon Frith describes early punk as, in part, "a challenge to the multinationals' control of mass music, an attempt to seize the technical and commercial means of music production" ("Art Ideology," 463). Frith's Marxian claim that punks seize the means of production correlates with Jacques Attali's concept of "composition" in *Noise: The Political Economy of Music* (1977). As Susan McClary explains in her 1984 afterword to this book, "It is this demystified yet humanly dignified activity [the creation of music] that Attali wishes to remove from the rigid institutions of specialized musical training in order to return it to all members of society. For in Attali's eyes, it is only if the individuals in society choose to reappropriate the means of producing art themselves that the infinite regress of Repetition . . . can be escaped" (156). For Attali, taking control over composition allows people to avoid Repetition and, with it, the reproduction of the dominant mode of production. The desire of the New York punks to be both audience members and performers suggests that they intuit what is at stake for them: if they cannot make music without passing through the commercial mechanisms that will condone their music making, then most of them will never make music at all, and each new musician or set of musicians will merely reproduce the already-existing mode of music production that the Big Six oversees.

In the conclusion to *Noise*, having built toward them gradually, Attali finally advances these conclusions on what "composition"/"composing," or seizing the means of music production, means or could mean:

> We are all condemned to silence—unless we create our own relation with the world and try to tie other people into the meaning we thus create. That is what composing is. Doing solely for the sake of doing, without trying artificially to recreate the old codes in order to reinsert communication into them. Inventing new codes, inventing the message at the same time as the language. Playing for one's own pleasure, which alone can create the conditions for new communication. A concept such as this seems natural in the context of music. But it reaches far beyond that: it relates to the emergence of the free act, self-transcendence, pleasure in being instead of having. (134)

The New York Scene did not bring to fruition all of the results that Attali imagines might grow out of composition, but it bore desires similar to Attali's and a partial enactment of his hopeful program. Beginning in 1974, punk tried to seize the means of music production within the context of its historical conditions of possibility: the New York Scene attempted to wrest the right to create music from the Big Six and thereby democratize that right. Describing the first punk scene, McClary comments that "[m]any of the original groups began as garage bands formed by people not educated as musicians who intended to defy noisily the slickly marketed 'nonsense' of commercial rock" (156).

Frith notes that, during the '70s, as the music industry became consolidated, the cost of producing rock albums rose until "the average 'rock 'n' roll album' cost between $70,000 and $100,000 in studio time, and any rock 'sweetening' (adding strings, for example) could add another $50,000 to the bill; promotion budgets began at around $150,000 and rose rapidly" (*Sound Effects*, 147). Although McClary claims that composition, as a force, attacks the "rigid institutions" of "musical training" (156), punk seeks to free music less from music schools and instructors than from the Big Six, the economic institutions that control the performance, recording, production, distribution, and promotion of rock music. In an interview in Legs McNeil and Gillian McCain's book, *Please Kill Me: The Uncensored Oral History of Punk,* Joey Ramone, the lead singer for the Ramones, invokes the economic desires that underlie punk when he congratulates himself and his band for how quickly and cheaply they recorded their first album *(The Ramones):*

Money wasn't tight yet—some albums were costing a half-million dollars to make and taking two or three years to record, like Fleetwood Mac and stuff. Doing an album in a week and bringing it in for sixty-four hundred dollars was unheard of, especially since it was an album that really changed the world. It kicked off punk rock and started the whole thing—as well as us. (229)

Despite Joey's hyperbolic claims, the first Ramones album and the cost of its production spoke to punk's desire to gain and democratize access to the means of production. Because the band's music could be produced so inexpensively, a small independent label such as Sire Records, run by Seymour Stein, could afford to sign the band in 1976 and release its first album without needing to sell millions of copies of it in order to recoup its investment in the band (Heylin, 254). Commenting upon Stein's reasons for fronting the money for Ramones albums, Craig Leon, the producer of *The Ramones,* notes that "they were very inexpensive records by industry standards, so why not?" (254). The specific set of economic conditions within the music industry that Frith describes explains why some of the New York scene's punk rock and especially the Ramones' music could be played, recorded, and produced cheaply enough to facilitate a shift within punk from music consumption to music production.[5] Punk bands and the independent labels that grew up around them did not require the outlay of capital that the major labels did.

Many of punk's commentators have also understood punk as an attempt to open up the possibility of performance to people not formally trained in music. Neil Nehring, writing on the English punk scene, makes a comment that also applies to the New York Scene: "Performance . . . was a possibility that virtually everyone involved contemplated, with the do-it-yourself aesthetic of the music; the barre chords on guitar, simple but versatile chord forms, were a staple of punk" (315). (A barre chord is played by pressing one finger flat against the fret board of the guitar and strumming the strings with the other hand.) In terms of difficulty, most guitar chords are no easier to learn than single notes; each chord or note requires a specific positioning of the fingers. However, chords, which are produced when several notes are played together, fill out a band's sound in a way that individually played notes cannot. In order to avoid the time and money needed to learn to play the guitar well, technically speaking, guitarists in bands such as the Ramones learned to play a few chords, thereby becoming capable of producing a full sound, and they eliminated solos in order to sidestep the need to play lengthy "riffs"— progressions of individual notes or combinations of chords and notes. What makes the first Ramones album an "unheard of" project, as Joey Ramone describes it, is its literally unheard aspects—its lack of solos. Instead, the Ramones popularized what has come to be known in punk—not pejoratively—as "three-chord punk."

The relative ease with which punk could be played contrasts with the "progressive rock"[6] that in 1975 nudged its way into the U.S. charts when Led Zeppelin's *Physical Graffiti* (Swan Song/Atlantic) was the eighth-best-selling album of the year. Progressive rock bands such as Led Zeppelin required musicians who could play solos, because the songs tended to be long and inevitably contained lengthy guitar solos and, occasionally, solos for each instrument in the band. Dee Dee Ramone, the Ramones' bass player, recalls that when the Ramones first formed, its members "didn't know what to do when we started playing. We'd try some Bay City Rollers [a pop, rather than progressive, band] songs and we absolutely couldn't do that. We didn't know how. So we just started writing our own stuff and put it together the best we could" (McNeil and McCain, 183).

Although Nehring stresses the underlying assumption of Dee Dee's comment—that anyone could play punk—the sort of technical proficiency that progressive rock signifies, with its lengthy songs (by rock standards) and solos, was not actually necessary or prominent in much of the popular music of the mid-'70s. Led Zeppelin was the only progressive rock band that had a best-selling album between 1974 and 1976, and no progressive rock single made the yearly top forty for those years (Theroux and Gilbert). In 1974, when the Ramones began to play regularly at CBGBs, the top-grossing LPs in the United States were John Denver's *Greatest Hits* (RCA), Elton John's *Goodbye Yellow Brick Road* (MCA),[7] and Paul McCartney and Wings' *Band on the Run* (Apple). The top-selling single was Barbra Streisand's *The Way We Were* (Columbia) (Theroux and Gilbert, 231).[8] In 1975, two Elton John LPs (*Greatest Hits* [MCA] and *Captain Fantastic and the Brown Dirt Cowboy* [MCA]) occupied the first and third slots in the list of top ten albums, Earth, Wind and Fire's *That's the Way of the World* (Columbia) was second, and the top single of the year was Captain and Tennille's *Love Will Keep Us Together* (A&M). In 1976, the year that Sire released *The Ramones*, Peter Frampton's *Frampton Comes Alive* (A&M), Fleetwood Mac's *Fleetwood Mac* (Warner Brothers), and the Eagles' *Greatest Hits* (Asylum) were the top-grossing LPs, while Johnnie Taylor's *Disco Lady* (Columbia) was the top single. All of these top-selling albums and singles required immense outlays of capital from their labels to cover performance, recording, production, distribution, and promotion costs. However, none of the acts was a progressive rock release; they were all pop, with the possible exception of *Disco Lady*. Looked at in terms of the type of proficiency that rock could require, it seems clear that the barriers that prevented a rock fan from becoming the next Elton John or Peter Frampton were tied to economics more than to skill.

As I will explain in more detail in relation to the Sex Pistols, what passes as skill in the music industry changes over time. Beginning with the New York Scene, punks interrogated notions of skill in rock and pop and demonstrated that the owners of the means of production produced the ruling definitions of skill (to paraphrase Marx). In other words, it was not Elton John's greater skill that differentiated him from punk but the fact that the music industry capitalized him to a greater extent than the Ramones.

Although the first two desires that I draw from CBGBs and the Ramones, treated as artifacts, relate to economics—punks' attempt to carve out a social space that is not governed by money and their attempts to situate themselves within that realm as active participants by seizing control of the means of production, both from the Big Six and from progressive rock musicians—I do not mean to suggest that economic concerns were the only obstacles separating the New York punk scene from the Big Six or that all of the scene's desires were economic. The first scene's aesthetic choices also signified a social desire.

The New York punk scene bore the desire to create a realm of music production not wholly governed by economics, and the scene thereby raises two questions: if punks sense that the commercial sphere of music production represses what I propose are certain non-individuated desires and felt needs, then what are those desires? Can they be read in their desublimated forms in punk cultural productions? I have derived the desire to erode the barrier between audience and band member from the size of CBGBs and the interactions between audience and band members that it encourages. A desire for collectivity can also be read in CBGBs and the Ramones. As I mentioned above, CBGBs is a small club whose size prevented punk bands from establishing the sheer distance from their fans that the best-selling pop and rock bands of the mid-'70s could maintain in their "arena-rock" performances. Because the major labels' costs for producing rock music escalated throughout the '70s, their bands needed not only to tour but to tour the largest venues that they could fill, so that the labels could recoup the huge investments that they had made in them. Popular bands such as Elton John and John Denver could not afford to play shows in clubs the size of CBGBs. In contrast to arena-rock, CBGBs expresses, in a material form, punks' desire to resist the physical distance between popular performers and their audiences, which precludes collectivity.

The social desire for collectivity also took on aesthetic forms within punk's sound and style. From 1974 to 1976, punk reacted not only to the Big Six but to the cult of the pop star (and glam and glitter rock star) that the conditions that I have outlined above foster. First, since supposedly anyone can perform punk, its audiences do not feel compelled to lionize its performers. Additionally, the lack of solos in the music of the Ramones signifies a further move toward group rather than individual production. A solo trains an audience's attention upon a specific performer and grants her or him a type of identity within the rock world by showcasing individuated skills. Without solos to guide its investment of interest in specific band members, the audience experiences a band as more of a collective, and band members seem more approachable and less like the distant prodigies that mid-'70s pop superstars had become. A lack of solos also allows an audience to experience music as a set of voices (instrumental and human), each of which can be picked out by the listener but all of which combine into a collective sound.

The clothing style of the Ramones also reflected a desire for communality. The Ramones played in matching T-shirts, leather jackets, jeans with holes ripped in the knees, and cheap sneakers. Pete Frame, author of *Rock Family Trees* (1980) (a two-volume study devoted to New York underground rock), understands the clothing styles prevalent in CBGBs as "glitter-backlash . . . jeans, T-shirts, leather jackets, ordinary" (27), and Hilly Kristal adds, in an interview in 1986, that "CBGB bands and audiences weren't style conscious in the way the glitter groups or the English punks were later on. The only style was torn T-shirts and torn jeans. They just came as they were—the way kids in the East Village dressed then. . . . Even though CBGB is referred to as a punk club, there was never much of that fashion here" (Henry, 58). Understood as "glitter-backlash," the Ramones positioned themselves against bands such as the New York Dolls, who performed frequently at the Mercer Arts Center in New York City until it closed in 1973. Rather than attempting to outdress and shock their audiences—as the Dolls had when they dressed in drag or in red, pseudo-Soviet uniforms—the Ramones emphasized their connections to their audiences. Henry comments that the "New York Dolls confounded traditional images of gender distinction in their stage performance," but their "[g]ender blurring and outrageous attire were simply means by which to shock the general public and show rock audiences something they had never seen before" (40). In contrast, the Ramones' clothing expressed an impulse toward anonymity, suggesting that they had emerged from the audience themselves, an effect that in turn suggested not only that they maintained ties with that audience but that other audience members might emerge as performers in their own right.

There is one final sense in which the Ramones' style signified a desire different from the high fashion or parody thereof embodied in the mystery, pretensions, and aloofness of glitter and Glam Rock performers, such as Lou Reed and David Bowie (Bowie's song, "Fame," was the third-best-selling single of 1975 [Theroux and Gilbert, 231]). Unlike the Dolls, whom Henry describes as following "the precedent set by David Bowie and Lou Reed in blurring gender distinctions," the Ramones rejected the ambiguously gendered clothing of glam and glitter rock and the forms of collectivity that might have emerged from that style. Instead, they opted for a more traditionally masculine and heterosexual style of clothing and its concomitant version of collectivity.

In the New York Scene, another desire ran alongside those that I have enumerated above: the music industry's desire, which was not sublimated, to commercialize potentially lucrative phenomena. The Ramones exemplified this occurrence in New York. According to Jon Savage, New York's most prominent zine, *Punk*, drew the seemingly varied trajectories of the scene together, enacting a "successful translation of CBGBs into a package that record executives like Seymour Stein [of Sire Records] could readily understand" (139–40). Stein signed the Ramones to Sire in January 1976, and the label released their first album, *The Ramones*, that February. The label quickly began arranging for the Ramones to tour in support of their album. The first tour began on July 4, 1976. Sire released the band's second album, *Ramones Leave Home*, in early 1977, and the supporting tour began in spring of the same year. A third album, *Rocket to Russia*, was released in late 1977 and was followed by a winter tour in 1978–79.

Although the Ramones did not entirely cease playing CBGBs between '76 and '79, their recording and touring schedule loosened their connection with the New York Scene and its home base of CBGBs. Additionally, as early as the autumn of 1975 the Patti Smith Group signed with Arista, while other key bands in the CBGBs scene—including Blondie, Talking Heads, Television, and Richard Hell and the Voidoids—were garnering record company interest. All of these bands signed with labels within a year: in 1976 Blondie signed with Private Stock, Talking Heads signed with Sire, and Richard Hell and the Voidoids signed with Ork. Television signed with Elektra in 1977 (Savage, 552). The push toward commercialization moved to the fore, the desires to resist commercialization, seize control over the means of production, and collectivize were momentarily absorbed, and the New York Scene dissolved by the end of '76.

THE ENGLISH SCENE

The English Scene arose in London in 1976, continued until 1978, and included several bands: the Sex Pistols, The Clash, The Damned, The Stranglers, X-Ray Spex, The Buzzcocks, The Vibrators, The Adverts, Generation X, and Chelsea. Similar to the manner in which the Ramones and CBGBs serve to exemplify artifactual evidence of the New York Scene's desires, the Sex Pistols and "punk style" will serve, here, as nodes where a set of specific desires, some carried over from New York and some new to punk, intersect and find cultural expression as commodities and social groupings.

Commentators on the New York Scene rarely link desire with punk, but those mapping out the English Scene frequently do so. Greil Marcus's work on punk exemplifies this tendency.[9] In *Lipstick Traces: A Secret History of the*

Twentieth Century (1989), he proffers Johnny Rotten, the lead singer of the Sex
Pistols, as the simultaneous culmination and degradation of the expression of
a type of desire, arguing that "an unknown tradition of old pronouncements,
poems, and events, a secret history of ancient wishes and defeats, came to bear
on Johnny Rotten's voice—and because this tradition lacked both cultural
sanction and political legitimacy, because this history was comprised of only
unfinished, unsatisfied stories, it carried tremendous force" (441). Marcus's
book invokes a utopian impulse that throbs through the avant-gardist projects
that he traces through the twentieth century and sees culminating in the Sex
Pistols. He finds this pulse gathering strength because it is not "sanctioned" or
"legitimate," suggesting a repressive logic to cultural desires.

Adhering to Freud's conceptualization of the repression of desire and its
ineluctable return, Marcus follows the force of avant-garde desire as it changes
in magnitude but not in terms of type or direction over the course of the twentieth century. In a succinct summary, he tracks the desire that he has identi-
fied and variously defined through seventy years:

> Measured against the demands its precursors made, punk was a paltry reflec-
> tion; measured against the records the Sex Pistols and their followers made,
> the leavings of dada, the LI [Lettrist International], and the SI [Situationist
> International] are sketches of punk songs; all in all it is the tale of a wish that
> went beyond art and found itself returned to it, a nightclub act that asked for
> the world, for a moment got it, then got another nightclub. In this sense
> punk realized the projects that lay behind it, and realized their limits. (442)

In short, punk becomes the most recent bearer of a transhistorical charge that
Marcus describes at different times as utopian, nihilistic, and negative
(negating), but punk falls short of the original energy that infused the
dadaists, Lettrists, and Situationists because it, more quickly than its prede-
cessors, disappears from history. Capitalism subsumes it; at least, Marcus
would have it so. Consequently, it is disheartening to find him complicit with
this process of subsumption in his admitted attempt to codify in particular
the Lettrists but also punk. He confesses: "I have tried to make the ethos the
LI claimed into a narrative to fill in the gaps, to make it at least half as clear
as it was to Debord, Wolman, Bernstein [all prominent Lettrists] and the
rest—inevitably to make their old papers into something *fit for rational consumption.* They didn't" (398, my emphasis).

Marcus's attention to punk proves useful in three ways: he links punk
with desire, capitalism, and history. In contrast to Marcus, I have been proposing that desire be thought not in transhistorical or individuated terms (as
belonging to Johnny Rotten exclusively, for example) but situated within the
specific historical, economic, and regional conditions from which it emerges.

Such a conceptualization of desire forces me to map and name the specific components of a scene in ways that Marcus's generalized and transhistorical notion of desire does not. The connection between the English Scene and capitalism and punk's links with history also require unpacking.

According to *New Musical Express* writers Julie Burchill and Tony Parsons's account of the New York and English scenes, *The Boy Looked at Johnny,* English punk emerged from a specific socioeconomic moment, the result of repressed forces and desires. In 1975, there was a "mood of economic crisis [and] depression prevalent in a UK torn by one million plus unemployed and legions of school-leavers swelling their ranks every day, the three-day week, teeming assembly-line education and the Tory mis-rule" that culminated in "miners' strike black-outs" (26). Against this economic background, Burchill and Parsons note that rock venues became "giant stadiums at which the opulent rock aristocracy occasionally deigned to play" (26). It is in the light of this context that the Sex Pistols' "fury made them innovators; for the first time a band was directly reacting against the music business monolith" (34).

The Sex Pistols and their manager, Malcolm McLaren, were not resisting the dominant economic mode of production for rock music, though. In *Sound Effects: Youth, Leisure, and the Politics of Rock 'n' Roll,* Simon Frith writes that "by the end of the 1970s . . . [w]here capital investment was important the majors still had no rivals. In Britain, EMI, Decca, Pye, Phonodisc, CBS, and RCA manufactured and distributed most of the records that were issued (EMI alone manufactured one in four of all records sold, and distributed one in three)" (138). The commercial system that CBGBs and the Ramones initially eschewed was still in place in 1976, but instead of resisting it, the Sex Pistols and McLaren courted the major labels, and the Sex Pistols signed with not just one but two of them. On October 8, 1976, the Pistols signed with EMI. On January 5, 1977, the label, tired of being connected to the several scandals that the Pistols had generated in a few months, dropped the Pistols (Savage, 285), but A&M signed them on March 10 of the same year, only to drop them six days later for vandalizing the company's offices and verbally abusing A&M employees. On May 12 the band signed with an independent label, Virgin Records.

The desire to avoid commercialization that ran through the New York Scene did not reappear in the English Scene, whose bands embraced the major label attention directed at them after the Sex Pistols had whipped up media attention around punk.[10] Within a few months after the Sex Pistols signed with EMI, The Clash had signed with CBS, The Damned with Stiff, and The Stranglers with UA, in addition to numerous other punk signings. However, although the disdain for the major labels evident in New York did not reappear in London, one component of the desire to democratize access to the means of producing rock did. The simplest and most famous expression of this desire appeared in a set of diagrams in the December 1976 issue of a zine devoted to the Stranglers, *Sideburns*. The diagrams demonstrate how to play three guitar chords—A, E, and G—and alongside them runs the text: "This is a chord. This is another. This is a third. Now form a band."[11]

Read as an artifact or constellation of artifacts, the career of the Sex Pistols also exhibits a mild thrust toward making performers of audience members. Originally, the Sex Pistols was composed of Johnny Rotten on vocals, Steve Jones on guitar, Glen Matlock on bass guitar (later replaced by Sid Vicious), and Paul Cook on drums. None of the band members ever took lessons, and they were not accomplished musicians. Three of the band's original members—Matlock, Cook, and Jones—had used stolen equipment (Jones stole it piece by piece over the course of two years) to teach themselves how to play and had formed a garage band called the Swankers. Malcolm McLaren, the owner of a King's Road clothing boutique called Sex that sold bondage wear, converted the Swankers into the Sex Pistols and persuaded Johnny Rotten to sing for the band.

According to Jon Savage's account in *England's Dreaming: Anarchy, Sex Pistols, Punk Rock, and Beyond,* for the Pistols' first show the band opened for Adam Ant's band, Bazooka Joe. Ant remembers their set: "There were no guitar solos, it was just simple songs. They did five and that was it: goodnight. The rest of my band hated them because they thought they couldn't play: in fact somebody said as much to Glen [Matlock] and he said: 'So What?'" (qtd. in Savage, 142). What Jacques Attali identifies as the will to composition surfaces here, understood as the desire to seize control over the means of producing music, but in England it took a diluted form compared to its earlier U.S. version. Technical proficiency prohibited both U.S. and English musicians to a much lesser degree than commercial music's institutions, and, while the Sex Pistols provided an English incarnation of the desire to produce music regardless of technical training, their manager, Malcolm McLaren, actively sought out commercial backers.

The Pistols' initial contract with EMI promised the band forty thousand pounds in non-returnable advance money: twenty thousand pounds upon signing and an additional twenty thousand pounds a year later. A&M signed the Pistols for seventy-five thousand pounds five months later, Virgin signed them for fifteen thousand pounds two months after A&M's signing (and an additional fifty thousand pounds a month after that), and Warner Brothers paid fifty thousand pounds in 1977 for the only LP that the Sex Pistols ever recorded, *Never Mind the Bollocks* (1977). Other bands followed suit; Julie Burchill and Tony Parsons comment that, by "the spring of 1977, there were four Pretenders to the Sex Pistols inviolate throne—The Damned, the Jam, the Clash and the Stranglers. Their names never became household-words synonymous with 'Punk Rock,' but all four consoled themselves with hooking a meal-ticket from a major label" (29). The Clash signed with CBS for an advance of £100,000. Especially when considering the fact that the monetary amounts above were only the advances paid and that numerous other punk bands were signed in addition to these five, the significant amount of capital that the majors invested in punk does not speak to the desire to shift economic control over music production from the major labels back to the producers themselves.

While the lack of solos and formal training that conditioned the music of the Sex Pistols can be read as traces of the same move toward anonymity and collectivity that the music of the Ramones signifies, little else about the Pistols echoes the New York Scene's investment in collectivity. In place of collectivizing, the Pistols aimed at antagonizing. Adam Ant describes their first gig, which exemplified the band's behavior over the course of its brief lifespan: "At the end Rotten slagged off Bazooka Joe [for whom the Pistols were opening] as being a bunch of fucking cunts" (qtd. in Savage, 142). Savage summarizes the Pistols' public stance in 1976: "It quickly became clear, as they moved out into the world, that the Sex Pistols were programmed for confrontation. McLaren was ambitious for his group: as his instrument, they would act out his fantasies of conflict and revenge on a decaying culture" (150). Although the English Scene maintained, in diluted form, only two of the New York Scene's three determinant desires, all three returned in later punk scenes. However, new non-individuated desires become legible within the artifacts of the English Scene, if those artifacts are approached as material objects and social structures that harbor imprints of the collective desires that punk produced. One such desire is a drive to create, or recreate, history as a narrative in which punks could feel that they actively participated.

The subtitle of Greil Marcus's *Lipstick Traces: A Secret History of the Twentieth Century,* warrants attention. Marcus explains in the prologue that two questions shape his book: "Is it a mistake to confuse the Sex Pistols' moment with a major event in history—and what is history anyway?" (4). He dispenses with the first question quickly, answering it in the negative, and, one hundred fifty pages later, proffers the beginning of an answer to the second question. He describes the secret history of "the performing space" as

> a place where revolution goes to die, where its spirit, to use a favorite situationist word, is "recuperated": *where the shout of what should be is absorbed into the spectacle of what is,* where the impossible demand is brought back into the fold of expectation and result, where the disease of collective vehemence is cured; where "revolution" means a moment in which people say no, enter into festival, are then in one way or another pushed out of history, their moment dropped down into a footnote. (151, my emphasis)

Marcus proposes to write the "secret history" of the Lettrists, Situationists, and punks—groups that have been pushed out of History proper; however, it is worth noting Marcus's implied concept of History. In his "Theses on the Philosophy of History," Walter Benjamin warns that "[t]here is no document of civilization which is not at the same time a document of barbarism" (256). Marcus's argument initially invokes what Benjamin would term the "History of the victors," and, consequently, events that "drop out of History" seem to Marcus to open up the possibility that "secret" histories could be written, oddly enough, in an effort to reinsert them into History. Marcus's project seems to violate the spirit of the "secret" history: if being pushed out of History is what allows a group to live a secret history, then to be recuperated would mean the opposite, for the Situationists especially but also for the Lettrists and punks; a recuperation would mean a reinsertion into official History that, by definition, must not include them. In a more generous reading of Marcus, I might highlight the possibility that he does not mean to recuperate punk for History but to destabilize the concept of History by forcing it to include and account for secret histories. However, he situates punk within the already existent history of the Lettrists and Situationists, as its final chapter. As such, it does not break with tradition and traditional means of representation that, as I will explain below, a destabilizing of History necessitates.

Instead, recuperation appears to be Marcus's project, and he fulfills it. He narrates the story of punk's desires, and his narration enacts their closure; he renders them consumable, a part of History, and shepherds them into the "fold of expectation," thereby sheltering them and us from confronting or learning from them as unfulfilled desires. In Marcus's narrative, punk's translation from utopian impulse ("what should be") into spectacle ("what is") marks the site at which History contains punk and makes a footnote of it; History itself becomes a spectacle. In contrast to Marcus, I propose that the Sex Pistols exhibited the will, prominent within the English Scene, *to live historical time*, in Guy Debord's words. In *Society of the Spectacle*, Debord describes the rise to power of the bourgeoisie and explains that the "victory of the bourgeoisie was the victory of a profoundly historical time—the time corresponding to the economic form of production" (104): official History becomes "economic history" or the History of the economy. He adds that "history, which had hitherto appeared to express nothing more than the activity of individual members of the ruling class, and had thus been conceived of as a chronology of events, was now perceived in its general movement—an inexorable movement that crushed individuality before it" (105). It was the desire to retain the notion of a history that could be participated in that flowed through the English Scene.

One response to this problem of history/History appears in McLaren's attempt to figure, along with the Sex Pistols, within official, economic History. It appears in an unrepressed form—since this desire is in no way inimical to the commercial production of music—in McLaren's pursuit of the major labels and the series of contracts that he and the Pistols signed with them. The manager and band obtained an at least momentary place within the economic History of the commercial record industry.

More in line with my project here, however, is punk's method for mediating between economics and some other method of formulating history. Punk's mediatory strategy is negation; it is the attempt to live history by negating Historical tradition through breaking with it and thereby clearing a space for a new form to emerge.[12] As Peter Bürger writes, "[T]he historical avant-garde movements cause a break with tradition and a subsequent change in the representational system" (63). Although punk might occur too late to be considered avant-garde, its negation does cause a shock which creates a break that marks the vanguard of a new "representational system." Bürger adds that in "contrast to the constant change of individual *means* of representation, which marks the development of art, the change of the system of representation . . . is a historically decisive event" (116). I attribute this "decisiveness" in part to the *collective* rather than individual aspect of the change. The Sex Pistols alone were not enough to constitute a real break, nor have I been arguing that they were, but the will to history that they bore, and that eventually informed the English Scene as a whole, constituted a shift in mass culture's means of representation.

As Bürger indicates, the shift begins with a break made possible by a shock. Before punk and the Sex Pistols, mass culture and especially its music component had become reified and remote from what Dick Hebdige considers "working class concerns." According to Hebdige, in the mid-'70s Glam Rock held sway in England, with fans who were over twenty adhering to David Bowie, Lou Reed, and Roxy Music (62). He adds that glam "tended to alienate the majority of working-class youth" because of its musicians' "extreme foppishness, incipient élitism, and morbid pretensions to art and intellect" as well as their "lyrics and lifestyles" that became "progressively more disengaged from the mundane concerns of everyday life" (62). Hebdige credits the most financially successful glam rocker of the mid-'70s, David Bowie, with "opening up questions of sexual identity which had previously been repressed, ignored or merely hinted at in rock and youth culture" (61) but closes down the possibility that those questions could figure among English youth culture's "everyday concerns," which he describes as characterized by a "working classness," a "scruffiness and earthiness" (63), and focused upon how "the passage from childhood to maturity was traditionally accomplished" (62). Hebdige elides the gendered aspect of what he reads as punk's rejection of ambiguously constructed sexual identities in favor of heterosexually constructed ones.

Although the popularity of glam is debatable, as I have indicated above, by the mid-'70s the commercial record industry (the Big Six) in the United States and England was investing large amounts of capital in primarily pop and rock performers: John Denver, Elton John, Paul McCartney and Wings, and Barbra Streisand in 1974; Elton John and Captain and Tenille in 1975; and Peter Frampton, Fleetwood Mac, the Eagles, and Johnnie Taylor in 1976. In the arena, the space in which these acts performed, the distance between the audience and the stage dramatized the class differences between the two. Arena rock fits the model for the spectacle that Debord describes, with reference to "cultural centers," as capable of recapturing "isolated individuals as individuals *isolated together*" (122). He adds that, in the spectacle, "[a]ll that once was directly lived has become mere representation" (12). The spectacle radically separates the few performers from the immense audiences and denies the possibility of interchanges between them, producing "a flat universe bounded on all sides by the spectacle's *screen*, [so that] the consciousness of the spectator has only figmentary interlocutors which subject it to a one-way discourse" (153). The pop and rock stars stood alone and at a great remove from their audiences and performed as the spokespeople for the Big Six that lurked, invisible, in the wings behind them.[13] The names of the bands from the '70s also emphasize the cult of the rock "artist"/"musician": of the ten groups that I list above, seven were named after the principal performers, encouraging audience members to cathect these individuals while regarding the rest of the bands' members as back-up musicians.

In my description of the relations between major label performers and their audiences, I do not mean to shut down the disruption that audience members have the potential to embody at a major label artist performance or the possibility that a single person, group of concert goers, or entire audience might create readings of performances that the music industry neither intends nor condones. Such disruptions and readings would, again, fall outside of the History of the music industry. In short, I do not mean to construct a rigid opposition between active performers and passive audiences. However, while I have attempted to leave open the possibility of active major label audiences, in examining the material arrangements of punk and major label shows, the punk venues strike me as much more likely to facilitate active audiences, while major label shows seem calculated to prevent them.

The pop and rock music industry as a spectacle was punk's target. In order to enter into the history of mass culture, punk had to assault and break with the tradition put in place by the creators of that history—the commercial music industry. To change the means of representation, the old means had to be attacked and exposed as false and contradictory. Toward this end, English punk attempted to negate the spectacle itself, but its attack upon the spectacle assumed the paradoxical form of hyper-spectacle, of endeavoring to push all the way through the spectacle in order to expose its contradictions in an unconscious effort to come out the other side of it and arrive at something that was *not-spectacle*.

A question now arises: What aesthetic form did the music of the spectacle take in the realm of mass culture and music? Even if accomplished with extremely broad strokes, the task of sketching the aesthetics of mid-'70s pop and rock looms as a daunting project that I will not undertake here.[14] However, the *form* of the music industry's major product of that era can be quickly delineated. As I mentioned above, the capital investment in rock and pop, the arena venues that that investment necessitated, the consequent distancing of musicians from their audiences in the social and material spaces of class, and the immense salaries that performers garnered all combined to establish the apotheosis of the singer-songwriter as the creative "artist" doing "important work" in the mid-'70s. Such work supposedly warranted the large advances that the major labels paid performers. In short, the very form of the arena-rock spectacle served to guarantee that the audience maintained the proper attitudes of awe and respect toward the spectacle of the performer. As Simon Barker, an early member of the Sex Pistols's fan club, the Bromley Contingent, says about Glam Rock in England, whose labels trafficked in similar means of representing their artists: "It became a lifestyle. Roxy [Music, an English glam band] perpetuated that: seeing [Brian] Eno have tea with Salvador Dalí. Bowie had paved the way but they took it a little further" (qtd. in Savage, 145). Barker's comment suggests that Brian Eno, as a representative of the music industry, deliberately and publicly demonstrated the differences between himself and his fans, who presumably could not arrange to have tea with an iconic surrealist painter such as Dalí. Punk might also constitute a range of lifestyles, but for Barker these "styles" would not hinge upon differences between the social mobility of the performers and the audiences. Additionally, punks would not publicly attach themselves to a representative of an already-established form of high art, such as Dalí.

In 1976, the year before A&M signed the Sex Pistols, the label had the top album of the year: Peter Frampton's *Frampton Comes Alive* sold more than thirteen million copies. Frampton was a singer-songwriter and guitarist who established himself in the late '60s in two bands, the Herd and Humble Pie (Theroux and Gilbert, 242). On May 10 of the next year, hard on the heels of its success with Frampton, A&M signed the Sex Pistols outside of Buckingham Palace. Although the history of the Sex Pistols offers numerous examples of the hyper-spectacular, the signing of the Pistols to A&M serves as a moment in which the desires underpinning the English punk scene became visible, especially in relation to Peter Frampton's work, if this staged signing is read as an expression of collective desires in an encoded form. Signing a "talent" such as Frampton, whose singles "Show Me the Way," "Baby I Love Your Way," and "Do You Feel Like We Do" carried his album to the top of the charts, maintained the arena rock spectacle: although Frampton's performance was pure spectacle, it did not acknowledge itself as such. Instead, it leaned upon the music industry's rationalization of the spectacle, which was that the artist was worth an impressive advance because of his talent and proficiency. No doubt Frampton's most impressive talent, for A&M, was actually his ability to move more than thirteen million units.[15]

The signing of the Pistols signified something else: it publicly demonstrated that a major label[16] would sign a band to a two-year, £150,000 contract *solely on the basis of its spectacular image,* hoping and trusting that spectacle would translate into sales. The signing reads as the English Scene's desire to pierce through the fiction of the spectacle and show it for what it is: the Pistols demonstrated that, when tempted, the same apparatus that, to sell its products, mobilizes the fiction of a depth model, of a real talent or artistry behind a band or artist's image or appearance, will also forsake that model and all claims of quality or aesthetics in order to sell a band that announces itself as nothing but spectacle, nothing but appearance. In this exposure of the spectacular character of the music industry, the money becomes foregrounded and attached directly to spectacle rather than to aesthetics: A&M was obviously not signing the Pistols for any reason other than to fashion them into commodities. This signing therefore falls back, retroactively, upon all signings to taint them with their spectacular character, with the fact that the spectacle itself is the commodity, perhaps even the newly dominant form of the commodity, as Debord claims.

The signing itself demonstrated, in microcosm, the type of spectacular behavior that the Pistols had already become famous for by March 1977 and maintained, on or off stage, from the beginning to the end of their short career. The actual signing of the papers in front of the palace was uneventful, although the juxtaposition of a punk band with English royalty suggests some parallels: both lack depth and are figureheads, for an industry or a nation. Both are types of spectacle. Later, after a press conference at which the band drank heavily, the Pistols arrived with McLaren at A&M's offices. Paul Cook and Sid Vicious fought in the limousine on the way over. McLaren describes their subsequent arrival: "When we arrived at A&M Records, they all got out, Sid without any shoes, Paul with a black eye and blood dripping down his shirt. Steve was carrying bottles in his jacket and in his inside pocket, and the same went for Sid who was catatonic" (qtd. in Savage 317). They visited the offices to discuss their first single for A&M, to meet the people with whom they would be working, and to celebrate the signing. None of these events occurred, but Sid cut his foot, swore at a secretary, smashed a toilet bowl and a bathroom window, and then bathed his foot in another toilet. Cook and Johnny Rotten threw wine around the offices and at Sid, and Steve Jones went into the women's bathroom by mistake and propositioned the women whom he surprised there (Savage 319). Jon Savage concludes: "The Sex Pistols were supposed to be bad but they were stretching the limits of the playpen.

Although Green [the A&M executive who oversaw the signing] had expected a certain wildness, the spectacle at the New King's Road offices was both excessive and squalid" (318).

While the show that the Pistols put on for the A&M employees only accounts for one of the registers in which they performed, I have concentrated upon it because it marks a point at which the English punk scene directly encountered its primary target: the commercial music industry. McLaren's strategy was to attack it from within its ranks, as a member, not in order to replace it with another option but to expose its contradictions. The English punks' collective desire to create a type of history in which they could participate surfaced at A&M's offices when McLaren and the Pistols attacked the music industry's official History of what rock means and what its means of representation signify. In order to establish an unofficial history, the English Scene's punks created a moment of shock in which they broke with the spectacle of the History of rock, which is the spectacle of rock's *economic* history—the history of the most popular and best selling albums and singles—masked as the History of "rock as art." The break took the shape of a hyper-spectacle, a spectacle that acknowledges itself as spectacle, an image and an appearance that does not pretend to correspond to anything beyond itself. Specifically, the English punk scene foregrounded its spectacular character in order to disavow the deeper meanings that might adhere to commercial rock sold as the art of singer-songwriters. However, in announcing that the rock industry was just economics whose History was the narrative of its labels' financial successes and failures, English punk can be read as expressing the desire that rock could mean something besides economics, that it could represent something besides sales. The English Scene's attempt to push beyond spectacle without ever arriving there itself betrayed a desire for an outside to economics.

A further desire emerges from England's early punks, the desire for an identity that was neither founded upon nor represented by appearance. Again, punks attempted to face down spectacle but this time in the form of fashion, and, again, they turned the spectacle back upon itself in their hyper-spectacular clothes. Dick Hebdige takes a different tack in approaching punk fashion. He describes it as a "rendering" of "working classness metaphorically in chains and hollow cheeks, 'dirty' clothing (stained jackets, tarty see-through blouses) and rough and ready diction" (63). For Hebdige, punk fashion can be read semiotically as a system of signs that represents the working class. In response to English Glam Rock in particular, punk renders visible, for the cultural theorist at least, contradictions between the upper class that Glam Rock fashion represents and the working-class significations of punk. In short, Hebdige locates in punk the expression of a cultural desire to reassert the existence of the working class within the field of commercial rock, where upper-class trappings were privileged and signs of the working class were for the most part invisible.

If I extend Hebdige's semiotic approach, I might argue that English punk fashion represents not just the working class. Safety pins and clothespins for fastening clothes, threadbare, hole-filled, and dirty garments, as well as trash can liners used as clothing could all serve as stylized reminders of the lumpen proletariat living at or near the poverty level, a group that mass culture forms such as Glam Rock in England and mid-'70s arena rock in general ignored in favor of valorizing notions of art, glamour, and beauty. With these signs of poverty and of the working class, punk is demanding that someone recognize and acknowledge the existence of the working class and the lumpen proletariat. But who would do the acknowledging, and what forms would that acknowledgment take? Would a mediated demand emerging from a mass culture group require a mediated response from another such group? More importantly, why does punk style need to be understood in Hebdige's strictly indexical terms, where signifier x represents y, a signified class position? These questions seem particularly troublesome in light of the English Scene's relations with the spectacle that I have outlined above. If punks' bad and shocking behavior correlates less with authentically bad and shocking acts than with the exaggeration of those acts as spectacle, then why would style obey a different logic? What I propose, instead, is that a variety of often conflicting markers that work in a number of ways constitute punk style. Two sets of markers in particular—Nazi paraphernalia and sexual bondage gear—suggest a reading different from Hebdige's.

Following the logic of Hebdige's index, punk's adoption of Nazi accoutrements—and the swastika in particular—and fetish-wear would represent Nazis and practitioners of bondage and sado-masochism. In contrast, Mark Sinker writes that English punks' styles reflected their desire

> no longer to be noticed. Dressing-to-shock (zips, rips, binbags, tattoos, the pretty-slut tease, fetish-wear taken casually public) is adopted against the instant society *stops* being shocked. Stops being shocked by surface gestures anyway. . . . [Punks] only wanted a world where what you wore was all just fashion: where how you look isn't who you are. (124)

He adds that "Sid and Siouxsie wore swastikas because they *weren't* Nazis. . . . The only acceptable function of fashion was the overthrow (for all time) of the very metaphysics of fashion" (125). Sinker's argument suggests that one of the desires reflected in fashion parallels those attached to spectacle that are legible in punk behavior. Punks adopt fashions that mix codes related to class, fascism, and sexual practices not to represent those categories but to exaggerate them, to demonstrate that the surface markers of fashion, and by association all clothing, are purely spectacle and, as such, do not correlate with their supposed social referents. In short, if punk fashion can be read as a critique of any of the categories that it invokes, it critiques them not by representing them as the signifier represents the signified, for Saussure, but by calling into question the material means too often understood as representing class, politics, and sexuality: fashion. However, as I will explain below, punks did not empty Nazi and bondage accoutrements of their signifying power, nor were these fashions, both of which deliberately displayed structures of dominance and subordination, coincidental choices.

To return to Bürger's assertion that shock and its contingent break with historical tradition allow for the possibility of a change in the means of representation: while punk evidences the desire for such a break, it does not mobilize shock in exactly the manner that Bürger employs it. He defines it as a "refusal to provide meaning" (80) and explains that this refusal "is experienced as shock by the recipient. And this is the intention of the avant-gardist artist, who hopes that such withdrawal of meaning will direct the reader's attention to the fact that the conduct of one's life is questionable and that it is necessary to change it" (80). This is a tall order. At best, punk's use of shock expressed the desire to break the signifying chain, the means of representation, that linked mid-'70s fashion with identity. For example, punks donned fetish-wear, working-class clothes (especially boots made by the Dr. Martens Company), and swastikas in public, wearing them when and where they were not engaging in sex, work, or Nazi politics. This sartorial gesture produces shock where it disconnects the markers of social groups from the groups that they are taken to signify. A break in the means of representation follows the shock, because the old means no longer serve: no longer do Dr. Martens represent working classness, nor does fetish-wear represent sexuality, nor do swastikas represent Nazism. Perhaps the next person whom one encounters wearing Dr. Martens comes from the working class but perhaps not.

Punks did not want their surfaces to be legible; they did not want their surfaces to contain them within traditional categories of sexuality, class, and politics. As Sinker suggests, this commentary on fashion does not attempt to replace the spectacle of fashion with the reality of an identity that hides behind it, but punk's attempt to cancel fashion as a reflection of identity, to cancel the idea that there is a representational relationship between style and identity by pointing up the spectacular character of fashion, preserves a potential but empty space for some not-yet-existing means of representing identity. Punk style raises the question of what forces construct identity besides style, and where does the negation of style leave identity as a construct?

Despite what I have been reading as punks' efforts to sever style from signification, punks do not wholly succeed in this endeavor. Nazi and bondage accoutrements produce more than shock and a clean break with meaning: they also make visible what is generally erased from but also constitutive of bourgeois culture—the social relation between the bourgeois and the working classes, the relation of the owners of the means of production to the workers. Greil Marcus explains the punk use of the swastika: "It meant, history books to the contrary, that fascism had won the Second World War: that contemporary Britain was a welfare-state parody of fascism, where people had no freedom to make their own lives" (118). Marcus's reading of the swastika, while perhaps generous to a fault, encourages an interpretation of punks' adoption of the swastika as an allegorization of the imbalance of power between the members of the ruling class and those working to support them or living on the dole. Donning sex clothing allowed punks to embody a similar allegorization.

It is worth noting that punks wore not just conventionally erotic clothing but bondage-wear and accoutrements associated with sado-masochism in particular, such as bondage straps and their accompanying rings, studded and spiked belts, bracelets, and collars (including dog collars and chains), etc. This paraphernalia explicitly raises the issue of power, while placing punks not in a dominating position but in a dominated one. To the implied question "Who is being fucked?" this punk scene seems to reply, "We are, we don't like it, and we will force everyone to observe us being fucked." The ripped clothes of this scene also suggest that the wearers have suffered a violent attack. In this instance, bondage-wear takes on an added nuance: it does not represent sex directly but a social relationship between two groups, one of which controls the other. Bondage-wear allegorizes the class system as a brutal one in which all of the power is on one side. In tandem with this desire, the masochistic impulse that the clothing bears indicates that a type of pleasure might also be attainable not in abject submission but in rendering this relation explicit and public. Just as masochists enjoy being dominated in contexts in which power relations are rendered explicit, punks take pleasure in rendering social relations similarly explicit.

In punks' appropriation of fetish-gear can also be seen their suspicion and professed hatred of the hippie movement and its co-optation of the idea of "free love" from the early twentieth century. Punks responded to the hippies' supposed liberation of desire as a form of what Herbert Marcuse terms "repressive desublimation": repressed cultural and sexual desires return, but rather than assuming liberated forms they are recodified into new repressive structures, in this case "free love," "open marriages," etc. In the semi-documentary film, *The Great Rock 'n' Roll Swindle* (1980), Malcolm McLaren claims that he invented the slogan "Never trust a hippie,"[17] and, whether he did or not, most punks did not trust anything connected to hippies. By coding sexuality not as liberated or liberating but as sadistic, masochistic, public, and shot through with power relations, punks negated it in its hippie incarnation, where it served as an extension of liberalism. However, punk again demands that the means of representation change by breaking with the traditional means without proffering new ones.

For the English Scene—as exemplified by the Sex Pistols and punk fashion—the initial three desires that ran through the New York Scene did not figure as prominently as new impulses to figure within history and to critique the commercial music industry and fashion as spectacles consisting of signifiers that lack signifieds (worth or value in the case of rock and pop; class, politics, and sexuality in the case of fashion). However, where the English scene did not revivify New York's specific forms of resisting commercialization, its hyper-spectacle served as a different sort of critique, a working-through and exaggeration of commercial and spectacular logic instead of the attempted disengagement from the commercial apparatus that the New York Scene attempted. The English Scene drew desires from the New York Scene but redirected them in order to stave off, at least temporarily, succumbing to the music industry. It targeted the commercial music apparatus more directly, because the New York Scene failed to do so and was eventually overwhelmed by that industry.

But, as with New York, the English Scene only existed for as long as its repressed desires could speak, for as long as it could prevent itself from being stamped into the mold of major label product by the dominant order's repressive apparatus, the Big Six. Despite the major labels' efforts in England to advance their commercial desire regarding the Sex Pistols, McLaren and the Pistols' behavior highlighted the spectacular character of the commercial music industry without falling under its control until the Pistols signed with Warner Brothers in 1977 and agreed to an American and European tour financed by the label. Commenting on the tour's commencement, Savage writes that, "although they had had no major hit," the Pistols came to the United States "not as underdogs but international celebrities backed by one of America's largest labels. As far as Warner Brothers were [sic] concerned, the Sex Pistols were Rock-stars-to-be, a position they had not yet achieved in England, where they were hamstrung by notoriety" (444). McLaren attempted to sabotage the label's desire by insisting upon a tour of the South, with some success,[18] but the publicity and notoriety that the band generated during its passage through the southern United States climaxed when it had to conclude its tour in San Francisco's Winterland Ballroom before an audience of five thousand instead of the much smaller hall, with a capacity of five hundred, into which it had originally been booked.

By most accounts, the Winterland show of January 14, 1978, that proved to be the Pistols' final show was terrible on two levels: the band failed as spectacle and as an attempt at hyper-spectacle. When faced with having to become a genuine arena-rock attraction, to perform the spectacle seriously *as spectacle,* the Pistols disintegrated. Aping the security guards outside the big top is one thing, but aping the circus itself is another. Vic Vale, the publisher of the early San Francisco zine *Search and Destroy,* comments upon that last show: "You had the very thing which the Sex Pistols set out to critique, you had a spectacle, and I don't know if there is a way you can defeat expectations by being a band playing on a stage about ten feet above the audience, with bouncers, burly jock-like characters hired to stop people getting onto the stage" (qtd. in Savage, 457). What Vale terms "defeating expectations" resonates with hyper-spectacle. At Winterland, it became impossible to create a hyper-spectacle in a commercial venue designed specifically for absorbing such a show and rendering it a consumable commodity for a distant and complacent audience.

In 1977, the Sex Pistols signed with Warner Brothers, The Clash with CBS, The Damned with Stiff, The Stranglers with UA, X-Ray Spex with Virgin, Buzzcocks with UA, The Vibrators with RAK, The Adverts with Stiff, Generation X with Chrysallis, and Chelsea with Step Forward, and these bands were only the most famous partaking in that year's business arrangements. By 1978, the fleeting moment in which the desire for hyper-spectacle—for some version of history, class, politics, and sexuality that might emerge beyond the spectacle—competed with the overriding music industry effort to commercialize the English Scene had passed. As the New York Scene had in 1976, the English Scene dissolved when its various desires were subordinated to commercial forces that originated outside of the scene itself.

THE CALIFORNIA HARDCORE SCENE

The third major punk scene emerged in 1978 as the California Hardcore Scene and dissolved in 1982. In Huntington Beach, L.A., and San Francisco, around Black Flag and the Dead Kennedys, a constellation of desires emerged that both revivified some of the earlier punk scenes' desires and added new ones to them.[19] In the mid- to late '70s, California had already spawned a Hollywood and a San Francisco scene, but both of these began to fade away after the Sex Pistols played their Winterland show, and San Francisco and L.A. venues began banning punk shows.[20] As Gina Arnold explains about L.A., "the [punk] venues began to disappear, busted one by one by the LAPD. . . . And then it was 1980 and there was a sudden influx of bands from the valley and southern suburbs, Redondo Beach, Orange County. Black Flag and the Circle Jerks and TSOL [True Sounds of Liberty] and the Descendants took over the punk scene" (36–37). Other important bands in the L.A. half of this scene include Fear, Social Distortion, China White, and The Minutemen. In San Francisco, the major bands were Dead Kennedys, Minimal Man, Flipper, Social Unrest, Crucifix, and Fang.[21]

According to Craig Lee and Shreader, who wrote the first half of *Hardcore California: A History of Punk and New Wave*, early in the summer of 1980,

"Patrick Goldstein, a writer with the *L.A. Times,* ran an article called 'The SLAM!' . . . that freely exploited and made media-meat out of the suburban Punk scene, citing that punks (especially Orange County kids) were criminal, vicious, and *dangerous*" (Belsito and Davis, 46). Lee and Shreader add that the response to this article "was a disaster for such bands as Black Flag, the Circle Jerks, Fear, China White, etc. It banned them from clubs, jeopardized any party they played, flyer they put out, and even fans that wore their stickers. The Huntington Beach PD began to refer to bands as 'gangs'" (46–49). Regardless of whether or not a direct causal link can be established between one newspaper article and the ensuing behavior of club owners and the Huntington Beach Police Department, the emerging hardcore bands in L.A. were prohibited from playing shows.

Consequently, Black Flag did not need to avoid commercialization; commercialization avoided the band. However, refusing to adopt a different aesthetic[22] in order to make their music more saleable and acceptable to club owners, the members of Black Flag picked up and advanced the New York Scene's desires to resist commercialization and seize the means of production. Gina Arnold writes that Black Flag was "really the first band to be called hardcore. But its main importance to L.A.'s scene was organizational: more than any other early punk band, they were adept at finding places to play, getting permits for outdoor concerts and booking one-offs [single events as opposed to periodic or semi-periodic events] into town halls. And they were immensely popular" (37). Mike Watt, the bass player and sometime vocalist for the Minutemen, credits Black Flag with founding the independent band national tour as well: "Black Flag really blazed a trail for us. . . . That's what they should really be remembered for, making a circuit. . . . They found every anticlub in the country, and everyone chased after 'em down the road" (43). Because the more commercial clubs closed their doors to them, the band members took it upon themselves to found a noncommercial circuit of venues, both in California and elsewhere. In early 1981, "[p]olice harassment makes it impossible to get a gig anywhere in LA, so Black Flag starts touring around the U.S." (41), explains David Grad in "Everything Went Black: A Complete Oral History," which he wrote for the national zine, *Punk Planet,* in 1997.

In contrast to the L.A. scene, and perhaps partially because San Francisco's major media linked violence with San Francisco punks less than their counterparts in L.A. did, San Francisco clubs did not ban punks. More importantly, picking up and advancing the desire to resist commercialization that surfaced first in the New York Scene, several small entrepreneurs operating apart from and against the major labels opened small clubs in San Francisco that catered specifically to punk shows. The most famous of these opened in 1976, when Dirk Dirksen began booking bands into the Mabuhay Gardens, a Filipino supper club, on Monday and Tuesday nights. He was interested in "an 'organic living nightclub' in which others would do their trip and he could attempt to document contemporary music" (Belsito and Davis, 68). By January 1977, Dirksen's small company, Dirksen-Miller Productions, had taken over all of the Mabuhay's bookings, and by 1978 the Mabuhay showcased almost exclusively punk acts (74). From 1979 through the early '80s, a whole series of small, noncommercial clubs that catered primarily to punk opened and closed, including 330 Grove Street, the Deaf Club, the A-Hole, Club Foot, Club Generic, Jet Wave, Temple Beautiful, and Valencia Tool and Die. For the first time in the history of punk, a supportive network of punk clubs existed that could resist the major labels to some degree by separating themselves from them. Although punks made a similar attempt to establish a material base for L.A.'s scene (the Hong Kong is the best example of an L.A. club engaged in this effort), they never had the success in L.A. that San Francisco enjoyed.

Hardcore bands made aesthetic choices that helped ensure the club situation described above. The punk rock that typified the New York and English scenes, such as the songs of the Ramones and the Sex Pistols, obeyed a different aesthetic than the rock and pop music of the mid-'70s. Both bands played at more rapid tempi than Elton John, John Denver, or Peter Frampton, avoided solos, and adhered to a minimal idea of instrumentation: they avoided keyboards and wind instruments in favor of a guitar, bass guitar, drum kit, and vocalist. Johnny Rotten's chanting and screaming and the Ramones' rapid-paced vocals that bore a distinctly flat affect replaced the emotive singing of the major label bands.

In keeping with the short punk song format that New York and English bands originated, Black Flag songs are extremely brief. While the commercial pop or rock song tended to clock in around three minutes, only three of the fifteen songs on Black Flag's first album, *Damaged,* are between three and four minutes long; the other twelve all last about two minutes, although one is only thirty-one seconds long ("Spray Paint"). All of the songs showcase short, simple lyrics, and the musicians play their instruments even more quickly than the Ramones and Sex Pistols did.[23] Greg Ginn, the band's lead guitar player, explains that "guitar leads didn't come into the music with early Black Flag because we didn't have a real rhythm section for about a year, so I couldn't drop out and keep a strong rhythm at the same time. That had a lot to do with the initial songs. We didn't have a problem with it being simple" (38). The band worked through four lead singers before settling on Henry Rollins, who sang/shouted for them on their first LP and continued as lead singer until Greg Ginn dissolved the band in August 1986. Rollins perfected an adolescent-sounding scream (in punk texts, "snotty" is usually the preferred word for classically punk vocal mannerisms), with which he attacked his audience. The Ramones were fast, Johnny Rotten was snotty, and Henry Rollins was both, in addition to sounding more brutish than most of the earlier scenes' singers. Frequently, he physically fought with audience members before, during, or after shows. The aesthetics of Black Flag's music and of their behavior (the band members understood attacking the audience sonically or physically as constitutive of their music's force) prevented most labels from considering them seriously and led MCA to drop them quickly after it released their first full-length album.

The Dead Kennedys' (DKs') aesthetic choices paralleled Black Flag's: the band played extremely quickly and aggressively, and Jello Biafra's vocals were both aggressive and snotty, although he added a taunting, self-righteous air to his delivery as well as chanting/screaming his words more than singing them. Craig Lee and Shreader describe the "thrash" sound of the bands that, in terms of musical style, inspired the DKs or were inspired by them as "any music that used jackhammer tempos which effectively turned the beat into a hum. The vocalist delivered a similarly paced diatribe about anything from McDonald's hamburgers to murdering bus drivers" (Belsito and Davis, 118). (Unlike Greg Ginn's guitar playing, though, East Bay Ray's was already fairly accomplished on the Dead Kennedys' first album *Fresh Fruit for Rotting Vegetables*, which was released in 1979 on IRS Records and re-released in 1980 on Alternative Tentacles Records.) As in the case of Black Flag, the DKs did not make aesthetic choices likely to endear them to the major labels.

In the summer of 1981, Black Flag recorded their first LP, *Damaged*, and Greg Ginn, the band's guitarist and founder, made a deal with Unicorn Records to distribute it. MCA then became interested in Black Flag and agreed to release the album under its name and logo; however, after the album was released in 1982 and the MCA employees in charge of the deal heard it, they withdrew from their deal with the band, claiming that the album was "anti-parent." Unicorn did not pay the band for the album, and the band attempted to terminate its deal with the company, but Unicorn sued the band and the judge issued an injunction against them that barred them from releasing records on their own (Grad, 41).

In the shadow (and because) of these legal wranglings, Greg Ginn formed a record label—Solid State Transformers (SST)—with the band's drummer, Chuck Dukowski, on which they began releasing Black Flag's music and that of other California bands, such as the Minutemen and the Descendants. Mike Watt describes the L.A. punk scene in an interview with Gina Arnold: "Punk was about more than just starting a band, it was about starting a label, it was about touring, it was about taking control. It was like songwriting: you just do it. You want a record, you pay the pressing plant" (40). Ginn and Dukowski's establishment of SST records in 1978 underscores the urge that Watt expresses as "taking control." While independent record labels (labels not affiliated with the six major labels of 1980—CBS,

Warner Brothers, MCS, RCA, PolyGram, and Capitol—that were responsible for 95 percent of the records released that year, according to Arnold) had existed before this moment, SST was one of the first labels run by punks for releasing primarily punk music. SST joined Slash and Frontier Records in LA, two labels that, with SST, manifest the desire running through the California Hardcore Scene to seize control of the means of production from the major labels, or at least from non-punk labels, that seemed to stand over and against the scene. Ginn strove to attain a modicum of control over his band's work and the instruments of its production and distribution;[24] hence, the small L.A. labels can be read as a movement toward the composition and production of independent music as opposed to the reception and consumption of commercial music. In order to express desires in this fashion, the California scene channeled its desires through the necessary aesthetic means: its abrasive, noncommercial aesthetic choices protected against the draining of punks' desires into the corporate music industry, producing punk labels instead.

A parallel move occurred contemporaneously in San Francisco. In November 1978, "out of sheer necessity, San Francisco's first independent record label catering to Punk was born" (Belsito and Davis, 93): Chris Knab and Howie Klein's 415 Records. By "necessity," Belsito and Davis mean that no label apart from a punk label was likely to take a chance on the aesthetic that was beginning to emerge in Northern California. In 1979, Steve Tupper founded Subterranean Records for punk releases, and the same year Jello Biafra, the lead singer and songwriter for the Dead Kennedys, began releasing Dead Kennedys material on the Alternative Tentacles (AT) label that he founded in 1978. AT emerged as a label partly in response to the decision of IRS Records to drop the Dead Kennedys after the band members claimed that the label was unfairly censoring their work.

While Black Flag and the Dead Kennedys employed similar means to produce their music, these bands also served to exemplify two opposing vectors that surfaced to face one another in the California Hardcore Scene. The members of Black Flag set out to confront and attack their audiences, both sonically and physically. Kira Roessler comments on the band's approach to performing: "I was trying with my bass to slam [the audience] against the back wall," and she adds that she and the band "were forcing the crowd to submit to our [sic] will of the band—for longer than they could stand it" (44). Bill Stevenson, one of the band's drummers (there was a series of four drummers during the band's career), observes that the "only part [of being in the band] that seemed like something to write home about was that we had to fight a lot. ... The music drove people to that extreme and it was an evolution in the way teenagers related to their rock music—not being as passive" (44), while Henry Rollins adds "that every show there was the possibility you were going to get into a fight—breaking peoples noses, knives pulled. I have cigar and cigarette burns all over me. People tried to stab me with Bic pens" (44).

In 1977, Sid Vicious, provoked by flying beer bottles, attacked an audience member in San Antonio, Texas, with his bass guitar. Black Flag's violence was different. While Vicious's attack was a random occurrence, Black Flag provoked its audiences, which responded accordingly. Stevenson comments: "We . . . had a very confrontational stage vibe . . . we were trying to play through the audience rather than to the audience" (44). The band's aggressive tactics testify to a desire not unlike the Sex Pistols' need to expose the rock spectacle for what it was, to reveal the lack behind it, but, unlike the Pistols, Black Flag did not try for hyper-spectacle; instead, the band attempted to draw meaning, in the form of the body, back into the space that the spectacle, as pure appearance, left unoccupied.

In 1979, Billy Joel's *52nd Street* (CBS) album and the Doobie Brothers' *Minute by Minute* (Warner Brothers) album occupied the top two chart positions, while in 1980 they were replaced by Pink Floyd's *The Wall* (Columbia/CBS) and (interestingly) Michael Jackson's *Off the Wall* (Epic), and in '81 by REO Speedwagon's *Hi Infidelity* (Epic) and Kenny Rogers's *Greatest Hits* (Liberty). Despite the New York and English Punk scenes, the major labels still dominated the commercial music industry and financed the continuing myth of the singer-songwriter in Billy Joel, Kenny Rogers, and Michael Jackson (to some extent, although other factors such as dance and his family's history as performers were also integral to his appeal). Additionally, progressive rock, with the technical proficiency that it demanded, came into its own with Pink Floyd. Like the commercial groups of the mid- and late '70s, all of these top acts performed in arenas that inscribed in space the differences in class between the performers and audiences.

In the shadow of the major label spectacles, Black Flag offered its fans a space in which they could affect and be affected by mass culture in material ways—through physical contact, through shouting and being shouted at. Although the band once performed for 4,500 people in Santa Monica, it mainly played small clubs in which Henry Rollins could scream at audience members inches from their faces or engage with them from the floor of the club when there was no stage. In place of the untouchable character of arena rock acts, Black Flag dared its audiences to become involved, and fights became components of the shows. In the interaction between the band and audience can be read the desire to institute a form of mass culture in which the audience can participate directly and forcefully. A space was created in which this desire could be expressed collectively, along with frustration over the spectacle that pop and rock music had become, and Rollins established himself as a lightning rod for absorbing the charge of this combination of desire and anger. His body became the surface upon which fans inscribed

with Bic pens their antipathy for the separation inherent in the lead
singer/audience split; after all, he was still a lead singer, and he rarely parted
with his microphone.

Black Flag harangued its audiences and fought with them, paradoxically,
in order to build a conventionally masculine sense of community and collectivity and to inject the material aspect of physical contact, the body, potential
danger back into the rock show. This practice was gendered in the sense that
it discouraged women from attending or participating in hardcore shows.[25] In
contrast to Black Flag, but achieving the same results, the Dead Kennedys
encouraged stage-diving and audience participation in place of fighting.
While Biafra sang, audience members would climb on stage and dance with
him briefly (often imitating his idiosyncratic writhing and gesturing in a
dance dubbed the "Biafra") before leaping or diving off the stage to be caught
(or dropped) by crowd members. DKs shows were interactive events at which
anyone could share the stage with the band briefly. Biafra also joined the audience on the floor frequently, where fans would pile on top of him, and often
proffered the crowd his microphone so that it could sing along with a song's
chorus or simply take over the singing duties from him.

In an effort to build collectivity, the DKs, and Biafra in particular, also
hearkened back to '60s and '70s notions of protest songs and grass roots political activism and tried to rally their audiences around specific social issues. In
1976, the Sex Pistols lampooned Queen Elizabeth's Silver Jubilee—and some
of its specific ramifications—in the song "God Save the Queen," but a clear
political position never evolved for the English Scene. The DKs revivified this
nascent impulse (which, for the English Scene, was actually slightly more
explicit in The Clash than in the Pistols). Biafra wanted the DKs to remobi-
lize what he understood as the best of American '60s and '70s activism. In an
interview in the on-line journal, *Bad Subjects,* in 1997, Biafra likens the "heart
and soul of punk" to the "heart and soul of hippies . . . when they were radical," and in the introduction to a re-publication of the San Francisco early
punk zine, *Search and Destroy,* he tells the zine's editor, V. Vale: "Spiritually, I
think punk was in tune with the *early* hippies. . . . I'd once had so much belief
in everything 'hippie' being so great: the Diggers with their free store concept
and serving free dinners in the park; watching the Vietnam war being brought
down; watching Nixon leave Washington in disgrace" (v). In contrast to Malcolm McLaren's early rejection of anything associated with hippies, Biafra
selectively recuperated a few ideas from hippie liberalism and retooled them
into punk practices.

The DKs' invocation of grass roots activism became apparent first in
Biafra's return to the protest song format of the '60s and '70s (and earlier).
Almost every DKs song protests a specific political issue or cluster of issues.
On the first DKs single, released on Alternative Tentacles in 1979, Biafra

sings a song that he and John Greenway co-wrote, "California Über Alles," that raises the problem of the possibility or lack thereof for progressive political action in the late '70s. Biafra rails against what he sees as the erosion of the early hippies' radicalness. He imagines a dystopian world in which Jerry Brown, who embodies both the "adult" and the "aging hippie" and was governor of California when the song was penned, is elected president of the United States and rules it as a despot intent on converting the entire nation to what Biafra terms "orgo-deco." In the interview with Vale, Biafra adds that after the radical hippies became prominent, he watched "everything slowly turn into this mellowed-out, New Age (the term came later; I called it 'orgo-deco') 'all-natural ingredients at twice the price while you're listening to James Taylor' bullshit" (v). In the song, Jerry Brown announces to U.S. citizens: "Your kids will meditate in school . . . Zen fascists will control you / 100% natural / You will jog for the master race / And always wear the happy face. . . . Mellow out or you will pay . . . DIE on organic poison gas." The song conflates fascism in its '30s and '40s German incarnation with what Biafra feared might be the end of the possibility of progressive politics, which would be replaced by a forced and monolithic optimism belying the terror that was needed to keep it in place, in this case, the governmentally dispensed *organic* poison gas.

This song appears on the DKs' first album, along with songs aimed at raising consciousness about the neutron bomb ("Kill the Poor," an update of Swift's "A Modest Proposal"), the Cold War ("When Ya Get Drafted"), rent control ("Let's Lynch the Landlord"), chemical warfare ("Chemical Warfare"), and Cambodia/Pol Pot ("Holiday in Cambodia"). On all of their albums, most of the DKs' songs address political issues that Biafra seems to have transposed from the late '60s and early '70s to Northern California in the late '70s and early '80s. Along with these issues, he adopts some of the same political techniques of that historical moment: he attempts to generate punk collectivity through consciousness-raising. And although Biafra's protest songs employ irony and bitterness in places, they are never ironic about the possibility that music can wield political influence by binding people together around perceived problems.

Biafra also ran for mayor of San Francisco in 1979.[26] Marian Kester describes his attempt: "So what was the Punk Program for San Francisco? Here again the DKs unfurled the banner of 60's [*sic*] radicalism: like SDS [Students for a Democratic Society] before him, Biafra merely took seriously America's self-image as liberal paradise with opportunity for all" (17). His platform consisted of what Kester considers demands drawn from "liberal common sense," such as "rent control, public works programs, fixing standard rates for city services, [and] electing police" (17); however, it also demanded that businessmen on Market Street wear clown suits from nine to five, and it called for a "Board of Bribery" that would set rates for businesses and individuals wishing to purchase political influence. Biafra came in fourth in a field of ten candidates, with 4 percent of the vote (6,591 votes).

Biafra's campaign marked the place where two of the desires that constituted punk's California Hardcore Scene collided and conditioned one another. First, the impulse toward collectivity evident in Black Flag's attempt to construct a form of mass culture in which the audience could readily participate reappeared not only in stage-diving at DKs shows (and other California hardcore shows) but also in Biafra's mayoral ambitions: he attempted to establish himself as a medium through which punks could enter into the official History of their particular geographic region. His refusal to spend more than $1,500 on his campaign evidenced his desire, as well as the scene's, to crack History open to interests that are not well-backed financially. In short, Biafra and his supporters attempted to shift the official channel into History away from economics so that it might become a history of another sort, a history not wholly determined by moneyed interests. This desire is reminiscent of the Sex Pistols' attack upon the History of the music industry.

Where the Sex Pistols employed hyper-spectacle to pierce through the façade of that industry, Biafra similarly mobilized spectacle in his approach to local politics, attempting to render it ridiculous by forcing it to encompass the planks of his platform and thereby demonstrating that if he could earn votes with such a platform then the platforms and substance behind the spectacles of real politicians must be equally specious and spectacular. But Biafra's adherence to liberal common sense (as well as to the protest song) marked a tempering of the desire in punk to attack specific institutions by exposing their spectacular character. Although he ran for mayor as an underage candidate using a false name (his given name is Eric Boucher), Biafra refused to abandon completely the earnest modes of representation that New Left groups such as SDS employed in their attention to local and national politics as well as cultural forms of "protest." Black Flag bore the California Hardcore Scene's desire to re-inject material forces into the spectacle—to make the spectacle dangerous again, even if only to its participants—and the DKs' interest in grass roots and local politics combined with their refusal to treat politics as pure spectacle bore this scene's desire to transform the spectacle into a political force. The new impulse that emerges here is the will to sidestep postmodern misgivings related to representation. Rollins and Biafra were not convinced that the human body and politics had disappeared behind the spectacle, that the sign no longer denoted the relation between the signifier and the signified. This punk scene advanced a desire to return to the possibility of a material reality that can be represented and addressed culturally and politically. Although this desire originated in California, it became more salient in later scenes.

Fashion also took on a new significance in California. It no longer bore the English Scene's desire to shock and thereby alter the means of representation. In San Francisco and Los Angeles, fashion now evidenced the possibility of representing identity rather than critiquing the attempt to do so. Classic hardcore style consisted of "obligatory black leather, for those who could afford it, while torn jeans and plaid shirts sufficed for others. Headbands, leather wristbands with threateningly pointed studs, black motorcycle or combat boots and tattoos rounded out the look" (Belsito and Davis, 119). T-shirts, often with punk bands' names and logos, were popular. Hardcore punks shaved their heads or wore their hair short and all one length. These signs denoted membership in the L.A. or San Francisco punk scene, and punks' adherence to this communal style that marked its bearers as punks and made them recognizable to one another as such expressed a will to collectivity. The anonymity of the New York Scene's sartorial choices reappeared in a slightly modified form on the West Coast: punks looked fairly anonymous within their communities, but they could also be distinguished from non-punks, which was not always true in New York.

Punks in California forwent bondage gear in favor of the punk uniform that I have described above, which connoted a movement away from the problematization of sexuality and power that the English Scene invoked, in favor of a regression to the masculine and heterosexual stance that the New York Scene adopted as it moved away from the ambiguous constructions of gender that David Bowie and the New York Dolls embodied. Craig Lee and Shreader write: "Though some early punks were gay, they kept it to themselves. If you didn't have the right degree of street cool, you'd find yourself pogo'd[27] to the floor" (Belsito and Davis, 17). In terms of sexuality, "street cool" translated into conventionally masculine modes of heterosexual dress and behavior with little room for maneuvering, as the threat of violence in Lee and Shreader's comment implies. The intensified degree of physical contact between male scene members, however, foreshadowed the homoerotic elements that came to fruition in the subsequent Straight Edge Scenes.

The California Hardcore Scene inherited the remains of the New York and English scenes and redirected some of those scenes' desires, revivifying them in new forms in San Francisco and L.A. Each scene learns from past scenes and attempts to avoid their capitulations to commercialism. In California, the punk scene melded together desires from the two earlier scenes to create new strains, more resistant hybrids. The New York Scene's will toward collectivity as it appeared in CBGBs was preserved in California but brought into a relation with the English Scene's desire to transcend the spectacle in an effort to avoid commercialization. The sexuality and fashion of English punks were shunted to the side, but the desire to live historical time, and to refigure history as not-just-economics, reappeared in

California but not as hyper-spectacle. Instead, San Francisco punks tried to elect a punk mayor and raise consciousness.

But by 1982, California Hardcore had waned and almost disappeared. Regarding the L.A. contingent, Chris Morris writes that what "we think of today as 'L.A. punk rock' had atomized by 1982. Under law-enforcement fire, the beach-punk bands largely disappeared from L.A. venues" (22). More importantly, the scene's desires were gradually pressed into ready-made molds. Scene members adopted the already-established and available channels of communication. Protest songs, consciousness raising, and local politics existed as historical practices in their own right, and when punks accepted those practices as legitimate, the possibility that punk could transcend those forms or negate and transcend them disappeared. Instead, punks had to adapt to the logic underpinning the social institutions they set out to oppose. Protest songs did not seem to end wars or police actions, and new ones began. Biafra did not win the election. History appeared no less economically determined. In the California Hardcore Scene's infusion of a means of representation and resistance familiar to the institutions of local politics and the record industry, its desires took on familiar forms and could be contained as such.

THE WASHINGTON, D.C. HARDCORE SCENE
(FIRST WAVE STRAIGHT EDGE)

Existing contemporaneously for a time with the California Hardcore Scene, the Washington, D.C., Straight Edge Hardcore Scene arose in D.C. in 1979 and endured until 1985.[28] The cluster of bands that partially constituted this scene includes Bad Brains, Minor Threat, Government Issue (GI), S.O.A. (State of Alert), Rites of Spring, Scream, Beefeater, Faith, Void, Embrace, and Gray Matter, among others. The major venues, all of which were in D.C., included Madam's Organ Artist's Cooperative in 1979 and 1980 and the 9:30 Club, the Ontario Theater, The Chancery, d.c. space, and the Wilson Center from 1979 to 1985. Three structures, carefully interpreted, should reveal the dominant desires that ran through the D.C. Scene: the Dischord Records label, Revolution Summer, and the band Minor Threat. In a nutshell, here are the relations between the three. Minor Threat, which released all of its albums on Dischord Records, attempted to whip its audiences into a frenzy with aggressive songs composed of short, shouted lyrics and extremely rapid tempos. This aesthetic eventually appealed to and attracted a small contingent of neo-Nazi skinheads, who began attending Straight Edge punk shows in 1984 and 1985 and brought forms of racism and violence to the scene that had not existed there previously. In 1985, the neo-Nazis and the D.C. Scene's response to them, a movement that the scene's participants named "Revolution Summer," drew the scene to a close of sorts.

A loose idea of DIY (do-it-yourself) has been with punk since its beginning, but the D.C. Scene adopted the DIY approach from the earlier three scenes and pushed it farther. The Dischord Records label, founded by Ian MacKaye and Jeff Nelson in 1980, remains the paragon (in 2003) of punks doing it themselves. Both MacKaye and Nelson emerged from the D.C. punk scene and played together in the early straight-edge band Minor Threat that released all of its recordings on Dischord. In contrast to Ginn and Biafra, Ian MacKaye and Jeff Nelson did not initially understand their label, Dischord Records, as opposed to a commercial recording industry that stood over and against them. Instead, they envisioned it as a small label upon which they could release what MacKaye describes as "completely non-commercial music" (MacKaye, *All Ages*, 96). The point, he claims, was not to compete with the major labels but to produce music for which he and Nelson did not anticipate a large audience—primarily the music of their friends' bands. Regardless of their professed intentions, MacKaye and Nelson's label serves as a material signifier of the D.C. Scene's desire to resist commercialization.[29]

In the May/June 1999 issue of *Punk Planet*, MacKaye speaks about DIY as it applies to his current band, Fugazi, but his description also explains the concept in terms of how his earlier band, Minor Threat, embodied it, because he has adhered to roughly the same business practices since he first co-founded Dischord: "One aspect of do-it-yourself is that you really have to do-it-yourself. It's work! We manage ourselves, we book ourselves, we do our own equipment upkeep, we do our own recording, we do our own taxes" (38). MacKaye lays out his rationale, which was also the rationale of his bandmates in Minor Threat, for adhering to a DIY business strategy:

> I think that the reason we take the approach to music that we do is that then we ultimately have complete control over how we do our music and how we operate the band. We don't feel compelled by *anyone* to do *anything* that we don't want to do. We're not indebted to anyone. When a band signs to a major label, no matter how good a contract they think they have, no matter how much control they think their contract provides, it's unavoidable that you are conscious of being an investment. Somebody puts money into you and you have to pay off somehow. And you *want* to pay off. (38)

Minor Threat also distributed and sold its recordings, through Dischord, via mail order to individuals and via direct sales to record stores, while eschewing corporate investors. Through Nelson, MacKaye, Dischord, and Minor Threat, the desire to seize control over the means of production that Greg Ginn and Jello Biafra had set in motion out of necessity reemerged. It is no coincidence that Dischord was founded two years after SST and a year after Alternative Tentacles, although it did not become a strong presence in punk before the early '80s. These three labels point to the emergence of a specific desire's appearance in the United States in response to the absorption of the first two punk scenes by the music industry.

A further impulse picked up from earlier scenes and pushed forward in D.C. is the will to collectivity. Dick Hebdige claims that the English punk scene celebrated "in mock heroic terms the death of the community" (79), and the New York Scene demonstrated some cohesion but also a fair amount of bellyaching from some of its members when it became too large for them. Legs McNeil, the former writer and "resident punk" of *Punk* magazine (McNeil credits himself with naming the magazine and the punk movement itself), ponders the final Sex Pistols show and complains that "[o]vernight, punk had become as stupid as everything else. . . . It felt like this phony media thing. Punk wasn't ours anymore" (McNeil and McCain, 334). Commenting on California Hardcore, Gina Arnold lauds Black Flag as "the band that linked Hollywood and the beach . . . its nucleus was located geographically between the two . . . [and Greg Ginn] put together bills with the Orange County bands" (37). However, the New York and L.A. scenes' embryonic economic collectivity matured in the D.C. Scene and the cooperation among its bands, as evidenced in part by Dischord Records and its creation, Revolution Summer, in 1985. MacKaye describes the D.C. Scene just prior to that summer:

> We thought that these shows were disgusting and that this community was fucked because you go to a show and everyone just ends up fighting and getting beat up. . . . My friends and the original punk kids started to drop out because they were finding it dumb and no longer wanted to be a part of it anymore. We all got together and talked about it. We decided to reclaim this, but instead of trying to reclaim the punk scene, we decided to start our own fucking punk scene, another one. That's the way Revolution Summer started. . . . We decided everybody has to get a band and start playing and create this new scene, a new community . . . and we fucking did it. (MacKaye, *All Ages*, 104)

Of the nine bands that congealed around this notion of community, six of them released music on Dischord Records, and Nelson and MacKaye endeavored to grant the same control over the means of production that they had enjoyed in Minor Threat to the bands whose music they released.[30] The move toward an economic collective that I am reading in MacKaye and Nelson's approach to signing their friends' bands in order to form a label provided a base upon which a corresponding movement toward a more interpersonal collectivity and cooperation could be established and focused upon a specific cause—retrieving a scene from violent and racist hangers-on in 1985.

One additional form of communality characterized the D.C. Scene. Straight Edge adopted the idea of "friendship" as an important element of its lyrical content but invoked it almost exclusively as, first, failed and, second, between males. In the 1983 Minor Threat song "Look Back and Laugh," Ian MacKaye sings "about some friends growing up / And all the things they tried / I'm not talking about staple shit / They went for something more. . . . One day something funny happened / But it scared the shit out of me / Their heads went in different directions / And their friendship ceased to be." This song remains the epitome of the "friendship song," a Straight Edge trope that encompasses literally hundreds of incarnations. In the majority of them, the male singer/narrator recounts the story of a close friendship, almost always with another male, and expresses his anger and disappointment with that male for betraying him. In almost all songs of this type, the singer neglects to expatiate upon the exact quality of the lost friendship and includes no details about the form of the betrayal.

Although I will return to this desire below, where it intersects with other practices, I want to note that Straight Edge bears a desire for a community of males and for homoerotic relations between men. The community is successfully created, but the relations, although much sought after, remain out of reach for unmentioned (unmentionable?) reasons. One of the reasons is an implicit homophobia in the scene, to which the lyrics to "Look Back and Laugh" attest. It is not difficult to read the song, and its reliance upon euphemism as it situates itself within homophobic U.S. mass culture, as a narrative about two young men crossing the socially constructed boundary between homosocial and homoerotic desire together.[31] The narrator explains that the men matured together and emphasizes the intimate nature of their relationship, which involved experimentation that was unlike the "staple shit" of growing up. The structure of the narrative seems to mirror the structure of the experiences that two young men would share who matured sexually together and experimented with homoerotic behavior in a predominantly heterosexual as well as homophobic culture. Eventually, "something funny" happened: someone discovered the young men together or learned of their desires or behavior and chastised or abused one or both of them, which "scared the shit out of" the narrator. Or, perhaps one of the men believed that the relationship had suddenly transgressed the boundaries of male heterosexual friendship and conveyed his "discovery" to his partner. Such a realization might carry both "funny" and "frightening" qualities for one or both of the men. Subsequently, one of the men rejected the other: "Their heads went in different directions." In this song, and in the Straight Edge Scene in general, a close attention to homoerotic desire accompanies an unwillingness to acknowledge or accept that desire explicitly, and it is this avoidance that points to homophobia in the scene.

WHOA! IAN WAS TALKING ABOUT DRUGS AND MATURING, NOT HOMO LOVE.

In an effort to establish a form of history apart from the economy, English punks and California punks (to a lesser degree) rendered major label business practices and San Francisco politics hyper-spectacular in an effort to critique and consequently alter the means by which these institutions represented themselves (their musicians and their candidates). These punk scenes endeavored to expose the spectacle for what they understood it as—depthless surface. However, the Dead Kennedys' effort to write themselves into economic History by establishing their own label and to reinject depth into the means of representation available to them as a band reappeared in more developed forms in Minor Threat and First Wave Straight Edge. Learning from the absorption into the commercial music industry of the New York and English scenes and the California scene's economic semiautonomy, the D.C. Straight Edge Scene prevented its desire to produce noncommercial music from becoming trapped within the major labels and instead directed it, and the concomitant desire to enter into History, into the formation of an economic institution fit to express these two aims: Dischord Records. After the California scene, the desire to resist commercialization that first arose in New York in the mid-'70s—and that undergirds, in some form, the entire punk project—produced a new economic base for each new punk scene. Each scene's economic underpinning was different, but each testified to the lesson that the California scene seems to have taught all punks: a scene only begins to free itself from the capitalist economy after it controls aspects of its own economic production and distribution. Beginning with California hardcore, punks understood their scenes' economic groundings as the material base beneath their cultural productions, as a set of social and material relations that supported a no-longer-purely-spectacular system of performing, recording, touring, distributing, etc.

Having begun to establish itself economically with Dischord Records, the Straight Edge Scene turned a skeptical eye on the English and Californian spectacle and hyper-spectacle and resisted both. Rather than investing energy in staged contract signings, protest songs, and mayoral races, the D.C. Scene focused on the politics of the body rather than the body politic. The scene's method was anti-spectacle. Understanding the spectacle as excess, and the hyper-spectacle as more of the same, Straight Edge mobilized a minimalism that attested to a desire for anti-spectacle that was also a desire for a social reality that could be represented, that could be reached if only the layers of spectacle around it were peeled away.

There is a particular constellation of desires for which Straight Edge is most famous. The move toward minimalism and anti-spectacle produced a form of asceticism in the scene that began with an attack upon the punk song's form and content. Minor Threat in particular sped up hardcore and shortened its song lengths, also dispensing with much of the irony that the Dead

Kennedys had employed. Comparing Ian MacKaye's early band Teen Idles to Minor Threat—MacKaye's next band—rock commentator and D.C. punk Howard Wuelfing attributes Minor Threat's sound to the influence of seminal D.C. punk band Bad Brains. (The Teen Idles were friends of Bad Brains and shared their practice space and equipment for a time.) Wuelfing comments: "The difference between Teen Idles and Minor Threat was Bad Brains. They [Bad Brains] set the example of how to play extremely fast but with extreme precision" (qtd. in Andersen and Jenkins, 73). Minor Threat and Straight Edge songs served as radically compressed manifestos, announcing the beliefs of a person, band, or scene with complete earnestness and, consequently, voicing a desire to represent the conditions of living directly, to reattach the lyric to a transferable and relatively stable meaning.

The 1983 song "Out of Step," from the Minor Threat album of the same name, has only one verse and is less than two minutes long. It served not only the first Straight Edge Scene as a manifesto but also the Second and Third Waves of Straight Edge. Its lyrics are simple: "(I) don't smoke / Don't drink / Don't fuck / At least I can fucking think." The chorus is also marked by brevity: "I can't keep up / Can't keep up / Can't keep up / Out of step with the world." First Wave Straight Edge marks the first time that a punk scene consciously began to turn back upon punk itself to negate specific parts of earlier scenes. By 1983, excessive drug, tobacco, and alcohol use were widely associated with punk rock not only in the media and public consciousness but also in punk's awareness of itself. After the English Scene, sex was also linked to punk, especially heterosexuality and more specifically male heterosexuality. As a scene, Straight Edge became a countervailing force that closed down specific forms of desire embraced by earlier scenes: First Wave Straight Edgers fostered sobriety and clear thinking and wanted to open a cultural space in which such behavior would be not only tolerated but celebrated. If the drinking and drug use that earlier scenes engaged in was hyper-spectacular in its professed purposelessness (in contrast to the higher state that some of the hippies were allegedly trying to reach through drug experimentation), then Straight Edge established the anti-spectacle of the teetotaller.

One sphere in which the Straight Edge stance could be appreciated was that of law and order. Guy Picciotto, a member of the early Straight Edge band Deadline in 1981, recalls a police officer pulling the band over for making an illegal turn: "He says, 'Don't you see, you made an illegal left turn?' We're all, 'uuh. . . .' We were all drinking orange Nehi. He looked in and says, 'Oh, man, I can't believe that, I gotta let you go. You're all drinking orange Nehi. I've never seen anything like that'" (Connolly et al., 48). In contrast to earlier scenes, a desire to live within the structure of the law manifests itself in the D.C. Scene; consequently, fighting with the police (which occurred on a semi-regular basis in the English and California scenes) plays a minimal role in this scene.

Although Straight Edgers were law-abiding, the scene also developed as a strategy for allowing D.C. youths to situate themselves in relation to the law, while extending their sphere of social mobility by publicly displaying their adherence to laws governing the sale of alcohol. Ian MacKaye recounts an early show that Minor Threat played in San Francisco:

> We were in San Francisco, and we played a place called Mabuhay Gardens. They asked if we were going to drink and we said, "no," and they put an "X" on our hands. So we came back to Washington D.C. and went to this night-club, the 9:30, and said, "Hey look, we're not going to drink and we will put this 'X' on our hand. If you see us drinking, you can throw us out forever. We are not going to drink, we just came to see the music." (Lahickey, 99)

The publicly worn *X* expressed a self-imposed adherence to the law but also allowed teenagers into clubs that would have turned them away previously. The entire scene's survival can be understood as predicated upon this Straight Edge tactic, because bands and audiences composed of minors first had to get in the door of over-twenty-one nightclubs before they could establish a scene and before they could assemble the economic clout to push for the "all-ages" shows that eventually became one of the hallmarks of the D.C. Scene. Through the establishment of an all-ages scene, D.C. Straight Edgers also created a channel through which youths could enter into economic history as not just consumers of older punks' work but as producers of punk themselves.

I have been describing the D.C. Scene's desires primarily as responses to, and critiques of, the practices of punks in earlier scenes. In contrast to New York, London, etc., D.C. punks stayed sober, embodying a refusal to be sedated or medicated; however, cultural tendencies existing outside of punk might have reinforced the scene's notions of ethical and bodily "purity" and a certain fascism of the body. Although a 1981 study sponsored by the National Institute of Drug Abuse (NIDA) found that the use of illicit drugs had lev-eled off, or, for some drugs, declined, (Reinhold, A1) by 1983, NIDA had launched a public service campaign aimed at twelve to fourteen year-olds (Sweeney, 9) that had evolved by October into the "Just Say No" campaign (Doherty, D22), spearheaded by Nancy Reagan (Carmody, D9). In 1984, a new study sponsored by NIDA indicated that, in '84, 3 percent fewer high school seniors had experimented with illicit drugs than in '83 ("Fewer High School," C9).

Although the D.C. Straight Edge Scene was already established when hysteria about HIV and AIDS exploded in the United States in the mid-'80s, the growing attention to both probably served as a cultural undercurrent reinforcing the scene's stance on heterosexual intercourse. According to Tom Flynn and Karen Lound, "[I]n the last three months of 1982, only fifteen stories on AIDS appeared in all the nation's leading magazines and newspapers combined" (13), but, by February 1983, it had become clear that sexually active male homosexuals were not the only people vulnerable to AIDS (Biddle and Slade, 7). However, even as late as 1985, Mervyn Silverman, the former health director of San Francisco remarked: "I tell people that I don't think straight people who have been immensely active with a wide variety of sex partners need to start worrying yet, but they will need to if they keep it up" (W. Turner, B7).

Both of these cultural currents that arose outside of the immediate sphere of punk—Washington's campaign against drugs and the spread of fear and information on HIV and AIDS—followed the emergence of the D.C. Straight Edge Scene, but it is not difficult to imagine that they reinforced the scene's strict policing of bodily fluids. In place of the mixing and spilling of blood (in fights, during sex, and when giving or receiving tattoos), saliva (during sex and early punks spit—"gobbed"—on bands while they played), and sweat (while dancing and during sex) that characterized the earlier punk scenes, D.C. punks attempted to avoid exchanging or intermingling their bodily fluids, with the possible exception of sweat (again, while dancing). However, if these extra-punk exigencies inflected punk desires, they did so by being unconsciously internalized by punks before they were subsequently expressed in the scene's behaviors and artifacts, because punks' antiauthoritarian stance prevented them from openly or consciously adopting behaviors that the federal government, as authority incarnate, promulgated, whether in the guise of Nancy Reagan or C. Everett Koop. Along with other authority figures, the government took a beating in punk lyrics in the '80s, and it is a punk truism that punk music of the '90s suffered without the conspicuous target that Ronald Reagan provided from 1980 to 1988. (A New York hardcore band even took the name Reagan Youth.)

Avoiding alcohol, tobacco, and illegal drugs, and thereby maintaining a "Straight Edge," also denotes a desire to inscribe upon the body the opposition that punk establishes between the spectacle and the reality. A photo that captures this desire appears in *Banned in D.C.* Its caption reads, "Thomas Squip on his bed 1–84" (Connolly et al., 138) and shows Squip, the lead guitarist and singer for the Dischord band Beefeater, crouching naked on a folded Mexican blanket, holding his guitar in front of him. In the background, a rock and a walking stick are visible. The white wall behind him is blank. This photo succinctly illustrates Straight Edge's incorporation of the logic of spectacle and anti-spectacle into the realm of identity. In an effort to arrive at identities that were not based upon spectacular surfaces, Straight Edgers stripped away what they read as the detritus of punk. In Squip's case, the only necessities would seem to be a musical instrument, a place to sleep, and a walking stick for transportation.

Straight Edge pared down the punk fashion of earlier scenes. Although D.C. punks initially developed a style that amalgamated elements from previous and contemporaneous punk scenes, they gradually set aside more and more of these characteristically punk trappings. In place of them, they wore the jeans and T-shirts that had marked the New York Scene. Rather than the spectacular hairdos of English punk that potentially pointed up the artificial and constructed character of all notions of beauty and style, they shaved their heads, leaving about an eighth to half an inch of hair that marked them as punks but non-skinheads, at least for other punks. The Straight Edge Scene fostered antifashion (or, if early punk fashion was antifashion, then anti-anti fashion) not because its members opposed commercial fashion with noncommercial fashion but because they attempted to disassociate themselves from fashion altogether. The perfect Straight Edge look did not call attention to itself *as a look* but as resistance to the idea that one must have a look. Although haircuts marked Straight Edgers as punks, they also expressed a refusal to engage in hair styling: it was a DIY cut that D.C. punks gave one another with shared electric razors. Taken together, these ascetic elements of Straight Edge attest to the scene's desire to arrive at or create a nonsuperficial identity that could emerge after the earlier punk scenes' investments in surfaces had been negated and transcended.

The single verse of Minor Threat's song "Out of Step" (quoted above) concludes with the line, "Don't fuck." This Straight Edge statute combined with a desire for a community of males established a masculine and homoerotic atmosphere for the scene. Although the scene's members often professed that they opposed sexism, racism, and homophobia, women were marginalized within it. While the young men did almost all of the performing (there were *no* female Straight Edge bands or singers), the women tended to be relegated to the role of girlfriend, fan, club worker, label worker, or photographer. Women also performed the majority of the work of recording the scene's history (*Banned in D.C.*'s four editors are all women). Eve Sedgwick theorizes a "homosocial continuum" for males that runs from "homosocial" behavior, including "such activities as 'male bonding,' which may . . . be characterized by intense homophobia, fear and hatred of homosexuality" (1), and homosexuality, while understanding all points along the continuum as related to desire. With Sedgwick's model in mind, I want to argue that the participants in the D.C. Scene understood their behavior as homosocial when in fact it was homoerotic. Although sexual intercourse was forbidden, male band and audience members engaged in various modes of homoerotic behavior. In place of the often violent slam-dancing and stage-diving of the California scene, straight-edgers "moshed" (although the term did not exist yet): they purposely brushed and bumped against one another but without attempting to cause pain, as they did in San Francisco and L.A. Band members also leapt off the stage to be caught by the audience, but audience members were not encouraged or allowed to do the same. The D.C. Scene also created the "dogpile": the lead singer would enter the crowd in order to stir it up emotionally through his proximity, and when the emotional charge in the audience had reached a certain point its members would pile upon the singer, who often continued to shout out the lyrics from under the mass of writhing young men on top of him. Although the homoerotic quality of these acts was rarely explicitly acknowledged within the scene, it testifies to a desire for intimate relations between men that would fall somewhere between the poles—heterosexuality and homosexuality—of the homosocial continuum. In short, Straight Edge males cannot be easily subordinated beneath traditional constructions of "gay" or "straight" identity.

The Straight Edge Scene understood refraining from intercourse as a necessary component of maintaining a "Straight Edge," but, while songs expatiated upon how avoiding drugs, smoking, and alcohol allowed a person to stay focused, the logic behind swearing off sex remained tacit. For example, Minor Threat's song "In My Eyes" devotes most of its two verses to the benefits of avoiding alcohol, before making one of the scene's few lyrical comments upon male-female relations: "You tell me that you like her / You just wish you did." Assuming that the same logic governs the scene's stance on the four acts that it forswears, sex, and heterosexual sex in particular, must threaten the scene in the same ways that drugs, alcohol, and tobacco do: it forces a "Straight Edge" to deteriorate, meaning that an individual loses focus and becomes dissolute, scattered, lethargic. Sex also seems to threaten the scene's sense of male collectivity; girls or women are dangerous because they could distract the young men and draw them away from the scene. These reasons for avoiding sex all stem from within the scene, but the fear of HIV and AIDS could also help shape Straight Edge constructions of sexuality, although the scene has left behind few direct references to AIDS or HIV. In conclusion, in place of the English Scene's highlighting of the spectacular character of sex, participants in First Wave Straight Edge attempted to abolish sexuality and avoid intercourse but nevertheless engage in risk-free expressions of homoerotic desire.

Planets affect one another, condition one another's orbits, and, obeying this logic, people in the D.C. Scene were sober and consequently focused upon their work enough to be able to embrace the DIY concept of maintaining economic control. Perhaps this initial link between DIY and Straight Edge proves Jello Biafra's frequently expressed suspicion that, in the '70s, major labels preferred to have their musicians addicted to drugs and would even supply the drugs that both made the musicians malleable and kept them dependent upon the label in an extremely tangible way. The members of the D.C. Scene strove for a form of personal autonomy—control over their minds and bodies—that paralleled and produced conditions fruitful for the control that they sought in their business practices. Within the scene, two sets of influences overlapped and reinforced one another, one from outside of punk and one from within it. Broad cultural tendencies toward sobriety and sexual abstinence melded nicely with the economic lesson that earlier scenes taught D.C. punks: to avoid co-optation and death, a punk scene must establish an independent economic base. By avoiding personal dissolution at the level of the individual, D.C. Scene participants held off economic dissolution as well, and, as a result and unlike the fate of some of the previous scenes, the D.C. Scene was not appropriated by the major labels.

Nevertheless, in 1985, two events occurred that disbanded the D.C. Scene. Violent and racist neo-Nazi skinheads had begun coming to Straight Edge punk shows in 1984 and 1985, and, in response, the D.C. Scene members rallied together to establish what they named Revolution Summer, an organized effort to create a group of new bands that openly discouraged violence at their shows. In place of Minor Threat and other bands' aesthetic efforts to incite their audiences into angry masses, bands such as the Rites of Spring, Gray Matter, Scream, and Embrace (Ian MacKaye's new band after Minor Threat broke up in 1983) produced slower, more melodic punk designed specifically not to appeal to racist and violent hardcore enthusiasts. MacKaye became famous in the scene for halting shows when audiences became too boisterous. It is possible that racist skinheads were also drawn to Straight Edge punk because of its fascination with moral and bodily "purity" that might have served skinheads as an analog for racist notions about "pure" blood and "pure" races that could be inscribed at the level of the individual body. But the D.C. Scene maintained its "Straight Edge," regardless, and the skinheads lost interest in the music.

On September 6, 1985, the Straight Edge community rallied together again to form the Punk Percussion Protest. More than one hundred members of the scene set up drums and other objects that could be played as percussion instruments on the sidewalk across from the South African Embassy in D.C. In reaction to apartheid, the scene members pounded out their protest for hours, beginning in the late afternoon and continuing into the evening. Ironically, these two events served to unify the scene and bring it to a climax from which it could not recover. As in the case of the California scene, the channeling of various competing desires toward specific goals, both linked to countering racism in the case of D.C., meant canceling some desires in order to bring the scene under the sway of others. This directing of desires also subordinated them as means beneath specific ends, and when the ends were met or the moment to meet them passed, the desires ceased. When Revolution Summer had discouraged racist skinheads from participating in the scene and the scene's members had expressed their outrage over apartheid, the scene, which had become oriented toward these particular goals, did not die but faded away.

Scene member Kenny Inouye commented, in 1985, that "everyone was bummed out at how stagnant and elitist everything had become" (Connolly et al., 165). Although several of the scene's bands, including MacKaye's band, Embrace, broke up around 1985, many continued performing, such as Government Issue and MacKaye's new band that formed in 1987, Fugazi. Rather than being appropriated or dying altogether, members of the D.C. Scene seemed to recognize that their movement had peaked; additionally, by 1986, a new wave of Straight Edge had absorbed D.C.'s charge and was taking it in new directions.

THE NEW YORK HARDCORE SCENE
(SECOND WAVE STRAIGHT EDGE)

The second Straight Edge Scene emerged from the same locale as the first New York scene—CBGBs in New York City—which became the ground zero of what came to be called New York Straight Edge (NYSE), New York Hardcore (NYHC), Youth Crew punk, or Second Wave Straight Edge. However, while New York punk initially appealed to young urban men and women, NYHC, like First Wave Straight Edge, was composed primarily of white suburban boys, many of whom were from Connecticut suburbs of New York City. This scene began in 1986 and ended in 1989. The bands included, most famously for punks, Youth of Today, Bold, Gorilla Biscuits, Underdog, Supertouch, Uniform Choice, Judge, No For an Answer, and Insted.[32]

Aesthetically, NYHC differs significantly from early punk and from early Straight Edge. While the D.C. Scene stripped its sound down and played an extremely minimalist version of hardcore, the Second Wave sound is a hybrid of the D.C. hardcore sound combined with "metal," a broad rock and roll category that includes death metal, black metal, heavy metal, speed metal, and myriad other subgenres. When used to describe a punk band's sound, "metal" denotes the guitarist and bass guitarist's co-opting of chord progressions, or "metal breakdowns," typical of the metal subgenres. The term also implies that a band grants the guitar more prominence than is typical for punk: short riffs—series of single notes or combinations of single notes and chords—are tolerated or encouraged rather than eschewed in favor of chords alone. The NYHC scene organized itself around multiple desires for control that expressed themselves aesthetically in a greater apparent mastery, or control, over musical instruments than previous scenes demonstrated.

In the mid-'80s, Hilly Kristal, still the owner and manager of CBGBs, began allowing hardcore punk bands to play all-ages matinees during one of his least lucrative time slots: Sunday afternoons. By this time, the hardcore scenes of California and D.C. had dissolved, and the genre did not garner much attention in New York City's clubs. Inspired by the few hardcore bands that endeavored to nurture a hardcore scene in New York, a small group of white suburban high school youths began catching Sunday trains to New York from their middle-class suburbs in New Jersey, New York State, and Connecticut to see shows and, eventually, to perform in Straight Edge bands. Clinton Heylin described the first New York underground music scene in terms that serve to describe Second Wave Straight Edge ten years later: the scene was made up of "bands supported by cult followings developed through live performances at local nightclubs rather than recording contracts and mass media hype" (135). Although Kristal had raised the cover charge for Sunday matinees to five dollars—from the one dollar of the mid-'70s punk shows—the club and NYHC bands were "self-consciously aligned with noncommercial popular music trends" (135), as were the original New York punks. However, NYHC was aesthetically and economically different from the first New York Scene.

As with the first Straight Edge Scene, NYHC established an economic base for itself fairly quickly. Jordan Cooper, many of whose friends were involved in playing Straight Edge hardcore, founded Revelation Records in New Haven, Connecticut, in 1987, later moving it to Huntington Beach, California. For its first couple of years, Revelation released almost exclusively the music of NYHC bands. As in the case of SST, AT, and Dischord, Revelation provided a scene with an outlet for its products, so that its participants did not have to meet commercial expectations or business practices in order to have their music released.

In terms of groups, the band Youth of Today (YOT) is to NYHC what Minor Threat is to First Wave Straight Edge: YOT was the first and, for punks in general, the most famous Second Wave Straight Edge band. Hence, YOT, its lead singer, Ray Cappo, and CBGBs will serve as points with which to triangulate the desires underpinning NYHC. A drive toward collectivity underscored the scene and found expression in new variants of the "friendship song" that Minor Threat established. YOT's song, "Stabbed in the Back," adheres to this hardcore trope's expectations. As with most Straight Edge friendship songs (First or Second Wave), it expresses anxiety over the fear of losing a friend more than it exhorts its listeners to strengthen or maintain bonds. It begins, "We were brothers, you and me / Loyal to our hardcore scene. . . . Then something happened to you / You changed." As the use of the word *brothers* suggests, almost all Second Wave friendship songs concern specifically male friendships. To reinforce this idea of friendship—or unity as it comes to be called—NYHC co-opts "crew" from rap and hip-hop, and the term comes to mean a group of male Straight Edgers who have formed a subgroup within Straight Edge in general, usually organized around a sense of loyalty to a specific band, suburb, neighborhood, club, or some combination of the three.

As I have argued for several of the earlier punk scenes, the establishment of a record label and its sale of a scene's products and tour support of a scene's bands marks the non-repressed desire within any scene to enter into History, understood as the history of the economy. Because of the low economic costs of entering the punk field, punk offers youths an opportunity to begin to understand themselves as producers and subjects of a sort of history, rather than as its objects. Instead of working in the service or heavy industry sector of the economy, where many youths work during high school and afterward, and whose histories tend to reflect the biographies of corporate business owners and executives rather than accounts of individual workers' lives, youths see in punk the possibility of taking an active role in producing the history of punk, either as label owners or performers. This desire to figure within history, to create a history in which the individual could figure, takes on material forms for ever-younger youths. While girls, boys, women, and men ranging from their late teens to middle age constituted the first New York Scene, by the mid-'80s, NYHC participants were almost all less than eighteen years old.

Also geared toward the goal of creating a Straight Edge history—as a component of the more extensive history of punk—Straight Edgers attempted to construct an identity for themselves, based loosely upon the D.C. Scene's similar project. But, while First Wave Straight Edgers tried, through asceticism and anti-spectacle, to hold a space open for a not-yet-existent identity that would not depend upon spectacle, NYHC attempted to fill that space with a set of rules. In addition to forbidding drugs, tobacco, and alcohol, one of the Second Wave's new tenets was mandatory vegetarianism. Avoiding meat suggests an ascetic effort to avoid consumption, but the lyrics of YOT's song "Youth of Today" also link meat to the slaughterhouse and invoke the desire to take a "morally straight" stance toward animals. In broad and vague terms, racism and sexism are also decried. All of these "rules" of Straight Edge became understood by NYHC participants in moral terms, so that violating them amounted to blasphemy, to losing a "moral Straight Edge." Taken at face value, these morals seem to rank alongside slogans such as "Be All That You Can Be" in terms of complexity. For example, offering his audience advice in "Break Down the Walls," Cappo suggests, "Look beyond the fashion to the crowd that they are in / Look beyond their riches or the color of their skin / Look beyond appearance and the truth you will find / Look for what's inside before you make up your mind!" Many Second Wave Straight Edge bands espoused similar morals, but, regardless of how simple, they still betrayed the desire for an understandable and above all knowable set of tenets that could guide a person interested in creating a moral life. In this sense, NYHC participants resembled the Parisian wrestlers that Roland Barthes describes in "The World of Wrestling": "[W]restlers remain gods because they are, for a few moments, the key which opens Nature, the pure gesture

which separates Good from Evil, and unveils the form of a Justice which is at
last intelligible" (*Mythologies*, 25). In Straight Edge, the desire surfaces not
only to participate in history but to understand that participation through ethical categories.

Just as the D.C. Scene twisted back upon earlier scenes to disavow certain aspects, NYHC rejected portions of the First Wave. The D.C. Scene, and
most of the other punk scenes, turned away from constructions of masculinity that praised athleticism and the muscular male body, both of which were
anathema to most punks before the mid-'80s. It is difficult to imagine a buff
Sid Vicious, for example. In direct contrast, NYHC proclaimed the joys of
male physical fitness. Band members kept the short hair of the First Wave but
performed in hooded Champion brand sweatshirts ("hoodies"), athletic
footwear, and muscle tees. They also wore baseball caps, shorts, sweatpants,
and T-shirts bearing the names of sportswear manufacturers. While the D.C.
Scene had mistrusted all fashion as spectacular, the Second Wave enthusiastically embraced a particular notion of fashion that highlighted a cluster of
desires centering upon sexuality.

First, NYHC's acute attention to what enters the male body and, more
importantly, what does not enter it, established that body as a privileged site
and bearer of desires. YOT's song "Free at Last" sums up the NYHC desire
to police the body's boundaries. Cappo sings, "This world is filled with competition and greed / A disgusting way of life / But we'll try to break . . . Free! /
Free at Last! / From the animals in the slaughterhouse / To the drugs on the
streets / They'll pollute our minds, our bodies." Together with establishing the
importance of the male body and understanding it as besieged by a set of
immoral and external influences, NYHC expressed a strong admiration for a
specific construction of the male body. In "Youth of Today," Cappo sings
"Physically strong / Morally straight / Positive Youth / We're the Youth of
Today." An abundance of NYHC lyrics deal with male physical strength, and
the whole scene celebrated the fit male body that it pictured as young, muscular, broad-shouldered, small-waisted, and free of body and facial hair. On
the cover of one of the pressings of "Break Down the Walls," an early YOT
album, the figure of Cappo, dressed only in running pants and basketball
shoes, dominates the photo. The cover's composition accentuates his sweaty
and well-defined muscular upper body. Countless subsequent Straight Edge
album covers displayed the same exhilaration over the male body. Such explicit
attention to the male physique suggests at the very least the desire for a cultural zone in which male physicality and partial male nudity can be sensually
enjoyed. Not surprisingly, Straight Edgers' involvement with the physical
extended to participation in athletics (NYHC fashion specifically referenced
this involvement). Weightlifting in particular served as a further sign of the
importance of the body, because it is perhaps the sport most invested in a strict

attention to the shaping of the physique both as a whole and as a set of particular, fetishized parts. Punk shows also became more athletic than ever before: the dogpile and moshing return with added intensity.

Like other scenes, NYHC can be schematized as a set of interlocking desires: the lyrics, dogpiles, moshing, celebration of male friendship, and appreciation of the male body all feed off one another. Connected to the scene's core desires and running alongside them is, as in First Wave Straight Edge, the sense that women pose a threat to a cohesive male community of punks. In spite of its songs' constant admonitions to its members to refrain from racist, sexist, and misogynistic behavior, New York Straight Edge was probably the most male-dominated subgenre of punk rock thus far. In *All Ages: Reflections on Straight Edge,* a collection of interviews with members of the Second Wave of Straight Edge, two women who were involved as fans and friends of band members relate their memories of the scene. The first, Susan Martinez, recounts how

> being a girl at shows was extremely alienating at times. Girl bands or even girls in bands were so rare, and even then, mocked by boys. . . . Girls were displayed lots of times by boys as ornaments or prizes. We were not taken seriously for who we were, but by what we looked like. . . . Girls were always the supporting cast, never the stars. (112)

It is no coincidence that a woman, Beth Lahickey, did the interviews that, combined, constitute the book from which this comment comes. Lahickey served as a sort of secretary to a scene that boys created. Tellingly, the only other woman whose memories appear in *All Ages* is Becky Tupper, Ray Cappo's girlfriend in the mid-'80s, whose interview is one of the shortest in the book.

Regardless of Straight Edgers' supposedly nonsexist stance toward women, they succeeded in creating a space in which women were almost nonexistent. If Martinez is correct, then the few women who did attend shows had to be aggressive in order to avoid being victimized but, in turn, paid a price for that aggression. She comments, "I rarely left the front of the stage at shows and remember punching and/or kicking more than a couple of boys who groped me. . . . It freaked out a lot of boys that girls could be aggressive, or have energy, or be in the pit, or jump off the stage" (112). It is difficult even to know whether Martinez's experiences were typical of this scene, because so few of the female voices that might have emerged from it have been recorded. Beth Lahickey, who worked at Revelation in the mid-'80s, comments on the scene in her introduction to *All Ages:* "I definitely tout the motivation behind the Straight Edge Scene, but in the same breath denounce its male-based egocentricity. At any rate, I chose to stand at its sidelines and support its players" (xvii). Holly Ramos, a participant in the scene, adds that NYHC "was a real guy thing; I think it was a real gay thing, too. Girls weren't involved whatsoever in bands. . . . There was that whole male bonding/sweating/being-naked/doing-that-dancing going on" (Blush, 34).

Despite the "True to Death" slogan of NYHC, the scene dissolved fairly rapidly. As Lahickey explains, there was the "problem of clubs booking over 21 shows [that] hindered bands whose members were often underage. The fear of a lawsuit caused club owners to discourage 'aggressive dancing'" (xxii). Hilly Kristal stopped booking Straight Edge shows at CBGBs in the late '80s, noting that in "the early 80s, up through '87, it [the Straight Edge Scene] started getting rougher and rougher. I had to hire people to keep others from stage diving because they'd break ankles and arms and legs. I had to stop it because I didn't want people to get hurt and also insurance reasons, too. I started getting people suing" (93). Lahickey believes that more important to NYHC's decline was the fact that "soon enough, as people got a little older, the once united scene began to unravel, and people began going their separate ways in life" (xxii). Unlike the other scenes—even First Wave Straight Edge that evolved into a new D.C. Scene that still exists in 2003—the core desires of Second Wave Straight Edge quickly calcified until they paralleled a juridical and conservative social construction of the middle-class, American, suburban, male youth so perfectly that as soon as the original participants in NYHC aged a little they no longer fit the profile. They were excluded when they no longer professed their intolerance for alcohol, drugs, cigarettes, meat, and sex. It was one matter for scene participants to swear off alcohol and sex while underage and living with their parents or guardians but quite another as they grew older. The demand that scene members live according to the rules of NYHC, rules that codified and sanctioned legal and social pressures already in place for structuring teens' lives, choked off Straight Edge as a scene by 1989.

THE RIOT GRRRL SCENE

In the late '80s, Calvin Johnson, the founder of small independent label K Records, began the International Pop Underground (IPU), a record club whose members would periodically receive 7"s ("seven inches," the contemporary equivalent of 45s) with an Olympia, Washington-based band's song on one side and an internationally known band's song on the flip side. The club culminated in a five-day IPU Convention in 1991 in Olympia (organized by Johnson), and the convention's first event was dubbed Love Rock Revolution Girl Style Now. Four all-female bands from the area played: Olympia's Heavens to Betsy, Vancouver's Jean Smith, British Columbia's Mecca Normal, and

Eugene, Oregon's, Bratmobile. The audience's energetic, positive responses to the bands—particularly the girls' and womens' enthusiasm—led audience and band members to recognize in themselves a nascent collectivity, which eventually became the Riot Grrrl Scene. The scene's backbone consisted of Bratmobile and Heavens to Betsy together with Bikini Kill and Calamity Jane in the United States and, later, Huggy Bear and Skinned Teen in the U.K. The scene lasted from 1991 until roughly 1995, although Riot Grrrl chapters continue to function throughout the United States as well as internationally in 2003. While the Riot Grrrl Scene bore many of the previous punk scenes' tendencies, it differed significantly from other scenes in terms of its explicit attention to gender and feminism. Riot Grrrl was also more dispersed than preceding scenes, first crystallizing in Olympia but soon spreading out across the United States and beyond.

Although Riot Grrrls refused to be constrained by an immutable or monolithic set of tenets, this fact did not prevent them from distributing numerous manifestos. The most famous, the collectively authored "Riot Grrrl is . . . ," appeared in the zine *Riot Grrrl* in 1991. It lists seventeen reasons that necessitate Riot Grrrl, several of which evidence Riot Grrrl's adoption of previous punk scenes' anticommercial impetus. Here is the thirteenth: "BECAUSE we hate capitalism in all its forms and see our main goal as sharing information and staying alive, instead of making profits or being cool according to traditional standards" ("Riot Grrrl is . . ."). Riot Grrrl's positioning of itself in opposition to capitalism took material form in the labels on which the scene's bands released music, the most important of which is Kill Rock Stars (KRS). Slim Moon founded KRS in 1991, and the label's first release was a spoken word single featuring Kathleen Hanna, the lead singer of Bikini Kill, on one side and Moon on the other. The same year, the label released a compilation that included Bikini Kill and Bratmobile, two Riot Grrrl groups that would later release full-length albums on KRS. Moon comments on KRS's beginnings: "One night, I decided that a compilation of all the good bands in Olympia would sell pretty good if I could get it out by the IPU convention" *(Kill Rock Stars)*. Despite his attention to sales here, the label has maintained noncommercial status since its inception. Its web page explains that

> Kill Rock Stars is an independent record label . . . based in Olympia, WA. . . .
> Unlike all major labels and many indie labels, profit is not our primary motivation. Kill Rock Stars is dedicated to releasing high quality meaningful recordings in a manner that is fair and respectful to the artists. . . . KRS just wants to give you some good stuff to listen to that actually means something to counteract the empty and boring stuff you see on TRL [Total Request Live, a popular MTV show] or whatever. *(Kill Rock Stars)*

The label's stated aims dovetail nicely into the Riot Grrrls' efforts to resist capitalism, at least in its major label, primarily for-profit forms.

Mass media attention to Riot Grrrls began to threaten their anticommercial, anticapitalism stances shortly after the formative IPU Convention. *Sassy* magazine wrote on the movement that same summer, and the media's attention to the grunge rock phenomenon in Seattle included a careful scrutiny of the geographic region in search of the Next Big Thing. A Riot Grrrl Convention occurred in Washington, D.C., in the summer of 1992 and drew more media attention to the grrrls. Chérie Turner notes that "[g]rrrls saw the media alter and repackage their powerful vision and they stepped up to protect it" (20). It was not so much the "repackaging" of the Riot Grrrl movement that was troublesome but the packaging, period. The mass media was not overly dismissive of the movement. Turner points to *Newsweek*'s questioning of "the seriousness of the girls' convictions in a 1992 article: 'There's no telling whether this enthusiasm of the Riot Grrls, their catchy passion for "revolution, girl style," will evaporate when it hits the adult real world'" (20). But the article's author, Farai Chideya, introduces Riot Grrrl with an anecdote about a scene member's confident resistance to sexual harassment, and while Chideya characterizes the scene as "feminism with a loud happy face dotting the *i*," she adds that the Riot Grrrls "may be the first generation of feminists to identify their anger so early and to use it." Similarly, the *Houston Chronicle*'s Michalene Busico, commenting on the scene's emergence in San Francisco, hopes that "someday the San Francisco Bay Area girls will rule the way they do in Olympia, where girls will join arms and charge through the boys slamming in front of the stage, or in Washington [D.C.], where about 150 riot girls from all over the country . . . gathered last month for a convention." Busico then quotes Riot Grrrl Sam Ott, who describes joining the scene: "It's like coming out of the closet," and Busico finishes her thought: "As a girl."

In response to the media attention, many of the scene's members imposed a commercial press blackout on themselves in 1992 and would only grant interviews to zines and independently run media outlets. When Busico asked Kathleen Hanna for an interview for the *Houston Chronicle* story, Hanna replied, "Our integrity is being taken away by the media and the powers of exploitation. . . . You should respect us as an underground movement. The nicest thing you could do is not write an article about us. Or have a blank space where the article would be—that would be even nicer." Busico adds, "And then she hangs up." What troubles Hanna is *Newsweek*'s or the *Houston Chronicle*'s appropriation of Riot Grrrl in order to move more magazines or newspapers. While the Riot Grrrls, and especially the founding mothers, refused to define Riot Grrrl, preferring to leave it open for individual members to define as they saw fit, the commercial press's short, catchy articles necessarily molded the movement into digestible forms for readers. The slotting of the articles into particular sections codes them for readers and prepares them to receive the articles in particular ways. the *Houston Chronicle*'s article appeared in the Lifestyle section of the Sunday paper, as did *Newsweek*'s. *USA Today* ran two short articles on Riot Grrrl in August 1992, both in the Life section, and Montreal's the *Gazette* ran a short article in September 28, 1992's Woman News section. The disconnect that Hanna points out lies between an experience that parallels "coming out" for its participants and its use as grist for Sunday Lifestyles sections, the light reading on recent trends that follows the "real news"—local, international, and business.

The Riot Grrrls' backlash against the media—their refusal to allow themselves to be commercially publicized in that manner[33]—also granted materiality to Hanna's conviction that there is "a message in terms of how you make something or how you run your business or how you create a product or a musical sound" (Hanna, *Punk Planet*, 38). Reason number three from the "Riot Girl Is . . ." manifesto is "BECAUSE we must take over the means of production in order to create our own meanings." In place of the corporate media, Riot Grrrls substituted their own means of production and representation. In terms of production, they turned to Slim Moon and KRS Records, with whom they enjoyed a degree of control over their music. In parallel with their U.S. cognates, the English Riot Grrrl band Huggy Bear founded its own label/mail-order service, Famous Monsters of Filmland, on which they released their early 7"s. In terms of representation, Grrrls turned to zines.

Stephen Duncombe defines zines as

> noncommercial, nonprofessional, small-circulation magazines that their creators produce, publish, and distribute by themselves. Most often laid out on plain paper and reproduced on common Xerox machines, zines are sold, given away, or, as is common custom, swapped for other zines. They're distributed mainly through the mail and are advertised through the grapevine of other zines and in the pages of zines containing reviews of other zines. . . . Filled with highly personalized editorial "rants," "comix," stories, poems, material appropriated from the mass press, hand drawn pictures, and cut-and-paste collages, the zine world is vast. . . . The printruns of these zines are small, averaging about 250, though the phenomenon, while hidden, is much larger. Anywhere from 10,000 to 50,000 different zine titles circulate in the United States at any moment. (427)

Duncombe traces zines back to science fiction fans of the 1930s—although earlier precedents include underground newspapers as well as surrealist publications—and adds that in "the 1970s, this zine stream was joined by punk rockers" (428). Zines assume an importance in the Riot Grrrl Scene that they lacked for earlier punks, though. Duncombe writes that "[b]y producing zines

and networking with one another, Riot Grrrls become producers instead of
merely consumers, creating their own spaces rather than living within the confines of those made for them" (446). The DIY logic of zines predated Riot
Grrrl and was one of the movement's generative forces. Before becoming the
drummer for Bikini Kill, Tobi Vail published the zine *Jigsaw* while living in
Olympia. Kathleen Hanna was attending Evergreen State College (also in
Olympia) and contacted Vail after reading *Jigsaw*. Shortly thereafter, the two
formed Bikini Kill. Molly Neuman, who eventually drummed for Bratmobile,
was attending the University of Oregon when she first encountered Vail's zine.
She comments, "I read Tobi's fanzine and I was like wow, these ideas are really
exciting, and they're really well put, and they're just so smart. . . . It was as simple as someone going, 'You should do a fanzine' or 'You should start a band.' At
that point it was like, 'Okay, that's what we should do'" (Experience Music).

The DIY impulse first nurtured in zines eventually permeated the Riot
Grrrl Scene, spreading well beyond zine making. The Experience Music Project (EMP)—whose curators describe it as a "music museum combining interactive and interpretive exhibits to tell the story of the creative, innovative and
rebellious expression that defines American popular music"—write that the
"DIY ethic had long been an essential element of the alternative music scene,
but it took on a special significance with Riot Grrrl. Young women were not
only encouraged to play rock instruments . . . they also were encouraged to
produce shows, become DJs, start record labels, publish fanzines, design
posters, [and] organize protests" (Experience Music). At the 1992 Riot Grrrl
conference in Washington, D.C., workshops covered self-defense, rape,
racism, "fat oppression," and domestic violence. Riot Grrrls also taught one
another how to play punk rock. At the D.C. conference, "it was not unusual
for a band to play their first show the same week—or even the same day—that
they first picked up their instruments" (Experience Music). In 1995, Amy
Raphael writes that "[r]iot grrrl has excited some, left others cold. Much of
the criticism has fallen upon the 'clumsy' music they make, the apparent irrel-
evance to musicianship. Courtney Love has been quoted as saying she'd 'like
to have a Riot Grrrl in the band [Hole], but [she] can't find one that can play'"
(148). In defense of grrrls, Kim Gordon (of Sonic Youth) says, "'They're
showing girls they can make their own culture and their own identity during
those tender teenage years'" (148). Just as zines inspired Riot Grrrls to publish
their own writings, Riot Grrrl bands bore within their aesthetics the DIY
logic that would inspire grrrls to form bands even if they lacked technical proficiency. The music's simple, punk rock structures are legible traces of the
material conditions of their production, conditions that can be imagined and
replicated at home, in the basement or the garage.

The early punk that Riot Grrrl bands, and especially Bikini Kill, most
resemble aurally is the music of the X-Ray Spex, a late-'70s English band

that lead singer Poly Styrene (Marion Elliot) fronted. In 1985, Dave Laing wrote that "[n]either the Sex Pistols or Poly Styrene's X-Ray Spex . . . were easily assimilable to the norms of the musical mainstream" (39), but Riot Grrrl bands achieve a rawer sound than the X-Ray Spex ever did. Most importantly, Bikini Kill and Bratmobile largely forgo melody, a move akin to shunning narrative in filmmaking. Just as films that lack a tight narrative structure sacrifice their commercial prospects, musicians who refuse to offer melodic hooks limit their audiences to listeners who demand more than catchy choruses from performers. Kathi Wilcox's bass guitar lines establish simple, repetitive figures that drive many of Bikini Kill's songs, while Billy Karren's repeated chords yield a buzzsaw whine that fills out the band's sound. Behind them, Tobi Vail beats out the rhythm in straightforward 4/4 time, while Kathleen Hanna's vocals strike the ear as rhythmic chanting punctuated by occasional screams. Bratmobile's aesthetics closely parallel Bikini Kill's, although lead singer Allison Wolfe's lyrics are farther up front in the mix, while Kathleen Hanna's do not stand out as clearly from the dense music in which they are enmeshed. Even compared to the female "alternative," grunge bands—Babes in Toyland and L7—that recorded on Sub Pop Records in Seattle in the late '80s and early '90s, Riot Grrrl's aesthetics proved more abrasive and less commercially viable.

While zines carried the scene's explicitly anticapitalist commentaries, song lyrics contributed to the critique as well. In Bikini Kill's "Alien She," Hanna articulates the two valences of the consumption that she feels is demanded of women, its appeal and repugnance for her: "She wants me to go to the mall / SHE wants ME / To put the pretty, pretty lipstick on / She wants me to be like her / She wants me to be like her / I want to kill her / But I'm afraid it might kill me." The song's narrator finds herself trapped between "alien" demands to consume cosmetics that will render her conventionally pretty and other subject positions/labels/voices that strive to counter the *Alien: Feminist/Dyke Whore*. Later, on Bikini Kill's final album, Hanna sings "Reject All American," a song that begins, "regimented/designated/mass acceptance/over rated," continues with "If you work hard / You'll succeed / A starring role / on Nothing Incorporated," and concludes, "Reject sportscar . . . Reject all American / Reject ALL American." In concert with Bikini Kill, Bratmobile offers up the song "Flavor of the Month Club," in which Allison Wolfe intones, ironically, "You got your new clothes and your new friends to match / And too many dishes and a boyfriend, what a catch . . . Gimme gimme gimme more things! more things! / Does it really make you happy, is that really what you mean?" The fact that both bands address subjects calculated to be radio-unfriendly further guarantees that this music will not appear on commercial radio heavy rotation lists. Perhaps to comment on that exact fact, Bikini Kill's song "New Radio Lyrics" seems to be fit only for "New Radio," some future, more liberated incarnation of radio. The lyrics describe female homosex, and the song's penultimate line is "let's wipe our cum on my parents' bed." Similarly, Bratmobile interjects the word *fuck* into their lyrics whenever possible. On their first album, *Pottymouth*, the songs "Fuck Yer Fans" and "Fük U." feature the word repeatedly, while "The Bitch Theme"'s only lyrics, which recur several times, are, "yer such a bitch / Do u really think so?"

Words such as *bitch, dyke, feminist, whore, slut,* and *rape* held special power for Riot Grrrls and foreground two desires, one familiar from previous punk scenes and one peculiar to the Riot Grrrl Scene. Kathleen Hanna remembers writing: "Go to shows! Write stuff on your hands and arms so that other women will know that you're into feminist stuff too, and they'll come talk to you and then maybe you can hang out" (Turner, 28). Hanna's words evidence the profound desire for community that the scene fostered and met in numerous ways. Zines helped found a virtual community for the scene before the Internet was widely available: Grrrls could plug into the scene from any location that was accessible by mail. As Stephen Duncombe writes, commenting on one of his interviewees, "Looking for roots, a way to feel connected and supported in a world where her ideas and ideals seem out of place, Arielle and other misfits have created what she calls 'a community.' The community they've imagined and fashioned is an odd one, not situated in a region or specific place, but spread out across the country, often invisible from the outside. It's a community brought together and defined primarily through a medium of communication that Arielle and her fellow citizens make themselves: zines" (427).

Riot Grrrls also took steps to secure material space for themselves. Niki, from the band Huggy Bear (whose members preferred not to divulge their last names), writes, "We did women-only shows to challenge the acceptance of violence against women on all levels. The woman as the centre of things. Separatist shows do not *revolve* around stopping boys coming to shows—they are a way of bringing women/girls together and actually feeling different for our pleasure" (160). Creating women-only mosh pits was also a common practice at Riot Grrrls shows and marked an effort to allow women to dance with one another without fear of injury from aggressive male moshers. Huggy Bear collectively authored some thoughts on moshing at most non–Riot Grrrl punk shows (although the band adopts the first-person singular pronoun): "There is a very real threat that you will be crushed while the opportune scumbag will squeeze you, press his dick up against you. Girls have been fingered, had their breasts elbowed, and the way you get made to feel you are drawing attention to the fact you are close to his body . . . I mean, like it has some sexual significance" (157).

Meetings were also integral to the scene. Soon after the 1991 IPU Convention in Olympia, Bikini Kill moved to Washington, D.C. Kathleen

Hanna comments, "We were . . . talking about starting a widely distributed fanzine, so I said, 'Let's have a meeting about skill sharing.' . . . We had the first meeting and about twenty women showed up. A lot of them had never been in a room with only women before and were blown away by what it felt like: everybody had so much to say. That felt like an overwhelming response, so we continued our weekly meetings" (Hanna, "Kathleen Hanna: Bikini Kill," 99). Corin Tucker, who attended Evergreen State University and accounted for half of Riot Grrrl band Heavens to Betsy (H2B), recalls meetings she attended: "Some meetings were very organizational; if someone had an idea for an event they wanted to do, we would figure out who would do what in order for an event to happen. . . . And some of the meetings were really personal, talking about people's feelings, or things they were going through, or how feminism was relating to their personal lives. There was never really any set agenda" (Experience Music). Tucker's comments suggest that the need for a community upstaged meetings' particular concerns. Although earlier punk scenes were also shot through with the wish for community, Riot Grrrl expressed it more directly, in "Riot Grrrl Is . . ." for example. Reason number eleven is: "BECAUSE doing/reading/seeing/hearing cool things that validate and challenge us can help us gain the strength and sense of community that we need in order to figure out how bullshit like racism, able-bodyism, ageism, speciesism, classism, thinism, sexism, anti-Semitism, and heterosexism figures in our own lives." In the other punk scenes, community evolved fairly organically; in Riot Grrrl, it was planned but no less powerful for this reason, as Hanna's comments about the first meeting in D.C. indicate. Predominantly male collectives might emerge organically and spontaneously in U.S. popular culture, but an all-female collective had to clear space for itself by encouraging females to come to shows, posting signs announcing all-female mosh pits, etc.

The words written in felt-tipped marker on Riot Grrrls' arms, hands, and stomachs not only signified membership in Riot Grrrl; they also expressed an animus new to punk. Farai Chideya describes the practice as "an MTV-era way of saying, 'That's what you think of me; confront your own bigotry.'" Kathleen Hanna seems to confirm this interpretation. Speaking about being photographed at shows, she says: "I felt that if I wrote 'slut' or 'whore' or 'incest victim' on my stomach, then I wouldn't just be silent. I thought a lot of guys might be thinking this anyway when they looked at my picture, so this would be like holding up a mirror to what they were thinking" (Hanna, "Kathleen Hanna: Bikini Kill," 100). This is certainly one possibility, although I think that this use of language is more complicated than Chedeya's reading allows for. Instead of "confront your own bigotry," the labels place a more disturbing injunction on spectators: "confront your own fantasy." Bratmobile's song "Love Thing" begins, "Admit it—innocent little / girls turn u. on don't they? / u.

like to make them cry / u. like to tell them why / u like to grow them up." The literally embodied words direct the same accusation at the audience but employ a different tactic: they force the audience to "traverse the fantasy," in the language of Jacques Lacan and Slavoj Žižek. The point is not to admonish the audience for harboring scurrilous fantasies but to concretize those fantasies in order to move through, attenuate, and thereby dispel them. In order to combat sexism, Riot Grrrls wear tags that force audience fantasies existing at the level of the imaginary into material and symbolic form: your (symbolic) reality depends upon imagining (fantasizing) that all girls and women are sluts, whores, and bitches? Look, then, at your fantasy in symbolic form, in corporeal form. The idea at work is that the contradiction between the sexist fantasy of woman as whore, slut, etc. and the symbolic embodiment of that fantasy in the shape of a living Grrrl explodes the fantasy and shatters the reality that it supported by shifting it from the realm of the imaginary into the symbolic order, where it no longer holds the allure of fantasy. When the strategy works, the audience members have "traversed the fantasy," witnessed it taking on symbolic form and thereby leaving the realm of fantasy. No longer will it serve as a tacit, imaginary support for sexist behavior, for treating women as if they are, in reality, bitches, etc. Instead, what is left is "that which remains of reality after reality is deprived of its support in fantasy" (Žižek, *Ticklish Subject* 51). A similar strategy obtains intermittently throughout punk, for example in the California Hardcore band Fear's song "Let's Have a War," in which Lee Ving sings, "Let's have a war! Jack up the Dow Jones!" and the chorus is simply the words "There's too many of us" repeated numerous times at breakneck speed. By bringing the fantasy into the light, Ving shows it for the despicable thing that it is. However, only in Riot Grrrl does the attempt to traverse specific fantasies about femininity and sexuality become formalized as a method.

Riot Grrrl fashion echoed this method with its tartan skirts, girlish barrettes, bobbed hair, and tights. The little girl clothing materializes a set of fantasies in order to stretch them until they tear, revealing a different reality beneath. Nevertheless, the strategy risks being interpreted in less generous ways. Interviewing Lois (Lois Maffeo), a musical collaborator with Riot Grrrls but not one herself, Andrea Juno observes that "[s]ome aspects of Riot Grrrl need to be critiqued; sometimes I wonder why there's so much of an emphasis on girlhood—to me, it's like, 'Wait a minute, let's be women. Let's break the hymen'" (131). Lois defends herself ("I never wore short skirts and knee socks and pinafores" [132]) but also interprets the fashion more forgivingly:

> You can go on and on about what the possible primary meanings are for dressing this way. The adult criteria for beauty are very severe, but more pliable for young girls. Cute is defined in more ways than glamorous or beau-

tiful is, and a lot of adolescent girls who are searching for their own sense of allure don't necessarily define themselves as beautiful or glamorous; cute is a closer possibility for them. (132)

Lois counters the possibility that Riot Grrrls' fashion will encourage outsiders as well as scene members to infantalize grrrls, arguing, instead, for the fashion's functional and pragmatic properties.

However, a close reading of Riot Grrrl fashion suggests alternate readings. The cover photos from Bikini Kill's first, self-titled EP[34] and the Bikini Kill CD "The C.D. Version of The First Two Records" feature pictures from one of the band's shows. On "Bikini Kill," a black-and-white photo captures Tobi Vail in the left foreground. Her hair is bobbed, her bangs short (a cut made famous by Louise Brooks), and she wears a short black dress, slightly ragged at the edges of the sleeves and hem. Dark lipstick accentuates her mouth, which is open as she sings into the microphone. Dark sunglasses obscure her eyes. Fishnet stockings and a pair of clunky, sensible, old-fashioned women's shoes round out her outfit. Behind her, Kathleen Hanna stands playing bass and wearing an oversized white tee-shirt with "Riot Grrl" stenciled across it, white tights, and '70s-style white boots that zip up the sides and stop just below her knees. On "The C.D. Version," the cover image, a low-level shot—captures the women at a later moment in the same show. They're wearing the same clothing, but now they're sitting down next to one another on the stage, their legs flung out in front of and open. Hanna looks dazed; Vail continues to sing into the microphone clasped right in front of her mouth. Both images evoke the idea of girls dressed in their mothers' old clothing, girls playing "dress up" with adult clothing. Hanna's oversized shirt and '70s-style boots and Vail's frayed dress, fishnet stockings, and shoes bring to mind the somewhat formal, worn, and/or outdated clothing that a woman might allow her children to play with. The dark lipstick recalls girls' early attempts to apply makeup, migrating toward the not-so-subtle shades from their mothers' collections. These seemingly appropriated signifiers of mature female sexuality contrast with how Riot Grrrls deploy them, Hanna's childish barrettes, and the attitude that the musicians strike as they sit on the stage. Their body language resembles that of girls too young to be concerned that their dresses (or long T-shirt, in Hanna's case) have ridden up on their hips or that their underwear shows.

It's worth mentioning in this context that Hanna sometimes wore her underwear over her other clothing, as if to say "Do you want to see my underwear? Okay, here it is." This gesture traverses the fantasy not by countering it with its opposite—pants, perhaps, or a reproof: "Stop fantasizing about women's underwear!"—but by playing to the fantasy, moving directly into and through it in order to come out the other end. Analogously, in the environs of a strip club, this traversal might be dramatized by a stripper marching out from backstage already naked, walking to the center of the stage, turning around fully, and exiting. No slow tease, no pole dancing, no shaking or wriggling, just nudity. "You want to see nudity? Okay, here it is. Good night." The fantasy traversed would be that the nudity draws the audience and not the gradual metamorphosis from clothed to nude, a process that hinges on the fantasy that nudity might not actually be arrived at, that the entirely nude woman and her sexuality might not have to be confronted. After all, when she is finally nude the show is over.

Bikini Kill's cover art similarly traverses the fantasy of the female as naïf, as not sexually mature, as girlish, as not-to-be-taken-seriously. This fantasy materially serves men (and some women) within the institutional bodies of rock and roll—from musicians to club owners to booking agents—who benefit economically by policing the borders of the rock or punk sphere and maintaining its overwhelmingly male predominance. And, in another register—that of intersubjectivity—the same fantasy supports a sexist reality in which males are not required to respect or engage with female sexuality. "So you want your women girlish? Here's what your fantasy looks like—women who book their own shows, manage their own finances, and produce and publish their own music relegated to perpetual girlhood. Here is your fetish writ large and made public." The friction between Vail's and Hanna's maturity and the seeming lack thereof in their clothing drives this critique of woman as girl, like the growl added to "girl" to make it "grrrl." The same disconnect between women's sexuality and girlishness is evoked by the word "pussy," scrawled in large letters down Hanna's right arm on the album covers. Juxtapositioning this word with signifiers of "girl" confronts the spectator with an unresolvable tension: How can the word *pussy* be resolved with the evoked fantasy of prepubescence? As Žižek explains, the contradictions must be included in the fantasy: "[W]e identify with the work of our 'imagination' even more radically, in all its inconsistency—that is to say, prior to its transformation into the phantasmic frame that guarantees our access to reality" (*Ticklish Subject* 51). The fantasy's contradictions are precisely what allow it to support a particular construct of reality and subjectivity, and it is the unveiling of those contradictions within the symbolic—photos, in this case—that forecloses on one previously available subject position—a sexist one—by knocking out its "phantasmic" supports. The fantasy, like the dream that fulfills a wish, does not recognize contradictions, but the reality that is the symbolic order does.

If the dominant logic of History, understood as "the history of class struggles" (Marx and Engels, *Communist Manifesto*, 3), is the history of the economy, then the Riot Grrrl Scene will never successfully meld their history with official History. But there is another history that Riot Grrrl takes pains to record: the secret history of girls and young women in U.S. culture. As usual, Riot Grrrls express this desire—and the lack that produces it—explicitly. In 1992, in the zine *Riot Grrrl,* the editors wrote: "The Start: we are not quite sure what we're about—in a lot of ways we are a work in progress. But we do know that we're women and quite proud of it. We also know that we're tired of being written out—out of history, out of the 'scene,' out of our bodies. . . . [F]or this reason we have created our zine and scene" (Devosby et al.). For a channel into if not economic history then the history of social movements, Riot Grrrls chose Third-Wave feminism, with which they aligned themselves. Kathleen Hanna remarks: "[H]aving an analysis that had to do with oppression saved my life. If there wasn't feminist theory, I don't know what I would have done. This feeling of being pushed into invisibility is a product of oppression. It is a historical problem" (*Punk Planet,* 44). As with the Dead Kennedys, Riot Grrrls have organized their activism around liberal political precedents. In 2003, for instance, the New York chapter (RGNY, or Riot Grrrls New York City) have participated in New York City's AIDS Walk, hold weekly "counter-harassment parties" (during which they demonstrate in Washington Square Park that "there IS a consequence to disrespecting women, and women WILL confront them [their oppressors] in solidarity with other women" *[Riot Grrrl NYC!]*), and protested outside of the K-Rock Radio Station, where the playlist is 99.12 percent male. Commenting on the latter, Marisa Ragonese, a member of RGNY for the past three years, confesses that she "took up the decidedly liberal feminist project of challenging New York City's most popular hardrock station (and the home of Howard Stern)," even though she is "one of those wimmin who doesn't want a bigger slice of the male-dominated pie" (Ragonese, 27). In short, Ragonese will fight against patriarchal History where she finds it—an economically successful radio station in this case—but not merely to position women within a chauvinist system. The conviction that women should demand a qualitatively different social structure rather than more control over a patriarchal one has remained popular throughout Riot Grrrl's history but has not precluded the largely New Left politics that grrrls have adopted from Second Wave feminism.

Perhaps it is no surprise, then, that critiques of Riot Grrrl have mimicked historically earlier ones aimed at the Second Wave. Jessica Rosenberg and Gitana Garofalo observe that the

> fact that the vast majority of girls involved in Riot Grrrl are white and middle- to upper-class has caused outsiders to deride the movement and some of those involved to dissociate themselves from it. Although there has been much discussion recently [in 1997] of race as an issue within Riot Grrrl and society in general, no one seems to have conceived any viable solution to the racial homogeneity of Riot Grrrl. Most of the problem lies in the fact that

Riot Grrrl travels primarily through punk rock, a very white underground, zines, and word of mouth, which tend to go from white girl to white girl because of racial segregation. (811)

Despite this shortcoming related to inclusivity, which is no more prevalent in Riot Grrrl than in previous punk scenes, the Riot Grrrl Scene has succeeded in establishing a social field in which girls, including pre-teens, act as experts on their own lives and share their expertise with like-minded girls through zines and, over the past few years, over the Internet. Regardless of whether or not Riot Grrrl differs significantly from Second Wave feminism apropos of its telos or methods, it has constituted the youngest group yet of self-identifying feminists in the United States and generated a set of material relations between female producers whom History habitually takes notice of only as consumers.

The Riot Grrrl Scene continues in 2003, with active chapters in New York City, Philadelphia, and London, among other cities, but the majority of the chapters across the United States, Canada, and Europe have become inactive. A decisive split occurred in the summer of 1992, when commercial media publicized the scene, seizing on it as spectacle and surface more than content. In 1999, Corin Tucker recalls, "[m]ainstream media missed the entire point of Riot Grrrl. . . . They just completely trivialized the entire movement as being a fashion statement. The whole point of Riot Grrrl is that we were able to rewrite feminism for the 21st century." Tobi Vail remembers that, after the media blitz, "[t]he whole conversation became one of identity instead of one about activism or music or culture" (Experience Music). A rift grew between Riot Grrrls who had joined the scene before its national exposure and Grrrls who joined after it, with the earlier members suspicious of the new ones, who were, in turn, confused about that suspicion. Shortly thereafter, the original Riot Grrrl bands broke up, their members forming new bands, often on the same independent labels that had housed their earlier groups.

Ailecia Ruscin, writer of the Riot Grrrl zine *alabama grrrl*, comments that "Riot Grrrl has evolved and morphed into many different kinds of movements. Many argue that Riot Grrrl was co-opted by the media and others think that Riot Grrrls just became 'ladies' . . . Bratmobile's Allison Wolfe came up with the idea to hold a Ladyfest in Olympia, WA about 3–4 years ago and she used the word lady because she saw that many of the grrrls had grown up and evolved from their punk aesthetics into something a little different. [M]any folks still use this terminology, especially as Ladyfests have emerged all over the world in the years following the first one organized by Wolfe and others." While much of the original energy behind Riot Grrrl might have flowed into Ladyfest, Riot Grrrl itself has become one of the many subgenres of contemporary punk, with its numerous nodes and rhizomatic structure.

THE BERKELEY/LOOKOUT! POP-PUNK SCENE

The dominance of hardcore punk that began with the California Hardcore Scene finally waned in 1989, with the dissolution of Second Wave Straight Edge. Hardcore did not disappear in the '90s, and Riot Grrrl would figure as a feminine embodiment of it if the scene's members categorized their music as such, but Pop-Punk supplanted hardcore as the dominant genre of punk beginning in 1990 and enduring until 1995. The most concentrated nexus of Pop-Punk desires arose around Berkeley, California, Lookout! Records, and a Berkeley venue: the 924 Gilman Street Project. Pop-Punk bands seminal to this scene included The Queers, The Riverdales, Screeching Weasel, The Mr. T Experience, Pansy Division, Groovie Ghoulies, Fifteen, Lookouts, Green Day, Pinhead Gunpowder, and Blatz, all of which have recorded music for the Lookout! label.

In 1988, Larry Livermore founded Lookout! Records in Laytonville, California, before moving it to Berkeley a couple of years later. Loosely basing his business practices on those of Dischord, Livermore established a label in order to record, distribute, and encourage the music emanating from a newly burgeoning and noncommercially-based Pop-Punk Scene in Northern California, a scene in which he actively participated as a member of a band, the Lookouts. Livermore's economic support for the Pop-Punk Scene helped its members foster the same DIY approach that earlier punk scenes had advanced. In order to grant some control over their own production to the musicians on Lookout!, Livermore did not initially sign bands to contracts or determine which studios or engineers they could hire when they recorded, nor did he require bands to tour. He also practiced profit sharing.[35] In short, his business practices and label serve as material signifiers of the underlying desire of the Berkeley scene's punks to take control of their music's production away from the major labels that continued in the '90s—and continue today—to dominate the U.S. and world music industries.

The same desires found explicit expression in the 924 Gilman Street Project that Tim Yohannon helped found in Berkeley the same year that Livermore founded Lookout! (1988). 924 Gilman was, and continues to be, an "all-ages, non-profit, collectively organized music and performance venue. . . . It is (ideally) a violence, alcohol and drug-free environment" (*924 Gilman* June 2003) devoted to hosting noncommercial performances of all types but concentrating upon punk rock. Yohannon describes how he originally envisioned the space:

> I wanted it to be a place that would be run by the bands and the fans. Bands would meet and figure out what the bills would be. The bands would take responsibility for the whole show, for cleaning up, for every aspect of it. I

wanted it to be a cooperative effort amongst the different constituents within
that community. I wanted it to be something where people could take control of something that up to that point had been like a commodity that had
been something for sale. (Yohannon, 186–87)

To a limited degree, Yohannon's plan came to fruition, especially the economic
organization that he imagined for the club. It was and still is run by a collective that currently costs two dollars to join and meets on the first and third
Saturdays of every month to decide upon club policies, bookings, etc. Admis-
sion to the club was originally three dollars and is now five. Volunteers staffed
and continue to staff the club, and it was and is a nonprofit organization.

Ultimately, however, Yohannon was disappointed with 924 Gilman,
because the bands did not form the sort of community that he had imagined,
a community that would challenge the spectacular aspect of rock music shows
in which active producers played to passive consumers. Instead, he claims, "for
the most part the bands just wanted to make music. And for the most part people just wanted to be entertained" (187). He abandoned the project, but a new
collective of punks soon contacted him and reopened the space, and the club
began to serve not just as a performance space but also as a place that could
"hold benefit concerts for such varied organizations as Rock Against Racism,
Food Not Bombs, and Battered Women Shelters" (*924 Gilman* May 2000). In
Berkeley, the underlying desire to form a collective spread beyond the borders
of the punk community itself, making inroads into other social groups. The
Food Not Bombs chapter of San Francisco continues to be staffed partially by
punks. Within the punk community of Northern California, another collective
sprang up in San Francisco: the Epicenter Zone, a volunteer-run punk collective, opened in 1990 and was staffed entirely by volunteers throughout its existence (it closed in 1999). It was both a performance space and a punk store.

Yohannon hoped to engender a Berkeley scene that would attack the
spectacle of the rock concert, which had continued through the '80s, and especially the major label bands' polarization of performances into producing
musicians and passive fans. He remembers that, at 924 Gilman, he "placed an
open mic on stage where if someone didn't like what a band had just done or
sung, whatever, they could go up there and confront 'em, right there on the
spot" (Yohannon, 187), because he "wanted people to leave the show with
their brains working. Have fun, go crazy, and also come out of there with your
mind clicking instead of dead" (187). As he saw the situation, "the club and
the band conspire to try and turn the audience into a participant" (187).
Although this sort of exchange occurred occasionally, it remained the exception rather than the norm at 924 Gilman.

In fact, the Pop-Punk Scene turned against Yohannon, the Svengali-like
Jello Biafra of Berkeley, and against the formerly punk desire to counter the

spectacle or carve a place for punk in history. Comparing the mid-'70s poppy punk band the Zeros to the Ramones in the second issue of the *Search and Destroy* zine, V. Vale writes that the Zeros' lyrics "are really 'teenage'—as opposed to teenage 'concept' lyrics, such as the Ramones" (32). For Vale, "teenage" means silly and simple, descriptors that could certainly be applied to Pop-Punk, but a deeper drive was at work in Berkeley, the desire to create a space within punk rock for "nonpolitical" music, despite punk's tradition since the English Scene of being at least somewhat politically positioned. If, after London, punk has had an agenda of some sort, albeit a shifting one, if it has had something to do with change and with dissatisfaction, then Pop-Punk reveals, in its various artifacts, a desire to live without an agenda.

Aesthetically, Pop-Punk fell back upon Ramones-influenced three-chord punk and shared with the Ramones and the Zeros the desire to accept the spectacle as spectacle. Pop-Punk song forms and lyrics reflect this desire. While, by 1990, hardcore songs had dwindled in length down to only thirty seconds in some instances, Pop-Punk embraced the radio-friendly three-minute pop song with its verse-chorus-verse structure. This music aimed to please the audience more than to enlighten or collectivize it, and, as with the Ramones, songs tended to be lyrically simple and often deliberately silly. The Pop-Punk band Green Day's album *Kerplunk* (1992), on Lookout! Records, includes the songs "One for the Razorbacks," a conventional puppy love song (despite its title), "Dominated Love Slave," a send-up of the simple country love song, and "Words I Might Have Ate," a paean to unrequited teenage love. The Berkeley scene's bands also popularized the punk ballad that had become almost extinct during hardcore's reign. Pop-Punks drained the earnest and manifesto-like quality of hardcore from their songs and did not invest in the send-up of the spectacle that the English Scene instigated, either.

The Berkeley scene also turned away from the "jock" fashion of NYHC and deliberately and nostalgically reinstated the fashion of the New York Scene and especially the look of the Ramones. Leather motorcycle jackets returned, with The Queers adopting them as well as The Riverdales, and Screeching Weasel's logo, a weasel smoking a cigarette, also wears one, as do both Furious George's logo, Curious George, and the band's lead singer, George Tabb. NYHC punks were seldom tattooed or pierced, but the Berkeley scene enthusiastically embraced both forms of body modification. Although piercings were rare in early punk scenes, tattoos have surfaced sporadically.[36]

Reading the Pop-Punk Scene's sartorial artifacts reveals a nostalgic but tempered desire to revivify the impulses that ran through the New York Scene but did not reach fruition, while abandoning the desires that later punk scenes accrued. Pop-Punk initially seized a modicum of control over the means of its own production—through Lookout!, 924 Gilman Street, and the Epicenter (which extended the Berkeley scene into San Francisco)—that allowed its participants to resist commercialization. This resistance bound the scene into a loose collectivity, but Pop-Punks deflected the more radical gestures toward community that Tim Yohannon spearheaded, while setting aside questions of history, spectacle, and identity that other scenes invoked. For the most part, the Berkeley Scene also sidelined desires centering around sexuality, which means, in effect, that the predominantly patriarchal and homoerotic structure that emerged during Straight Edge reproduces itself but in a less exaggerated form in Berkeley. The scene's lyrical attention to adolescent heterosex does not necessarily speak directly to an underlying desire to engage in that form of sexuality, but it does suggest that participants in the Pop-Punk Scene want to absent themselves from the issues around sexuality that earlier scenes invoked, such as bondage, masochism, power, and homoeroticism. The scene betrays a wish to treat heterosexuality as a normative entity, while repressing homo-erotic practices more than the Straight Edge Scenes did.

Nevertheless, the scene is nominally opposed to homophobia. Since 924 Gilman opened, a set of rules has been painted on the wall facing the entrance: they explain that no racism, sexism, or homophobia will be tolerated within the club. Yohannon expressed rather than invented these rules for the scene, but their inscription at 924 Gilman marks their formalization. But rather than embracing the "non-homophobic" character of the Pop-Punk Scene as a social space in which various forms of sexuality could be practiced, most of the scene's participants accepted an almost desexualized construct of adolescent hetero-sexuality combined with a repressed male homoeroticism as normative. To con-struct sexuality along these lines, the Pop-Punk Scene melded Tim Yohannon's 924 Gilman Street "rules" with a conceptualization of adolescent heterosexual-ity best expressed by Aaron Cometbus in his zine *Cometbus*.

Although the fairly new zine, *Zine Guide*, has only been polling its readers for lists of their favorite zines and then publishing those lists for a few years, Aaron Cometbus's personal zine, *Cometbus*, which he produces himself but has distributed internationally, was ranked first in the "Favorite Zines Overall" and "Favorite Zines Among Boys" lists in 2003, and second in "Favorite Zines Among Girls." Aaron is deeply familiar with the Pop-Punk Scene, because he was and is a member of several popular Berkeley-based Pop-Punk bands, including Crimpshrine and Pinhead Gunpowder (both Lookout! bands). The most famous issue of *Cometbus*, 42, the *Double Duce* novel, recounts the time that he spent living in a collectively run house (Double Duce) in Berkeley during the early '90s. It narrates a partial history of the scene that emerged from its geographic epicenter as well as from one of its important musicians. For the most part, *Double Duce* concentrates upon relations between young men who live in the same house, play in the same bands, and participate in the same scene. It avoids mentioning homo-sexuality and describes women almost exclusively as potential or actual "girlfriends," who represent a threat to the house's male collective much as they did in the Straight Edge Scenes. Aaron describes this threat most explicitly when he bemoans his realization that, for the guys in the house, "it was obvious that our lives would be less flexible in the future, and the time was now to take on the world together, before everyone 'accidentally' got married, or got a career, or got dead." Heterosexual marriage, a career, and death are equated in terms of potential disruption to the Double Duce house.

The only form of sexuality that Aaron seems to approve of is the heterosexual and seemingly child-like relationship between his male friend Sluggo and Sluggo's girlfriend Sal. With great nostalgia, Aaron describes the couple and connects them to the house (and the room of Willey, one of the house's inhabitants) and to the Pop-Punk Scene in general:

> Sluggo and Sal were with us, too, half the time. They were in love, though no one even knew they were going out until one day they announced they had broken up. They were like two little peas in a pod, always running and riding and building and doing the most amazing things, then returning from their adventures and curling up together to sleep at their squat or in Willey's tiny closet.

> Although it wasn't that long ago, I always think of Sluggo and Sal in love as the time the world was young and nothing was impossible. It was an intoxicating feeling, but one we grew out of, out of necessity, and going back to it now would be about as much fun as going back to childhood. Only looking back on it does their romance sum up a whole era and the spirit behind it.

The "era" was the early years of Pop-Punk that Aaron describes, unironically, in the language of clichéd notions of an idyllic childhood completely divorced from even childish or adolescent forms of sexual desire. One of the best aspects of the relationship between Sluggo and Sal is that Aaron never witnessed a moment of it that struck him as sexualized in any way, because its sexual aspects were closeted. Even Sluggo's name (although the zine is autobiographical, Aaron gives his characters fictional names) conjures up a fictionalized and asexual relationship: the relationship between Nancy and Sluggo from Ernie Bushmiller's *Nancy* cartoon. Throughout *Double Duce*, the predominantly male and heterosexual Berkeley scene expresses a nostalgia for clichéd constructions of sexuality, or asexuality, that have never, in fact, existed. Yet, combined with this nostalgia is a yearning for two all-male interconnecting spheres, the "work" sphere, composed of bands and "the scene," and the "home" sphere that the Double Duce house represents for Cometbus.

Between 1993 and 1995, market forces altered the Pop-Punk Scene dramatically. The stage was set when Lookout! released Green Day's second

album, *Kerplunk,* in 1992. Unlike preceding Pop-Punk releases, it sold well
enough to generate major label interest, and a bidding war broke out that concluded with the band signing with Reprise Records, a division of Time
Warner, in 1994 and releasing a new album, *Dookie,* the same year. Based on
sales of that album, the band was offered a slot at the 1994 Woodstock festi-
val, and in the beginning of 1995 the fourth single from their Reprise album,
"When I Come Around," reached the number one spot in the U.S. modern
rock charts and stayed there for seven weeks. Currently, Reprise has sold more
than eight million copies of *Dookie* in the United States and more than eleven
million internationally. Following Green Day's deal with Reprise and the success of *Dookie,* major labels quickly signed contracts with a group of Pop-Punk
bands including the Offspring, who signed with Columbia/Sony in May
1996. In short, the Big Six capitalized upon the newly lucrative Pop-Punk
Scene. As in the cases of the New York and the English scenes, major label
contracts shattered the possibilities toward which Pop-Punk's core desires
militate. The Big Six prevent scene members from exercising control over
their means of production and consumption; they work against the mainte-
nance of punk scenes that are usually fairly small (numbering in the thousands) and regionally based; they contain punk within the official economic
history of the industry; they reproduce spectacle without critiquing it; and
they transform fashion, identity, and sexuality into superficial and purely spectacular commodities, incapable of interrogating the relations between surfaces
and depths that punks' desires investigate. Although Pop-Punk continues to
proliferate nationwide and globally in 2003, beginning in 1995 a backlash has
arisen against it in localized scenes, in all types of zines, among fans, and in
punk rock's forms and contents.

Evidence of an overall exhaustion with Pop-Punk is most apparent in the
record review sections of numerous punk zines between 1996 and 2003. For
example, in a 1996 *Punk Planet* review of an LP by Walker—a Pop-Punk
band from Lafayette, Indiana—Grant Gartland comments upon Walker and
Mass Giorgini, chief engineer and owner of the Sonic Iguana recording studio where several of the best-selling Pop-Punk bands of the '90s recorded:

> Mass Giorgini strikes again with Walker. I swear he should grab all these
> Pop-Punk bands he produces or engineers and start a revolution or some-
> thing. He could probably take over the world in sheer volume alone. That
> said, let me tell you that Walker, like many of the others, is extremely listen-
> able and very friendly. I really like the genre but I'm beginning to think that
> it's getting worn out. We need a change. (83)

By 2003, reviews have taken on a significantly more bitter tone. In an exemplary three-sentence *MaximumRockNRoll* review of the band Jack Fluster's

Disconstructed CD, Will Risk writes: "Shitty sentimental Pop-Punk which belongs on Honest Don's Records. The best parts made me go 'Whoa, that one line sounded like FUN PEOPLE,' not to equate this, in any way, with that band. The best part of this album is that the guitarist is wearing a cool NOFX shirt that I have never seen before." (Honest Don's Records is a label that releases almost exclusively Pop-Punk and is owned by Fat Mike, who plays in NOFX.)

CONCLUSIONS

The logic of Pop-Punk's incorporation might seem homologous to the logic that governs the dissolution of almost every punk scene: a set of desires flares out, assumes a set of aesthetic and economic forms opposed to consumerism, commercialism, and capitalism, and is recuperated or broken apart by the logic of the multinational, capitalist economy. In short, an escape and capture logic seems to map the general movement of punk history. Jude Davies, borrowing from Steve Redhead, identifies this structure as "the cycle of authenticity and recuperation that structures most academic discussions of the phenomenon known as punk rock" (3), and to his claim I would add that the same structure governs much of the discourse within punk itself. Debates about whether bands have remained authentic or sold out fill the pages of countless punk zines and have done so since punk's inception. The danger of the structure that Davies and Redhead highlight and militate against—and it is a heuristic that has gained popularity in approaching numerous phenomena, in addition to punk—lies in its apparent determinism and circularity. If analysis becomes nothing more than tracking cultural phenomena from birth to their ineluctable commodification and recuperation by capitalism, then that hermeneutic produces little more than repetitions of the same narrative: capitalism wins again. Sooner or later, everything becomes commodified. Give up now. But this is precisely why punk cannot be limited to its English Scene incarnation, which is what Davies and Redhead do. Looked at as a series of scenes strung together across time and geography, a different structure emerges. True, individual scenes escape from commodity culture and are captured, but, more interestingly, when the set of scenes is considered rather than a single scene, another structure emerges. A set of fairly consistent desires can be discerned acting as the engine of each scene, and each scene articulates those desires in a new configuration of relations between people and relations between people and objects. What matters is not that capitalists channel those desires along lines profitable to them. What matters is that the same core desires continually emerge and are continually becoming desublimated. These are the repressed desires that Raymond Williams argues must accompany any dominant mode of production; they are the impulses that the current mode of production cannot satisfy. What strikes me as essential is not that every punk scene seems predestined to recuperation but that punk renders legible the failings of capitalism in the guise of recurring, never-successfully-repressed wishes.

By way of summary, these desires can be named. Three emerge in New York: resisting commercialization, seizing control over the means of production, and fostering collectivity. The English Scene supplements these three with three more: interrogating History and the spectacular character of rock music; striving toward new constructions of identity and critiquing its links with fashion; and engendering predominantly male regions in which homosocial behavior is accepted, encouraged, and celebrated. All of the post-1978 punk scenes reimagine and rematerialize the same six core desires from the first two scenes with one new addition: Riot Grrrls express the desire to traverse sexist fantasies. One other difference distinguishes several of the scenes: hardcore, in all of its forms, is less prone to commercialization than other genres of punk, a phenomenon that I will return to in the next chapter. In looking at the groups of artifacts that punk's desires have produced, I have attempted to map the shape of those constellations and name the desires that constitute them. Punk performs a type of cultural work: it affords us the opportunity to recognize collective, cultural, and political desires as ours and to become conscious of them as such. The members of each scene strive to satisfy the desires that drive their scene. However, as punk's scenes demonstrate, the capitalist market economy cannot satisfy punk's core impulses. If Fredric Jameson is correct and our "political unconscious" harbors the desires that capitalism represses, then punk is one of the cultural fields in which repressed desires take material shape. It is worth remembering, at this point, the reason that particular desires must be repressed to begin with, which is that they cannot be realized within the parameters of capitalism. In short, "punk" is the name that can be assigned to an organization of radical desires that, combined, express a wish for a noncapitalist structuring of social reality. It is for this reason that punk's desires aim at an endpoint not dissimilar to one envisioned by Marx: "Let us imagine, for a change, an association of free men, working with the means of production held in common, and expending their many different forms of labour-power in full self-awareness as one single social labour force" (*Capital:* 1:171). Under these conditions, work means more than making money: "[L]abour is no longer just a means of keeping alive but has itself become a vital need" ("Gotha Program," 347). Buried within punk lie the same seeds that Marx identifies, the seeds of a society in which collectives own the means of production and produce for non-commercial ends. Furthermore, the history of this imagined society—punk, socialist, or both—would be the history of collectives and not the history of the economy.

In this chapter, I have described the seven largest punk scenes; however, numerous smaller scenes existed alongside the dominant ones. As of 2003, no new subcultural dominant has emerged within punk after Pop-Punk. Instead, punk has fractured into a multiplicity of small subgenres (participants number in the hundreds rather than in the thousands) that are not always linked to specific geographic areas. These subgenres include Garage, Glam Punk, Anarcho-Punk, Oi!, Queercore, Power Violence, Third Wave Straight Edge, Christian Hardcore (Christcore), Emo, Screamo, Crust, Street, Ska-Punk, Post-Hardcore, Grindcore, and '77–Style among others. Although none of these subgenres has grown large enough to dominate the field of punk, the past few years have witnessed an upsurge of nostalgia for the garage-rock roots of punk. The sound of many of these contemporary punk bands recalls the aesthetics of The MC5 (The Motor City 5) and The Stooges of the late '60s and early '70s. It remains to be seen whether a new scene will emerge around these neo-garage bands. Perhaps because no contemporary scene has congealed around a specific punk subgenre, several recent small scenes have advanced some of punk's core desires farther than any of the dominant scenes did. For instance, the most radical interrogations of the relations between punk and aesthetics occur in Anarcho-Punk and Crust. For this reason, in the next chapter I turn to these subgenres in order to map at least the vanguard of punk's current aesthetic project.

chapter two

Punk Aesthetics and the
Poverty of the Commodity

I had maintained intact my most precious human attribute—the
right to say no.

—Penny Rimbaud

PUNK VERSUS THE COMMODITY

Punk is structured around a fundamental contradiction between an anticommercial impulse constitutive of punk and punks' necessary trafficking in the commodity market. This contradiction has resulted in an economic, underground network of punk institutions that are more socialized than their corporate counterparts but that nevertheless circulate commodities. However, the punk/commodity opposition shapes the texts that these institutions produce; consequently, these institutions' practices speak not only to the violence and struggle of their existence as they resist the corporate model of production but also to the shortcomings of the commodity form itself, even when it is produced under the auspices of noncorporate punk enterprises. In the previous chapter, I argued that a desire to resist commercialization is one of the determinant desires constituting the seven largest punk scenes. I now turn to the punk institutions that express the strongest anticommercial sentiments in order to schematize the economic and aesthetic strategies with which they engage the major labels, the idea of the "commercial commodity," and the commodity form itself.

The two largest institutional forms of an early subgenre of punk, Anarcho-Punk—whose participants combine punk and anarchism—together with a punk collective that emerged from Anarcho-Punk in the mid-'90s, can be

81

understood as the material working through, on a limited scale, of the problem of imagining a cultural sphere that is not entirely determined by the capitalist economy. The particular and material form that this problem assumes for punks finds expression as a profound mistrust of, and resistance to, the commodification of punk.[1] This mistrust is conspicuous in three Anarcho-Punk institutions: the Crass Collective, the Profane Existence (PE) Collective, and the CrimethInc. Collective. Together, these collectives constitute the vanguard of punks' insistence on the possibility of opposing and negating the commodity market through economics and aesthetics.

Crass and PE exercise a set of negationist aesthetic choices: they experiment with song lengths and the form and content of punk songs and albums; they defer the consumer's expected forms of satisfaction; and they endeavor to negate and transcend the punk/commodity contradiction that structures these collectives as well as CrimethInc. and punk in general. Learning from earlier Anarcho-Punk collectives' aesthetic strategies, CrimethInc. mounts a new set of practices, including a different approach to negation, the use of irony, and an attempt to alter how punks confront the punk product in the marketplace. Both the early Anarcho-Punk collectives and CrimethInc. engage in similar economic practices aimed at opposing punk's entrance into, and circulation within, the commodity market. All of these institutions push DIY (do-it-yourself)[2] farther than other subgenres of punk have, favor punk enterprises over punk corporations, attempt to induce other punks to produce, and, whenever possible, give away what they could opt to sell.

Not surprisingly, neither the aesthetic nor the economic practices of Crass, PE, and CrimethInc. fully succeed, if success means a complete, if local or temporary, overthrow of the capitalist mode of production. Ultimately, the institutional critique that these structures bring to bear upon commodification cannot wholly transcend the clash between aesthetics and economics in the specific forms that punks find themselves positioned to negotiate. The critique absents neither a punk sphere from the commodity market in general nor an Anarcho-Punk sphere from the punk commodity market. Nevertheless, these collectives successfully, if often temporarily, establish spaces in which forces not bent upon profit making obtain and shape the lives of hundreds of scene members, and the turn away from profit enables other desires to come to the fore. Also, Crass, CrimethInc., and to some degree PE thematize and underscore their own failings, thereby at least partially negating these aesthetic forms of negation and economic forms of opposition as wholly viable punk strategies against commodification. By traversing these strategies and then reflecting back on their effectiveness or lack thereof, the collectives call into question the practices that they have mobilized, thereby gesturing toward other possible techniques for founding noncommercial cultural spaces, aesthetic spaces within the field of punk that economics does not determine or even significantly condition.

CRASS COMMODITIES

Anarcho-Punk, a subgenre that emerged in England in 1977 and contin-ues to exist in the year 2003, figures within punk as the most oppositional strand of punk's resistance to commodification. In 1976, an English hippie, Jeremy Ratter, and his commune-mate, Oscar Thompson, heard the Sex Pis-tols' "Anarchy in the U.K." for the first time. Ratter recounts their reaction: "[A]lthough we both felt that the Pistols probably didn't mean it, to us it was a battle cry. When Johnny Rotten proclaimed that there was 'no future,' we saw it as a challenge. We both knew that there was a future if we were pre-pared to fight for it" (Rimbaud, 216). Shortly after he first heard the Pistols, Ratter witnessed what he took to be the death of English punk, a death that he attributed to capitalism and, specifically, commodification:

> Within six months the movement had been bought out. The capitalist counter-revolutionaries had killed with cash. Punk degenerated from being a force for change, to becoming just another element in the grand media cir-cus. Sold out, sanitised and strangled, punk had become just another social commodity, a burnt-out memory of what might have been. (74)

In 1977, Ratter changed his name to Penny Rimbaud, Thompson's became Steve Ignorant, and together with some of the members of their commune and, later, people who trekked to the commune and expressed interest in the project, they formed a band, Crass, to attempt to push punk toward "what it might have been."[3] The band began in 1977, dissolved in 1984, and featured Ignorant, Rimbaud, Eve Libertine, and Joy de Vivre on vocals; Rab Herman helped found the band as the lead guitarist but Phil Free replaced him after a few months; Pete Wright played bass; Gee provided backing vocals and tape loops; and N. A. Palmer played rhythm guitar.[4] The commune that Rimbaud founded in 1965 in a decaying farmhouse in northern Essex, England, a few miles from London, was Crass's combined living and working space through-out the band's existence.

As Rimbaud admits, the members of Crass did not push the aesthetic nega-tion of the punk song in its major label, commodified, and English form (as exemplified by the Pistols' songs) as far as they might have. He comments that it is "true we have not greatly influenced music itself, but our effect on broader social issues has been enormous" (". . . In Which Crass Voluntarily"). Crass adopted a punk sound similar to that of the Sex Pistols: Ignorant sang in a snotty, nasal whine, while Rimbaud, Libertine, and de Vivre shouted most of their lyrics; the drums, guitar, and bass guitar parts did not require much technical profi-ciency to play, and there were few solos for any of the instruments. However, the members of Crass understood themselves as opposed to the major label form into which the Pistols' records had been stamped; consequently, their songs attempted to confront the commodified forms that the songs of the English Scene assumed. For example, Crass songs often lasted longer than the radio-friendly three-minute songs of the Pistols or the Clash, which meant that Crass songs could not be as readily commodified.

Additionally, while Pistols songs have simple lyrics and catchy, anthemic choruses, most Crass songs are simply structured but lyric-heavy tirades against war, consumerism, Repressive State Apparatuses, and Ideological State Apparatuses,[5] and about half of the band's songs do not contain choruses. In terms of content, Crass's lyrics differ somewhat from those of the Pistols. "Anarchy in the U.K." begins with, "I am an Anti-Christ / I am an anarchist / Don't know what I want but I know how to get it / I wanna destroy passers-by / Cos I wanna be anarchy." Crass's "Nineteen Eighty Bore" begins, "Who needs a lobotomy when we've got the ITV? / Who needs ECT when there's good old BBC? / Switch on the set, light up the screen, / Fantasise and dream about what you might have been, / Who needs controlling when they've got the cathode ray? / They've got your fucking soul, now they'll fuse your brains away." While the Sex Pistols invoked anarchy by name but did not engage in political activism, Rimbaud, who penned most of the lyrics for Crass, addressed the same sort of '60s and '70s liberal reform issues that the Riot Grrrls would take up, as well as Jello Biafra and the Dead Kennedys,[6] including the dangers of consumerism and apathy and their connections with the culture industry (specifically TV in the lyrics above), the threat of nuclear war and of war in general, corporate greed, etc.

However, where the Pistols' songs make a quick attack before beating a hasty retreat, a Crass song launches an attack and restates it repeatedly. "Nineteen Eighty Bore," which is not an especially lyric-heavy Crass song, contains thirty-six lines of roughly twelve syllables each, compared to "Anarchy in the U.K.'"s seventeen lines of roughly seven syllables each. While in much of the English Scene's music the lyrics and instruments command equal importance, in Crass songs the instrumentation serves as a vehicle for the lyrics, and the lyrics are so copious that the song structures seem incapable of containing them.

The length of Crass's rantings/songs combine with the bitter and mocking affect that Ignorant, Rimbaud, Libertine, and de Vivre's voices carry to produce a specific effect: the singers seem simultaneously gripped with both the need to condemn a particular social issue, or cluster of issues, and the realization of the futility of that effort. The band members play their instruments quickly, which adds to the sense that they have much to communicate but cannot possibly transmit it all within the limits of a song or album. This aesthetic approach militates against the commodification of Crass's music, if the commodity, as Marx claims, is "a thing which through its qualities satisfies human needs of whatever kind" (*Capital* 1:125). Instead of satisfying needs, Crass songs speak to their own inability to do so. Where most commodities promise at least the partial fulfillment of a need, Crass songs attempt to exacerbate need, adopting not the logic of the commodity but that of the advertisement, an advertisement for a product that does not yet exist. In a sense, all protest songs, and Crass songs are protest songs, are anti-ads; they try, with one hand, to produce a need where one did not exist but without offering, with the other hand, the remedy for the new need. This idea can be expressed another way: Crass songs do not forgo the effort to address needs, but the needs that they invoke without satisfying are qualitatively different from those that commercial commodities address.[7]

Crass also introduced sampling—in this case, the inclusion of found sounds—into punk. Between songs on albums, Gee would insert what she termed "tape collages" that were frequently short snippets of news from the radio, often related to English police actions or, after 1982, to the English conflict with Argentina over the Falkland Islands. To the end of a snippet, she would splice other snippet that seemed at odds with the first in terms of form, content, or both. Between the first and second songs on *Christ—The Album* appears this montage: a clip taken from a documentary on insects begins in mid sentence: "then they find their mate. The female climbs into the male, where she'll live the rest of her life. It's a simple life." This sample is fused to a second clip, in which a woman speaks to a baby and the baby's mother: "Come on now Ursula, come on, come on. She's lovely. Yes isn't she. I'm gonna pinch you, I am, I am." Gee's juxtapositioning of these two clips suggests a relation between them, although the subjects seem to be disparate: insect mating habits and human child rearing. This tape montage is sandwiched between "Have a Nice Day," a song about the "psychopaths" of Westminster, and "Mother Love," a song denouncing parenting as ideological brainwashing. In this example, the form of the Crass commodity militates against its own consumption as a commodity. In place of satisfaction, Crass albums present their listeners with a dialectical mix of media whose forms and messages seem to conflict with one another and that, when presented together, posit two implicit questions: What sort of social order could contain these contradictions within itself? And, how can these conflicts be resolved? In the above example, the tape montage and the songs that surround it ask how insect mating habits resemble the way in which an English woman raises her baby and how both of these phenomena are related to the British government and ideological brainwashing. An injunction, again directed at the audience, accompanies these questions: find a concept that can explain the interactions between these phenomena. Rather than satisfying needs, the album acts as an anti-ad; it attempts to create need and dissatisfaction without offering a cure.

There is another way to read Crass's use of tape montages, though, that partially negates their effectiveness as anti-commodities: Crass albums are themselves the resolutions to the oppositions that they pose. Gee does not attempt to splice her samples together seamlessly; she allows the sound of her recording apparatus's halting of one sample and starting up of another remain as proof of the apparatus's—and her process's—violence as it cuts off one speaker or sound and starts another, in order to force the two sounds into juxtaposition. Despite Gee's method, Crass albums materially demonstrate the power of the commodity to incorporate seemingly discordant elements into a whole. *Christ—The Album* resolves the conflict between its disparate elements by binding them together on a single vinyl (or aluminum, in the case of a CD) disk to suggest that within the form of the commodity no two sounds can be brought to bear upon one another in such a manner that they cannot be sold as unified—or at least contained—parts of a whole. In this sense, the Crass commodity stands as the reconciliation of a dialectic between the fragment or part and the whole.

There is a further way in which a Crass commodity cancels the aesthetic possibility of negating the commercial commodity through recourse to dialectics. Marx initially presents the commodity, in the first six chapters of *Capital,* as a fairly undeveloped economic form operating within the "sphere of simple circulation" (1:280), where it "satisfies human needs of whatever kind" (125). In the *Grundrisse,* he notes that in the market where a capitalist confronts potential consumers, the capitalist "searches for means to spur them on to consumption, to give his wares new charms, to inspire them with new needs by constant chatter, etc." (287). However, the capitalist rarely appears as a person in the market but sends the commodity in his or her place and relies, for the creation of needs, upon the contradictory nature of the commodity: the manner in which it functions both to satisfy desire by allowing desire to become invested within it and to defer indefinitely the complete realization of desire. The Crass commodity works through this logic materially, in the sense that Crass albums serve as ads, but not anti-ads, for other Crass albums. The perfect commodity never satisfies a need permanently; obeying a logic of eternal deferral, it only partially fulfills a need, while allowing for the possibility that a further commodity might satisfy the same need more completely or a new need suggested by the original commodity. As Kate Hinnant's poem "Superstore" expresses this idea, "Behind every / there is another." But even if a Crass album serves more to exacerbate a need than to meet it, it also prepares the way for subsequent Crass albums that bear with them the possibility that they might, finally, resolve tensions that the earlier albums left open. In short, each Crass album opens up on all the others, suggesting through its fragmentation its possible completion within the network of Crass's complete output.

Although Crass experimented with aesthetic strategies for negating the punk commodity in its English Scene forms, the band focused much of its energy upon economic forms of oppositionality. To begin with, the band recognized the commercial music industry as its enemy and refused to sign with a major label, despite EMI's offer of £50,000 in 1978. Earlier the same year, the band released its first 7", *The Feeding of the 5000*, on Pete Stennet's independent label Small Wonder Records but could not find a pressing plant willing to manufacture the record or a printer willing to print the cover that Gee had designed, as long as the record included as its first track "Reality Asylum," a song that attacked organized Christianity. Crass eventually substituted a minute of silence, entitled "The Sound of Free Speech," for the opening song and had the record manufactured. To avoid causing trouble for Stennet later in 1978, when the band members found a pressing plant willing to press "Reality Asylum," they founded their own label, Crass Records, in order to release it. They printed off five thousand covers themselves, rather than searching for a printer again.

Although necessity seems at least partially responsible for driving Crass toward a DIY approach to producing records, Rimbaud claims, in 1984, that by the time that DIY had become associated with punk in 1976, the members of the commune that he founded "had been doing just that" for "many years" (". . . In Which Crass Voluntarily"). Either way, Crass's appropriation of the means of production marks an attempt to resist the punk commodity in its Pistols and English Scene form: while the English Scene bands forfeited control over their means of producing commodities, in terms of both artistic freedom and the manufacturing process, Crass did so to a lesser degree. In fact, in order to maintain aesthetic control—specifically, in order to produce "Reality Asylum"—the band members realized that they had to find ways to bypass the dominant, or industry, mode of producing "punk commodities."[8] Having founded Crass Records, Crass never released their music on any other label. The band also managed itself, booked all of its own tours, distributed its own records, and designed and printed its own record sleeves.

The members of Crass also attempted to mediate between the two poles of the commodity, use-value and exchange-value, by deemphasizing their commodities' exchangeability expressed as a price. While reducing a commodity's price facilitates its exchange in one register, affordability, it also reduces the amount of labor that the consumer must exchange for the commodity, expressed as a portion of her or his wages. While the Sex Pistols and other English Scene bands could not control the prices of their 7"s and LPs, and, consequently, the bands' labels set the prices according to how much the market would bear, Crass controlled its pricing. The band members sold the "Reality Asylum" 7" for forty-five pence each, significantly below the market value of a 7" even in 1978. Since they first appeared on the market, Crass albums have always sold for less than major label products and, later, for less than most other independently produced punk products.

The members of Crass claimed that, unlike the commercial music industry that had engulfed the English Scene, they did not want to make a profit. Instead, they wanted to be able to sustain themselves and their commune, and, as Rimbaud claimed, their "prime purpose was the dissemination of information" (241). For this reason, even on their first 7" on Small Wonder, they included all six songs that they could play at the time, although the industry standard for a 7" was one song per side. Rimbaud claims that *The Feeding of the 5000* was the first multitracked 7" ever. In sum, the commodity served the band members not as a method for translating the surplus labor of others into surplus value for themselves but as a method for sustaining themselves as a small enterprise. Marx expresses this process of exchange as $C\text{-}M\text{-}C'$ (1:200), where C stands for commodity, M stands for money, and C' stands for a different commodity ("commodity prime"). The band exchanges commodities for money solely to purchase the other commodities that it needs. For the corporatized record industry, the process of exchange can be expressed, according to Marx's model, as $M\text{-}C\text{-}M'$ (248), where M' ("money prime") stands for a larger amount of money than M: the major labels purchase bands and their products in order to exchange them for greater sums of money so that the labels can grow as corporations. By adopting a different logic of exchange from that of the music industry, Crass replaced the corporate drive for profit as the force behind making music with the enterprising drive to transmit information and the possibility that money need not entirely determine the production of music.

Despite their low prices, Crass albums sold well enough for Rimbaud et al. to expand Crass Records in 1980. Rimbaud recalls that

[o]ver the years we were able to introduce an ever broadening cross-section of the record-buying public to the music of nearly one hundred different bands. Many of the records released on Crass Records barely covered their production costs, but as profit wasn't the aim, it didn't seem to matter. . . . [W]e had created an outlet for ideas and information which, apart from the small anarchist presses, had hitherto been unavailable. (125)

Commenting upon the process of production in general, Walter Benjamin writes, in "The Author as Producer," that "what matters . . . is the exemplary character of production, which is able first to induce other producers to produce, and second to put an improved apparatus at their disposal" (233). More important than the producers' attitudes toward the relations of production are their positions within those relations (222). Similarly, Crass Records induced other bands to produce by covering their production expenses, regardless of whether or not the bands showed a profit. The apparatus that the label placed at their bands' disposal was not improved upon technically (in fact, it was cruder than the industry model), but it was qualitatively different from the major labels' apparatus: it was socialized in the sense that it granted the bands a degree of control over their means of production similar to the degree that Crass exercised over their own.

Crass extended its efforts to establish a sphere of music production not entirely conditioned by commodification in its approach to performance. Rimbaud estimates that over the band's seven years it performed roughly three hundred shows, most of which did not make any money for the band (277). For their first gig, Crass played a benefit for squatters in a North London children's playground in 1977 (99), and their final gig was a benefit for striking miners in South Wales in August 1984 (273). Apart from their first few gigs, Crass did not play commercial venues, opting instead for what Rimbaud describes as "an extraordinary venue of far-flung places in the British Isles where no band had ever played before," including "scout-huts, church halls and sports centres" (124–25). During performances, the band dressed all in black and used only "domestic lighting" to create a sense of anonymity and avoid the "cult of personality" pervasive in commercial music (102). The band worked against the establishment of its individual members as commodified rock stars, a move that represents the possibility that audience members could become performers, because the difference in economic class between the two was not underscored by the rock star status that the commercial music industry manufactured for its artists.

Crass employed one other technique diametrically opposed to the form of commodification that the major labels engaged in: the band gave away all that it could for free. It printed leaflets on topics ranging from "industrial sabotage to breadmaking" (102) and distributed them at shows, and, in 1982, reacting to the British conflict with Argentina over the Falkland Islands, the band recorded a flexi,⁹ "Sheep Farming in the Fucklands," without identifying themselves on it and sent it to France to obscure its origins. From there, it "was smuggled into the country [England] and, with the aid of like-minded distributors and retailers, was randomly slipped into albums and singles of any label but our own" (220), recounts Rimbaud. The band proffered gifts whenever it could afford to, and the gift negates exchange between owners of commodities and owners of money, because no exchange occurs. Instead, an object—and a use-value—moves from one owner to another without generating a reciprocal movement of money.

In 1984, the band broke up. Rimbaud comments that "[a]fter seven years on the road, we had become the very thing that we were attacking" (254); "[w]e may once have had revolutionary potential, but somehow we'd been nullified, becoming merely another element of the grand social circus that I'd predicted could destroy us" (274). Two factors led to the band's end: first, as Rimbaud notes, Crass had become commodified, although not in the same way that the English Scene had been. While the Pistols never had much of an explicit political position to begin with, and signed with major labels three times, Crass explicitly promoted anarchism (although, Rimbaud and Ignorant admit, without any detailed knowledge of its history or practices) and never signed to a major label. However, as the English music magazine *Sounds* commented in 1986, "Crass became an unwilling legend. Their complete control over their records and their unbridled assault on all things authoritarian made them the reluctant leaders of an Anarcho-Punk movement that was about anything but leaders" (qtd. in Rimbaud, 303).

The band members discovered that they had become salespeople for anti-authoritarianism and their professed belief that all authority resides in the individual. Steve Ignorant remembers occasions when Crass "would be playing to packed houses of anarchist Punks who know all our songs, records, and ideas by heart. We were up there saying 'be individuals' while leading a movement full of followers. It's always 'Crass did this' or 'Crass said that'" (qtd. in O'Hara, 97–98). The members of the band believed that rather than giving Anarcho-Punks the impetus to become producers of their own ideas and lives they had produced fans that consumed Crass's ideas as they would any other commodity: Crass fans packed the band's shows and behaved much like other audiences at rock shows, fairly passively accepting their roles as consumers. In Rimbaud's words, "We were no longer convinced that by simply providing what had broadly become entertainment we were having any real effect" (". . . In Which Crass Voluntarily").

Commenting upon the youth subcultures prevalent in England just prior to punk, Stuart Hall, Tony Jefferson, John Clarke, and Brian Roberts claim that these subcultures "are not simply 'ideological' constructs. They, too *win space* for the young: cultural space in the neighbourhood and institutions, real time for leisure and recreation, actual room on the street or street-corner" (45). Participants also "adopt and adapt material objects—goods and possessions— and reorganize them into distinctive 'styles' which express the collectivity of their being-as-a-group" (47). Hall et al. temper this explanation of subcultures' material gains, though, when they insert the subcultures back into the geographical, historical, and economic context from which they, and punk, emerged: "There is no 'subcultural solution' to working-class youth unemployment, educational disadvantage, compulsory miseducation, dead-end jobs, the routinisation and specialisation of labour, low pay and the loss of skills" (47). Instead, youths "'solve,' but in an imaginary way, problems which at the concrete material level remain unresolved" (47–48). When Rimbaud et al. founded Crass, they were optimistic about their powers to do more than solve problems in imaginary ways. They set out to construct active fans who embodied a punk desire[10] to reshape the music industry along noncapitalist lines. Because they eventually became convinced that their fans did not embody that model, they dismissed the potential agency that their fans exercised outside of Crass's sphere of influence.

But fans of Crass did win space for themselves. In 1980, with a gift of twelve thousand pounds from Crass (but no actual participation from the band's members), a group of Anarcho-Punks and anarchists opened the Anarchy Centre in London and kept it open for a year. The Centre contained a bookstore, living quarters for punks without other homes, and a performance venue. It closed after numerous intra-Centre clashes between Anarcho-Punks and older, non-punk anarchists. The Centre did not win space in the same sense that Hall et al. invoke, though. Despite their assurances that youth subcultures gain "real time" for leisure and "actual room" on the street corner, Hall et al. are describing primarily symbolic victories that do not, in fact, translate into material ones. Can a public street corner, where the "possessors" can be shooed away at any time by the police, be owned more than symbolically, conditionally, and momentarily by members of subcultures? What material gains does "style" produce? The phrase "real time for leisure," suggests a leisure sundered from work and from the need to rest in order to work. I do not mean to imply that leisure does not exist but that the pure leisure of "real time" must be constructed as symbolic rather than actually existing within the capitalist economy that Hall et al. describe, and they admit as much.

Crass, and punk as a whole, are both underpinned by a desire for more than imaginary solutions to real problems, and, in this sense, the members of Crass were correct: they had not shaped fans who could restructure the capitalist mode of producing music in England, and they refused to be satisfied with anything less because they believed that radical, material changes could still be effected by cultural movements, by subcultures. Crass's question to Hall et al. might be: Why is a subcultural solution impossible rather than absolutely necessary? Crass also folded because it had become a business that forced its members into a single, nonindividuated unit. Although the band members had intentionally attempted to maintain their anonymity in front of their fans, by 1984, after an especially effective media prank, they became increasingly occupied with interviews (although they eschewed the commercial press) and the operation of the band and record label. Rimbaud remembers: "'There is no authority but yourself,' we said that, but we'd lost ourselves and become CRASS." Not only had the band produced consumers rather than revolutionaries, but it had fashioned the band's members into workers responsible for maintaining the producer of commodities that was the band. Rimbaud et al. had believed that Crass's distancing of itself from the major labels and the forms into which they pressed bands would grant the band's members some type of freedom but found, instead, that the economic basis of their band determined their lives. Marx writes that there is an economic "realm of necessity" but that the "true realm of freedom, the development of human powers as an end in itself, begins beyond it, though it can only flourish with this realm of necessity as its basis" (*Capital* 3:959). Ironically, the more economically successful Crass became, the more it relegated its members to the "realm of necessity."

In Rimbaud's writings on Crass, he decries the band's co-optation into capitalism and reads that subsumption as, ultimately, the band's failure. True, Crass did not wholly or permanently negate the sphere of commodification aesthetically or economically, but in its partial failure and Rimbaud's attention to it lies the cancellation of certain—but not all—strategies for combating commodification. And what about the collective's successes? Rimbaud discounts the fact that, for a time, two or three hundred people enjoyed a relation to capitalism significantly different from the one imposed on most people who live under capitalism's sway, which is to say most of the world's people. The Crass Collective and the bands that it helped foster exercised an impressive degree of control over the conditions of their existence and, furthermore, the members of later collectives that developed out of the English Anarcho-Punk movement learned, perhaps unconsciously, from the supposed failings of Crass, and those shortcomings shaped their attempts to resist commodification, again, aesthetically and economically. Not all Crass enthusiasts became the passive audience members that Steve Ignorant bemoaned. The band spawned an Anarcho-Punk movement that spread from England to Holland and the United States and adopted aesthetic and economic forms of negation of, and resistance to, commodification similar to and inspired by Crass's. Crass Records helped foster this movement, releasing material by many of the English Anarcho-Punk bands, the most famous of which is Conflict, which released its first 7" on Crass Records in June 1982. Other English Anarcho-Punk bands include the Poison Girls, Discharge, and Chumbawumba,[11] while, in Holland, BGK (Balthasar Gerards Kommando) and The Ex were the most influential examples. BGK existed from 1982 until 1988, while The Ex continues to tour and record in 2003. Crass has also influenced many U.S. groups to some degree, including hardcore bands such as the Dead Kennedys and MDC, but the Anarcho-Punk movement, in its European form, took root slowly in the United States, finally flowering into the Profane Existence Collective in Minneapolis, Minnesota, the most influential U.S. institution that Anarcho-Punks have formed so far.

A PROFANE EXISTENCE

The Profane Existence (PE) Collective began in 1989 and ceased in 1998, only to be reborn in 2000. Around the collective, and released by its record label, a new version of Anarcho-Punk music has grown up. While a single aesthetic dominated the Crass Collective, two aesthetics have shaped PE's project. *Profane Existence,* the zine, forms the base for one of these aesthetics, while the new sound of mid- and late-'90s Anarcho-Punk established the other. Rather than grounding itself upon a specific band, PE began as a zine and a record label, whose creators' aesthetic choices reflect the influence of Crass and the European Anarcho-Punk scene. In order to grasp *PE's* positioning of itself in relation to the field of zines in which it emerges, a more nuanced description of that field than I offered in chapter 1 is necessary here.[12]

For the sake of categorization and analysis, zines can be separated into two broad categories depending upon their modes of production, to which are wedded the sizes of the territories that they cover (although hybrids of these categories abound): first, the professionally designed, printed, and distributed national/international zine, written by a group of usually paid columnists and reviewers, with a distribution from one thousand to twenty thousand copies per issue, and, second, the individually designed, printed, and distributed personal zine (sometimes called a "perzine"), written primarily by one person and with a distribution of, at most, a thousand copies. *MaximumRockNRoll (MRR), Punk Planet,* and *The Big Takeover* are currently prominent national/international zines in the United States and are available from outlets (stores, shows, etc.) across the country, as well as internationally. The staffs of these zines are often responsible for their own layouts but contract out their printing and distribution needs (however, presumably anyone in any country can order a zine, whether professionally distributed or not, directly from the producer through the mail). The personal zine is written primarily by one person, who also designs it, prints it (often on a photocopier at a copy shop), and distributes it on commission or free at local shops and via direct mail. The most popular example of this category is Aaron Cometbus's *Cometbus,* although it is unusual, because, unlike most personal zines, Aaron has his zine professionally and nationally distributed, although he writes, designs, and prints the entire zine himself. A common subgenre of the national/international zine is the regional zine, written, designed, and often distributed by a collective of some sort. The only real difference between the regional zine and the national/international zine lies in the fact that the regional zine often does its own printing and caters to a smaller geographic area than a national/international zine. Popular regional zines include *Roctober, Heartattack,* and *Profane Existence.*

Over the course of its forty-two issues (so far), *PE* has been written by a shifting group of collective members and contributors, who send in material once, periodically, or regularly. In addition to writing, collective members edit the zine, procure its few ads, lay it out, and distribute it in the

Minneapolis-St. Paul region. However, they have the printing and the non-
local distribution done professionally. *PE* began as a black-and-white
newsprint tabloid; later, the collective had the cover printed in one color (in
addition to black-and-white); and, after issue #23 (Autumn 1994), the zine
shifted from a tabloid to an 8 ½ x 11" magazine format. Beginning with
issue #38 (Spring 2000), *PE* has reverted to tabloid size and added full
color to the front and back pages. This relatively new format suggests the
aesthetics of a newspaper, which PE functions as for many Anarcho-Punks,
especially those in the Twin Cities area.

AESTHETIC PROFANITY

One of the targets of the aesthetic choices of *PE* is the commercial music
magazine, such as *Rolling Stone, Spin,* and *Alternative Press Magazine.* The
other target is the national/international zine in its *MRR, Punk Planet,* and
The Big Takeover incarnations, because according to the Anarcho-Punk argument these zines—as well as commercial magazines—aim to entertain their
readers as pleasing and disposable commodities, while above all providing an
arena in which the major record labels can advertise their products. In viola-
tion of what Fredric Jameson terms a "taboo on the didactic in art (which we
moderns, we 'Western' moderns take for granted)" (*Brecht,* 3), *PE* endeavors
to instruct and inspire its readers, concentrating more on transmitting a message and disseminating information than pleasing its readers or advertising
commodities. *PE*'s two subtitles, "Making Punk a Threat Again" and "Anarcho-Punk Resource Magazine," encapsulate the zine's mission: it tries to be a
practical, hands-on guide to resisting capitalist state power.

Just as Crass overwhelmed its listeners with lengthy songs and copious
lyrics, the members of the PE Collective pack as much information as they
can into each issue of their zine, which is no longer than most in terms of page
length but carries, as a tabloid, four columns of tiny newsprint per page, and,
as a magazine, ran three columns of tiny newsprint per page. The density of
the information, made possible by the dearth of advertising, emphasizes the
zine's attention to text over design, while ads fill a significant percentage of the
pages of commercial magazines and national/international zines, both of
which also incorporate numerous design elements, such as readily legible and
varying fonts, numerous color photos, and pop-out quotes meant to facilitate
the skimming of articles and provide light entertainment. The few photos that
PE contains are usually taken by nonprofessionals and are always printed in
black-and-white, save the recent, full-color, two-page spread of Iraqi civilian
war casualty photos. (Written across them in red is "HOW MUCH SHOCK
AND AWE CAN YOU TAKE?")

Also in concert with the compressed and earnest rantings of Crass, *PE* offers its readers little of the fulfillment that the commercial commodity does. As in the case of Crass songs, *PE* does not satisfy the needs that national/international zines and commercial magazines set out to create and meet but endeavors to construct or address qualitatively different needs. Rather than speaking to a need to be reassured, placated, or entertained (where "being entertained" precludes critical thought), *PE* creates and partially fulfills its readers' needs for information and commentary on specific social issues. For example, issue #42 includes an article on "Recovering the Power of the Global Grass Roots in the Antiwar Movement." Additionally, updates on Mumia Abu-Jamal's imprisonment and impending execution appear frequently, coupled with suggestions for how readers might work toward rectifying his situation.

There is one further strategy with which *PE* resists commodification that resonates with the aesthetic of Crass and early Anarcho-Punk. Just as Anarcho-Punk strives against entertainment that delights without instructing, the early and recent tabloid format of the zine contrasts with other zines and the idea of the zine itself. A fanzine is nominally for *fans;* it is geared toward an audience that might interact with it actively and creatively—making its own zines, etc.—but that is also intensely and often obsessively interested in a specific, and often narrowly defined, topic. In contrast, the newsprint and tabloid format of early and recent issues of *PE* suggests that the zine should substitute or double as a newspaper, a source of local and international information and editorial commentary on a broad array of compelling topics. The format reneges on the conventional zine's promise to concentrate upon issues related to a dominant subject, because *PE* refuses to whittle down the scope of its coverage even to such broad categories as "punk," "anarchy," "politics," or "music." Instead, it documents the actions of any group of people whom the editors of *PE* believe are engaged in altering the world in a liberatory manner.

I do not mean to elide the active and participatory practices of fans of fanzines other than *PE* or of audiences of non-punk shows, nor do I mean to oppose active and critical punk consumers to passive and uncritical consumers of more commercialized forms of non-punk texts. However, there are different modes of activity, and punk's particular modes correlate more closely with Walter Benjamin's materialist notion of the "author as producer" than with what I take to be the more ideological and symbolic modes of Stuart Hall et al. and Henry Jenkins. Jenkins theorizes television spectators and "proposes an alternative concept of fans as readers who appropriate popular texts and reread them in a fashion that serves different interests" (23). He rejects "media-fostered stereotypes of fans as cultural dupes, social misfits, and mindless consumers . . . [and] perceives fans as active producers and manipulators of meanings" (23). Ultimately, though, Jenkins's fans, at best, get to keep what they produce from the materials they "poach" from mass culture, and these materials sometimes become a limited source of economic profit for them as well. Few fans earn enough through the sale of their art-works to see fandom as a primary source of personal income, yet, many earn enough to pay for their expenses and to finance their fan activities. This materiality makes fan culture a fruitful site for studying the tactics of popular appropriation and textual poaching. (49)

The fans that Jenkins describes are active and creative and practice an ethics of consumption not unlike the one that I ascribe to punk collectors in chapter 3.

However, as in the case of Stuart Hall et al.'s theorization of English sub-cultures, the ideological gains of Jenkins's fans are significant, but the material gains neither question nor establish an alternative to the dominant mode of production in which they are imbedded. Nor do Hall et al. or Jenkins offer reasons to believe that the cultural productions of Teds, Mods, and Skinheads or of television viewers employ strategies aimed at inducing other Teds, Mods, Skinheads, and viewers to produce. Unlike punks, these productions do not seem calculated to establish what Benjamin describes as an "exemplary char-acter of production, which is able first to induce other producers to produce, and second to put an improved [socialized] apparatus at their disposal" ("Author," 233). Instead, Hall et al. and Jenkins describe resistant and active strategies for constructing identities and surviving within capitalism. In con-trast, punk producers and cultural products express a set of desires aimed at materially altering the mode of production. Punks want something other than the ability to survive off the money that they make from punk: they want a mode of production in which survival would mean something other than what it means under contemporary capitalism, at least in a local context. For this reason, I privilege cultural practices that significantly alter the material, social relations of punks in liberatory ways over forms of consumption that serve only as means for constructing largely symbolic identities or subjectivities.

Despite its resistant aesthetic, however, *PE*'s frequent inability to bring the issues that it raises to conclusion (in 2003, the effort to revitalize grass-roots movements continues, and Abu-Jamal is still in prison and slated for execution in Pennsylvania), its deferral of satisfaction, obeys the same logic of deferral that underpins U.S. newspapers. While Crass's tape montages prof-fered the listener dialectical oppositions that might or might not be mediated on future albums, *PE*'s form and news content fail to offer the forms of satis-faction that the commercial newspaper also fails to provide in each issue but promises to fulfil eventually (an article on the status of the ongoing search for weapons of mass destruction in Iraq bears the implicit promise that the paper will eventually carry an article covering the conclusion of the search). Conse-quently, each issue of *PE* encourages readers to purchase the next issue, where what was not brought to resolution in the current issue might be concluded. In short, *PE* sacrifices the dialectical possibilities of early Anarcho-Punk texts in its partial subordination of its form to the logic of commercial publications.

A Second Wave of Anarcho-Punk bands began in the late '80s and continues in the present. The aesthetic of this latter wave has changed over the past fourteen years but is currently exemplified by the bands released on the Profane Existence record label that was founded with the zine in 1989. In 1990, the sound of the seminal U.S. Anarcho-Punk band, Nausea, from New York City, differs somewhat from the First Wave of Anarcho-Punk that began with Crass and Crass Records and ended in the mid- to late '80s. On Nausea's first LP *Extinction,* the band continues Crass's tradition of lyric-heavy tirades that often last longer than three minutes, but the band's singers (one male and one female) have lost the snotty tone that characterizes early Anarcho-Punk in favor of an earnest and depressive affect. Additionally, the bass drum and bass guitar are much more prominent, while the guitars are less so, lending the band, and subgenre's, sound a deeper, heavier tone. Learning from Crass, though, Nausea, which is exemplary of late-'80s and early-'90s Anarcho-Punk, addresses the same topics that the subgenre began railing against in the late '70s: nuclear war, war in general, racism, and organized Christianity. However, by the mid-90s the Anarcho-Punk aesthetic had changed radically. In the early to mid-'90s, Profane Existence released and/or distributed a cluster of new Anarcho-Punk bands, including Fleas and Lice, Hellkrusher, Misery, Naytia, Luzifers Mob, Angst, Anarcrust, One by One, Hellbastard, Counterblast, Warcollapse, Guts Pie Earshot, Dirt, and Health Hazard. Together with more than one hundred other bands across the globe, these bands make up a new subgenre of Anarcho-Punk, "crust," and the PE record label became ground zero for this movement.

Like other Anarcho-Punk songs, crust tracks vary in length from three to seven or more minutes, pitting them against commercial song lengths that hover around two-and-a-half to three minutes. Crust (or "crusty") bands also play some of the fastest hardcore that has yet emerged within punk but shift back and forth between extremely quick tempos and much slower ones. The lyrics focus on the same concerns that Anarcho-Punk has traditionally invoked, with the added additions of factory farming and animal rights. (Several early Anarcho-Punk bands, including Flux of Pink Indians, The Ex, and the Subhumans, popularized these issues for Anarcho-Punk.) Exemplary of crust lyrics, the 1995 Fleas and Lice album *Global Destruction* launches tirades against factory farming (in "Meatfactory"), commercialism (in "Squat Eurodisney"), nuclear testing (in "Chirac You Stupid Fuck"), and war (in "The War Will Never End").

Between early-'90s Anarcho-Punk and crust, the delivery of the lyrics also changes. Crusty lead singers growl and scream their lyrics, often drawing them from their throats in direct contrast to professionally trained singers. Crusty vocals are almost always aurally unintelligible to listeners unfamiliar with the songs (and sometimes to those who are), more so than in almost any other subgenre of punk.[13] While earlier Anarcho-Punk bands, from Crass to Nausea, held on to the idea of communicating a content or message through their lyrics, the aesthetic of crust bands seems to reject that earlier attention to content in favor of a new form. Regardless of their aesthetic choices, though, the members of crust bands still express a felt need to communicate.

In a September 1999 interview in *MaximumRockNRoll*, Alexei, the drummer for the crust band, Catharsis, salvages what he can from a show that the band had recently played in Salt Lake City and simultaneously expresses, in exemplary fashion, one of the most consciously promulgated ideas within crust about what needs to be important to crust bands:

> As suck ass as that [show] was, to me, it's that much more important that we go back and try again. There were a few seconds at that show where we connected with a few people. You can't get everybody in one fell swoop. You communicate, you exchange ideas, one person at a time, and as a result your ideas sort of evolve, as do theirs, and you benefit from each other in that respect.

But the form of Alexei's music contradicts his attempt to express ideas linguistically, because the delivery of the lyrics negates the exact path for communication that bands often rely upon—linguistic transmission. Even though Alexei acknowledges in the interview that communication and exchange need to occur both during and after shows (in discussions between band and audience members), it is the music and lyrics that presumably inspire those exchanges.

The conflict between the form and content of crust songs suggests a particular logic: the affect that each song must bear cannot be contained within its lyrics, and, consequently, the affect's charge overrides the lyrics and shapes the song into an inarticulate scream. The inability to communicate is ultimately what is communicated, an inability that mediates between the song's form and content. The songs communicate not specific or even general political insights but their own form's inability to contain their content; they underscore their own failure to represent something sensed but not articulated, or perhaps incapable of being articulated, through punk. The instruments, when played at breakneck speeds, aid in relating the impotence and distress of both attempting and failing to communicate, rather than promising or providing the fullness of a message. During the rapid tempo parts, the guitar (or two guitars), bass guitar, and drums seem on the verge of outrunning one another and the singer.

The urgency of crust suggests a situation apposite to the one that Adorno muses over, while considering Anatole France's "meditative" books; Adorno attributes his own "uneasiness" while reading these books to "the contemplative leisureliness, the sermonizing, however sporadic, the indulgently raised forefinger. The critical content of the thought is belied by that air of having all the time in the world, familiar from professorial pillars of the status quo" (99). Adorno concludes that France's "mode of delivery contains, beneath the poised humanity, a hidden violence: he can afford to talk in this way because no one interrupts the master" (99). Crust's form also expresses a "hidden violence," but with a difference: the aesthetic of the singer's voice can be read as a reflection of the hidden economic violence of the commodity market and the consequent need to push the critical content of the cultural product along as quickly as possible in the space of transmission that crust, as a new product, momentarily opens within the realm of the market before the next new product elbows it aside. The crust singer stands poised on the brink of having the plug pulled, the message shut off, and this situation is often literally true of crust musicians for economic and aesthetic reasons. There are economic prerequisites to playing punk rock as well as aesthetic expectations, and the crust band exists at the limits of both, ever on the brink of losing its economic base (because of Anarcho-Punk's profound skepticism of profit-making enterprises) or being shut down for not sounding punk enough (in punk scenes where punk is equated with some variation of punk's most profitable incarnations, such as Pop-Punk).

To summarize, crust bands do not transmit the fullness of a message but a representation of their failure and simultaneous need to transfer a content within the confines of the punk commodity market. At best, they manage to represent a perceived need. In short, crust does not provide the fulfillment that the commercial commodity promises any more than earlier Anarcho-Punk bands did. However, with a new urgency and desperation, the aesthetic of crust brings to the fore the effort to resist commodification to which Anarcho-Punk has always subscribed, partially in response to the early Anarcho-Punk aesthetic that failed to some extent. Penny Rimbaud comments that, by 1998, Crass had "achieved overall record sales of around two million" (277), and *Sounds* magazine notes, in 1990, that "the most celebrated thing about Crass these days is their phenomenal record sales. Theoretically, their walls should be covered in gold disks" (qtd. in Rimbaud, 315). The aesthetic of crust can be read as a tactical response to the seemingly inextinguishable potential for commodification always lurking in Anarcho-Punk and the eventual dissolution of the First Wave of Anarcho-Punk bands. Those early bands sold numerous records in spite of their long, lyric-heavy songs that took aim at nonconsumer-friendly social issues and drew upon dialectical oppositions—in form and content—without reconciling or transcending them, all in an effort to shut down the sorts of fulfillment that the commercial song proffers to its consumers. What the economic success of Crass demonstrates for punks of the late '80s through today is that even the forms of punk that are the most explicitly engaged in resisting commodification can be commodified. Even contemporary Anarcho-Punk and crust, the subgenres that set out to "make punk a threat again" after its initial sellout in England, are vulnerable.

It is an awareness of this vulnerability, coupled with a continuing perceived need to resist commodification, that have propelled crust toward its most recent aesthetic forms. One of the most obvious attempts to negate commodification appears in the names of crust bands. While the bands of the English Scene chose deliberately noncommercial names to oppose major label bands, Anarcho-Punk bands tried to negate, in their band names, the marketability that became evident in the English Scene. But in light of Crass's popularity and sales, crust bands endeavored to find monikers still more abrasive and less marketable than those of early Anarcho-Punk bands. In 1978, the year that Crass began releasing music, the three best-selling commercial bands were named after singer-songwriters: the Bee Gees (the Brothers Gibb), Billy Joel, and Andy Gibb had the top three albums and the top three singles of that year (Theroux and Gilbert, 267). Instead of naming themselves after singer-songwriters, bands in the English Scene adopted names reminiscent of adolescent sex jokes—the Sex Pistols, The Vibrators, X-Ray Spex— and words that connoted a spectacular degree of negativity or confrontation— The Damned, The Clash, The Stranglers. Following suit, but with less spectacle[14] and more earnestness, the early Anarcho-Punk scene sidestepped sex jokes in favor of confrontation: Crass, The Ex (a name calculated to suggest the crossing out of something), Conflict. During PE's existence, and continuing on after it, Anarcho-Punks and crusty punks ("crusties") experimented with whether a band's name could bear a charge shocking enough in its offensiveness to signify a genuine resistance to commodification of a type that the Sex Pistols and Crass could never obtain. In other words, in a contemporary setting crusties revivified the avant-garde strategy of shock. According to Peter Bürger, avant-garde artists employed shock to "direct the reader's attention to the fact that the conduct of one's life is questionable and that it is necessary to change it" (80). The specific conduct that crust aimed at in the '90s and continues to confront today was the practice of commodifying punk as pure, noncritical entertainment.

These '90s punks still had the major labels and their continuing success with singer-songwriters in mind to some degree. Of the best-selling music performers of the '90s, six are marketed as singer-songwriters, including Garth Brooks, Mariah Carey, Céline Dion, Kenny G (although he does not actually sing), George Strait, and Reba McEntire (Weisbard, 18). Of the other four, Metallica, the Beatles, Pearl Jam, and Pink Floyd (18), only one,

Metallica, suggests any degree of spectacular negativity and only to the degree that heavy metal carries a negative valence. The name also serves the purely functional purpose of situating the band within the metal genre of rock. Crust attempted (and attempts) to surpass, in terms of transgression, these commercial band names and those of all previous punk bands, including early Anarcho-Punk names, in an effort to carve out a cultural sphere upon which commodification could not encroach. The band names that resulted from this endeavor include Fleas and Lice, .fuckingcom ("dot fucking com"), Deadbodieseverywhere, Assrash, Anal Cunt (A.C.), Dropdead, Calloused, 9 Shocks Terror, Detestation, Children of Barren Wasteland (C.O.B.W.), Nausea, Asbestosdeath, Rash of Beatings, Carcass Grinder, Hellkrusher, Cattle Decapitation, Extinction of Mankind, Bleeding Rectum, Combat Wounded Veteran, Murder Suicide Pact, Scrotum Grinder, and Warcollapse, among many others. Couched within these names was a dare of sorts leveled at both the music industry and consumers—the dare to commercialize these band names and, perhaps, the fear that they could actually become commercial.

Behind this dare lies a logic similar to the one that I traced through the late-'70s English Scene's attention to style in chapter 1. Shocking punk clothing attempted to negate the idea that certain aesthetic choices bore specific meanings, that surface markers invoking structures of sexuality, class, and fascism represented subject positions corresponding to those markers. English punk style endeavored to cancel what punks felt were contradictory relations between signifiers and subject positions. The spectacular nature of the names of crust bands can be read similarly: the hyperbolically offensive names stand opposed to the bands that they signify, and this opposition reveals the contradiction between band names' referents (decapitated cattle, dead bodies, genocide, etc.) and the musicians themselves. Shock emerges from the distinct contrast between a punk band and the hyper-grisly referent of its name and, consequently, from the contrast between the commercial notion of a band that entertains its audience and crusty names that seem intended to disturb their audiences. This act of uncoupling to create shock sunders the supposed connection that early anarcho-bands such as Crass attempted to establish (the members of Crass set out to embody "crassness"). Early English punks tried to negate the aesthetics of clothing through shock, not necessarily to construct new types of identity but to cancel the identities related to style available in England in the late '70s. In a parallel manner, crusties exaggerated the offensiveness of their bands' names, not to establish a new conceptualization of what a band could be but to cancel the limited possibilities for punk bands in the '90s, a decade dominated by Pop-Punk.

The actual cancellation, or negation, worked in two registers and was not intentional. First, regardless of how offensive band names were, punks still purchased, and still purchase, commodified Anarcho-Punk and crust records, patches, stickers, shirts, etc., thereby demonstrating that shock no longer constitutes a wholly effective weapon against the commodification of punk: no punk product is so shocking that it shuts down the possibility of its own commodification or ability to entertain. As Bürger notes, "Nothing loses its effectiveness more quickly than shock; by its very nature, it is a unique experience: there is no such thing as expected shock" (81). Nevertheless, no band with a crusty name has appeared on a major label. (It's difficult to imagine PolyGram signing, for example, Asschapel.) Second, PE failed, briefly, as a business. The collective's economic failing—it went out of business for eighteen months for financial reasons—simultaneously denotes both a negation and an affirmation of sorts, a punk success. PE canceled, at least partially and momentarily, the commodification of crust by materially demonstrating that it could not be successfully sold, where the sustainability of PE would have denoted successful sales. Punk's antipathy for commodification frames the collective's economic failing as a sort of anticommercial success after all. The end of the collective bespeaks the possibility that Anarcho-Punk and crust resisted widespread commodification successfully enough to prevent their own sustainability, at least for a time. The shutdown also supports the notion that a punk commodity can be created that will not sell because of how offensive or shocking it is and raises the possibility that punk can successfully resist the commodity market, if only by failing within it. The failure also seems to denote that PE was focused on the correct goals that were not economic at root. Adorno expresses this idea—which takes material shape in punk—in a general way, remarking that "[h]e who offers for sale something unique that no-one wants to buy, represents, even against his will, freedom from exchange" (68). It is precisely this sort of freedom that PE brushed against when it closed shop.

Understood dialectically, Anarcho-Punk and crust employ an aesthetic that draws into opposition the commercial logic of the commodity market (and the concomitant logic of the sustainability of Anarcho-Punk and crust as movements) and the anticommercial vector of these subgenres of punk. This aesthetic's financial failure served to reject both terms of the opposition: neither a purely shocking and anticommercial punk seemed possible nor was a fully commodified Anarcho-Punk and crust. No new option, or third term, was proffered; rather, PE's failure laid an injunction before punks. Having negated aesthetic shock as a sustainable practice and rendered material that negation, the failure of PE implicitly demanded that the next wave of punks develop new options in the ongoing punk project, which is the negation of the punk product as a commodity combined, somehow, with the sustainability of punk itself. PE's failure pointed toward a third term without making it material, a form of punk that would transcend the opposition between punk and the commodity market to arrive at a new concept of punk.

It is in PE's failure, which gestured beyond the state of Anarcho-Punk and crust that maintained itself in the absence of PE and now continues alongside PE's return, that the collective can be considered utopian. In a published discussion with Adorno, Ernst Bloch explains that utopia "is not something like nonsense or absolute fancy; rather it is not *yet* in the sense of a possibility . . . it could be there if we could only do something for it" (*Utopian Function,* 3). Jameson directs us to a helpful passage from Bloch's *Principle of Hope,* vol. 1 that expands upon this idea: "Every great work of art, above and beyond its manifest content, is carried out according to a latency of the page to come, or in other words, in the light of the content of a future which has not yet come into being, and indeed of some ultimate resolution as yet unknown" (qtd. in *Marxism,* 149).[15] The utopian dimension of Anarcho-Punk and crust emerges in their references beyond themselves to a not-yet-existing zone within the field of punk, where producers could create not-wholly-commodified music in a realm that capitalism does not govern. The utopian vector also springs from Anarcho-Punk's and crust's refusal to resolve the contradiction between themselves and commodification through capitulation to the logic of contemporary capitalism. Instead, they hone in on the impasse that commodification represents for them, delineating it materially in their aesthetic responses to it and, in the case of PE, the occasional failure of those responses. Even though Anarcho-Punks and crusties cannot completely resolve the contradiction, they highlight and maintain its problematic nature for punks.

ECONOMIC PROFANITY

Through the creation of Crass Records, Crass attempted to resist the major labels' forms of commodification by assuming a degree of control over its own entrance into the commodity market. PE took this strategy several steps farther. Reminiscent of Benjamin's broad injunction that producers make "an improved apparatus" ("Author," 223) of production available to new producers, Anarcho-Punk, more insistently than any other subgenre of punk, promulgates the concept of DIY and its concomitant desire to establish a material and improved apparatus for producing music—a more socialized apparatus than the corporate one. An apparatus is socialized to the extent that it shifts the means of production out of the hands of a few dominant producers, the major labels in this case, and transfers it into the hands of a larger group of smaller producers, such as independent punk producers.

In 1997, having published thirty issues of its zine, PE printed and distributed a pamphlet, "At Present: What Is Profane Existence?," that described the zine's mission:

[T]he goal of our magazine is to spread communication of ideas and information, as well as help build a tighter, more politically active movement on
an international level. The magazine is distributed worldwide through punk
and underground channels, with a circulation of over 10,000 copies per issue,
and is enjoyed not only by punks, but other people who are looking for alternative sources of news and information.

In keeping with this statement, the collective helped found, organize, and
maintain an interlocking network of underground and socialized DIY punk
resources. Most importantly, in 1992, together with *MaximumRockNRoll,* the
collective published the first edition of *Book Your Own Fuckin' Life (BYOFL),*
an international DIY punk resource guide. It listed, by region, information on
bands, distributors, record labels, record and book stores, radio stations, promoters, venues, and zines, as well as miscellaneous items such as restaurants,
"crash pads" (where touring bands or traveling punks could sleep and sometimes eat for free), print shops, and websites. Only DIY entities were eligible
to be listed. The guide provided touring punk bands and punks in general with
a Yellow Pages of sorts to their own international network of businesses that
adhered to DIY policies. In 2003, the guide has passed through more than ten
editions and is currently available on the Web, although it is no longer published by Profane Existence.[16] The guide used to make a yearly attempt (and
on the Web that effort is continuous) to maintain an international punk community and eliminate the need for professional managers, hotels, chain restaurants, etc., thereby attempting to return control over touring to the bands
themselves and the DIY institutions that support them.[17]

   While the *BYOFL* guide remains a legacy of PE, other projects involved
with socializing the means of production have sprung from the same soil. The
collective attempts to make its readers conscious of ways in which they can
both imagine and resist their own relations to potentially oppressive forms of
authority. For example, the zine continuously provides "how-to" suggestions,
including how to begin an "anarchist collective," how to resist the police (in the
form of a "Why a No Pig Zone" flyer in 1991), and how to fight institutionalized forms of racism, sexism, and fascism (exemplary of this tendency is the
article "Anti-Racist Action" from *PE* #13). By 1997, the collective, operating as
a record label, had also released more than forty titles by primarily Anarcho-
Punk bands from around the world, thereby transforming an admittedly small
group of consumers into producers. The collective also established the Loin
Cloth Press for printing and publishing pamphlets in addition to whatever the
collective deemed literature, and Profane Existence Distribution was set up "to
spread materials within [the] movement, through an international distribution
network outside the normal corporate channels" (*Making Punk,* 133). In 2003,
the collective continues operating as a record label and distributor.

Penny Rimbaud and Crass proposed that the "dissemination of information" far outweighed any impulse to turn a profit from punk, and PE echoes this sentiment in its claim that the "goal of [its] magazine [was] to spread communication of ideas and information" *(At Present)*. Adhering to the belief that profit and punk are largely irreconcilable, PE institutes a $C-M-C'$ process of exchange similar to the one that Crass maintained. However, in their productions Crass rarely if ever alluded to their own relations to profit; on the other hand, PE's evasive action in its battles with commodification includes expressions of embarrassment, apology, and occasionally anger. For example, the cover of PE's *Blackened Distribution*[18] *Mail-order Catalog #3* (1999) reads:

> Blackened Distribution is an entirely worker-owned operation and is a paid, full-time job for those involved. We do recognize the inherent conflict having a paid staff creates when we label ourselves a part of the DIY (do-it-yourself) punk community. However, we feel that in order to properly and most efficiently run a large distribution service such as this, that full-time attention must be given. We have chosen to dedicate a vast amount of our lives to this project and we do not wish to be made slaves of it.

In the paragraph preceding the one above, the owners of Blackened Distribution reassure their potential customers: "Our only goal is to be a reliable distribution outlet for those who share our political ideals and do-it-yourself punk ethics." According to how these workers/owners understand their situation, punk concerns itself primarily with "political ideals" and "ethics" that oppose profit, and even a $C-M-C'$ process of exchange that allows workers to reproduce the instruments of production as well as their means of subsistence represents a disturbing complicity with capitalism. Blackened Distribution's decision to pay its staff a living wage meant making what it saw as a necessary capitulation in light of PE's fate in 1998: PE had proven a little too adept at avoiding profit and folded. In the letter announcing the decision to close, the editors explained:

> The problem is that the DIY scene exists in a little bubble where prices have to be kept lower than the realistic cost of production and labor. Each time we try to raise our prices to be a little closer to reality, we face staunch resistance from those who say we charge too much money or shouldn't be paid for our work in the DIY scene. This narrow-minded attitude doesn't allow extra money for food, clothing, and shelter, and therefore doesn't realistically support its own movement. (3)

Under the heading "The Pay Sucks" they added, "[W]e would also be liars to ignore the financial reasons for ending the collective. We believe in the DIY ethic that our products should be self-produced on a grassroots level and as cheaply and [*sic*] possible. However, we also believe that a fair day's work deserves a fair day's wage!"(4)[19] PE not only adopted the Anarcho-Punk stance on commodification that Crass initiated; it pushed it a step farther, to the point where sustainability was no longer possible.

Similarly, the Epicenter Zone, a volunteer-run collective in San Francisco something like PE but focused on punk in general rather than Anarcho-Punk in particular, closed in 1999 for financial reasons.[20] It was founded in 1990 and was staffed entirely by volunteers throughout its existence. Both of these closings, and the attention that punk zines (the news pages of national/international zines, primarily) paid them, serve to highlight the contradiction of the contemporary punk collective: the economic need to generate profit or at least sustainability militates against punk's increasingly desperate effort to avoid producing for profit, the effort to create a realm free from the commodity market. Punk collectives' failures are the guarantors of these collectives' fidelity to their punk DIY ethics.

PE's work on *BYOFL* marked an effort to socialize access to a specific sphere of the means of production. It was also an effort to "induce other producers to produce" (*Author*, 233), in Benjamin's words. *BYOFL* provided punks with the first mapping of the material resources available to them internationally; however, *PE*, the zine, does not function as such an inducement. The zine solicits from its readers and then publishes feature articles ("well-written articles of a social or political nature"), "news of resistance against fascism and all forms of oppression," scene reports, opinion pieces, letters, and "[a]rticles and ideas for the 'how-to' section of Profane Existence" (the section is called "Fucking Alternative-Fucking Punk Rock") ("Fucking Alternative," 2). As these guidelines for submissions suggest, the editors have a specific idea of what they want the zine to do, and even though they rely upon contributions from their readers, several of their contributors act as de facto collective members, sending in an article or lengthy letter almost every month.

To understand how the zine, as a mode of textuality, can provide its readers with the impetus to become producers themselves, and how *PE* does not do so, it is necessary to investigate the formal elements of the zine more carefully. In 1934, Benjamin pointed to the Soviet Russian press as the exemplar of a literary form that "induces other producers to produce," claiming that it "revises even the distinction between author and reader" (*Author*, 225). He remarks that this revision becomes possible because in the socialized Soviet press, "the reader is at all times ready to become a writer, that is, a describer, but also a prescriber. As an expert—even if not on a subject but only on the post he occupies—he gains access to authorship" (225). The press as a phenomenon "is, in a word, the literarization of the conditions of living" (225). In place of the newspaper, which in the United States occupies a thoroughly rei-

(SAME AS RUSSIA

fied zone in which even the letters to the editor must pass through a careful selection and editing process before they reach print, the zine occupies a place in punk somewhat analogous to the position that Benjamin affords the Soviet Russian newspaper. Writing in 1951, Adorno imagined the mimeograph machine occupying the same position: "If the invention of the printing press inaugurated the bourgeois era, the time is at hand for its repeal by the mimeograph, the only fitting, the unobtrusive means of dissemination" (50).

Despite the size and professional design elements of some zines, especially national/international zines such as *Punk Planet, Tailspins,* and *The Big Takeover,* a determinant characteristic of zines remains a socialized accessibility to the means of production, the sort that Benjamin finds when the line between reader and writer becomes eroded. In the zine racks in both corporate and locally owned record stores, the glossy-covered *The Big Takeover* sits next to personal zines, whose producers made them by stapling together photocopied pages of handwritten, typed, or word-processed pages. Although punks often read zines related (however tangentially) to some element of punk, it is understood within the realm of zine readers that no subject matter is off limits. It is in the zine that punks find a space in which to express and promulgate publicly their thoughts on music, politics, class, religion, gender, sexuality, race, education, etc. The zine can be the realm in which punk most successfully challenges the reign of the commodity, under which, for Jameson, purchasers of commodities only "consume the product in question, 'derive enjoyment' from it, become addicted to it, etc. Indeed, consumption in the social sense is very specifically the word for what we in fact do to reified products of this kind" (*Postmodernism,* 317). Perry Anderson, in an explication of this passage from Jameson, writes that subjects of contemporary capitalism ("late capitalism" for Anderson and Jameson, although the term might suggest wishful thinking) are "prisoners of an order that resists any other control or meaning" (57) besides consumption and its concomitant "euphoric highs" and "nihilistic lows."

But for punks, the zine can serve as a commodity that invites the reader to respond to it either by participating in an already established zine or by producing a zine oneself. A constantly reiterated refrain in punk zines comes into play here: "If you don't like a zine or a scene, start your own! Do-it-yourself!" The formal attributes of the zine encourage this participation, because they reflect the fact that zine authors do not need access to means of production more technically advanced than pens, paper, and copying machines (numerous zines offer advice on how to make copies without paying for them at chain copy stores). Part of the aesthetic of many zines and especially personal zines includes a deliberately unprofessional style. Some authors write zines by hand (such as Aaron Cometbus's *Cometbus*), and some type them out on manual typewriters, while spelling, grammar, and punctuation errors are often left uncorrected. These formal elements of the zine can be made to resist the reification of the commodity as Jameson describes it, when he comments that the contemporary "product somehow shuts us out even from a sympathetic participation, by imagination, in its production. It comes before us, no questions asked, as something we could not begin to imagine doing for ourselves" (*Postmodernism*, 317). In direct opposition to such products, the zine allows its readers to imagine exactly how it was produced and how they might produce similar texts. Unfortunately, *PE*, the zine, does not induce many of its readers to become writers, because the editors sacrifice the formal possibilities of the zine in favor of particular notions about content. By demanding that their contributors address specific issues—anarchism, antifascism, activism, politics—they shut down the option of fostering a community of punks in which each individual punk might feel qualified to participate as a reader and a writer, as an expert on—at least—her or his situation in life.

If PE's zine has done little to socialize the means of production, it has kept alive what, by 1989, had become an established Anarcho-Punk practice of negating the process of exchange through gift giving. Throughout its first life, barring issue 37, the zine was free in Minneapolis and St. Paul and, outside the Twin Cities, varied in price over the next ten years from one dollar to three dollars, depending upon the size of the particular issue and whether or not its purchasers bought it in stores or had it mailed to them directly from PE. PE's editors explain that, in its second life, "[t]hanks to the generosity of our advertisers and donations, you may be lucky enough to get a copy free at your local info shop, record store, or punk rock gig. The rest of you unlucky bastards are going to have to pay to have it delivered" ("Distribution Information," 2). (Throughout the PE collective's existence, it has only charged recipients for postage when the zine is mailed.) As in Crass's case, whenever possible PE does not demand that consumers exchange their wages, their dead and abstract human labor, for the zine.[21] PE thereby attempts to resolve the conflict between Anarcho-Punk and the commodity, on a local level, by giving away what it could have opted to sell.

CRIMETHINC.

The Profane Existence Collective is the largest, longest-lasting, and most influential collective in Anarcho-Punk so far. PE helped create a material base of punk collectives that have picked up and advanced punk's attacks upon commodification. CrimethInc., a more recently founded punk collective, is exemplary of a more contemporary and nuanced approach to Anarcho-Punk's possible forms of aesthetic resistance to commodification. Based in Atlanta,

Georgia, it began as Brian D.'s personal zine, *Inside Front*, and began operating as a collective only in 1996.[22]

The aesthetic choices of CrimethInc. regarding music do not differ substantially from those of the Anarcho-Punk and crust bands that PE released in the mid- to late '90s. CrimethInc. releases LPs, 7"s, and CDs by Brian D., the founder of CrimethInc.'s, band Catharsis as well as by Gehenna, Kilara, Timebomb, Trial, Ümlaut, Aluminum Noise, Ire What Seed, What Root?, Black Market Fetus, Breed/extinction, and Zegota. While none of these bands play crust or Anarcho-Punk, they all play variations on late-'90s hardcore that do not radically diverge from Anarcho-Punk or crust. As a collective, the economic practices of CrimethInc. also parallel those of PE, without qualitatively advancing or modifying them. However, while the aesthetic negation and economic opposition of the CrimethInc. collective's zine, music, and other publications do not break new ground, the collective confronts the commodification of punk more directly and attempts to negate it more desperately than any other collective has to date, through what could be considered a mediation between aesthetics and economics: advertising.

For Anarcho-Punks, advertising is by nature antithetical to punk. Ads aim to transform products into commodities by facilitating their exchange, by valorizing the labor that went into them; in direct contrast, punk in general and Anarcho-Punk in particular aim to resist commodification. Crass and the early Anarcho-Punk movement absented themselves from the problem of dealing with this contradiction: they rarely advertised, apart from posting and distributing flyers announcing upcoming shows or events. However, Crass did not face the option of advertising in ways that later Anarcho-Punk bands would; shortly after forming, the band ceased to grant interviews to nonindependent media and would not advertise in them either, but very few other outlets existed that might tempt the members of Crass to promote the band. By the time PE began, the situation had changed. Independent punk zines abounded, and the majority of them accepted ads from independent producers of punk products. PE placed its first ad in the booklet that accompanied a 1989 *MaximumRockNRoll* music compilation ("They Don't Get Paid, They Don't Get Laid, But Boy Do They Work Hard")—the ad was a black-and-white drawing. The upper half features a black helicopter shining a searchlight upon a brick wall, at the bottom of which lies a pile of skeletons. In the left foreground, a policeman stands facing the spectator, wearing a gas mask and carrying a rifle. Each of the lenses of the gas mask reflects an image of the grim reaper, holding up a skeletal hand with the middle finger raised. In the lower left corner, the ad's copy reads "From a Profane Existence to a Unified Resistance," and in the lower right appear the words, "The World Peacecore, Profane Existence, Anti-Copyright. All riots reserved." A small black-and-white photo is inset into the upper right corner of the ad: a punk wearing a leather jacket stands with her or his back to the camera. Stenciled across the bottom of the jacket are two words: "FIGHT BACK" (*Making Punk*, 5).

In its earnestness and lack of irony, this ad serves as an imagistic analog for the aesthetic of the collective's music and zine articles. It also invokes the idea of an evil police state at war with an innocent and oppressed population, an idea that figures in the lyrics of literally hundreds of songs on the PE record label. At this early point in the collective's genesis, the group's members did not yet know what products they would be selling, so the ad does not appeal to its audience to purchase anything; later, PE's ads in *MRR* dispensed with descriptive ad copy in favor of lists of the collective's record label releases, prices, and its mailing address. If the zine reader perusing PE's ads were not already familiar with the collective or its products, the ad would do little to persuade her that she should purchase them, although, like most ads, PE ads might begin to establish some degree of brand name recognition. In 2003, PE has become a frequent advertiser in *MRR* again.[23]

CrimethInc. adopts a different tactic in its ads than that of PE. CrimethInc.'s ads evidence a painful awareness of and attention to the contradiction implicit in advertising punk products. To combat this contradiction, CrimethInc. relies upon several strategies for mediating the opposition between the commercial onus that advertising bears and the noncommercial impetus borne by the Anarcho-Punk tradition from which CrimethInc. sprang. First, where Crass absented itself from the contradiction and PE ignored it, CrimethInc. positions fairly traditional sales-oriented ad copy side by side with anti-sales-oriented copy. The collective's ads present the spectator with both terms of punk advertising's dialectical opposition in order to attempt to cancel the terms and sublate the contradiction between them.

A print ad for CrimethInc.'s products appears on the third page of the May 1999 issue of its intermittently published zine, *Inside Front*. Across the top of the page runs the heading to a list of products: "Some of our latest attempts to spark world revolution by selling commodities." Halfway down the page, with the rest of the collective's small back catalog, is an advertisement for the band Timebomb's CD/LP entitled *The Full Wrath of the Slave*. Here is the copy that describes the album: "Anti-Capitalist, Anti-Authoritarian, Anti-Corporate, Pro-Animal, Pro-Environment, Pro-Human. Straight Edge. Black Metal. Hardcore from Italy . . . some of the fiercest, most powerful music we've ever encountered. Mercilessly focused on overthrowing the class system, and the oppressive social system. $8 USA/$10 world." The ad's earnest assertions about the force behind and essential attributes of Timebomb's music are at odds with the list's heading that ironically discounts the idea that any commodity could perform the cultural work that the ad copy ascribes to Timebomb's release, which is "[a]nti-capital" and "focused on overthrowing the class system." Because it cannot resolve this opposition, CrimethInc. mediates it by presenting both of its opposing terms on the same page, so that the terms condition one another. The reader cannot take either term at face value, because the collective insists on the possibility that punk can position itself as "anti-capital" and juxtaposes that insistence with its sense that a commodity can never be wholly "anti-capital." This move cancels both of the terms—purely anticommercial punk and purely commercial music—and thereby leaves a space for a third term, a utopian space in the sense that I have described it above with reference to Ernst Bloch, that it cannot completely fill. Instead, the CrimethInc. commodity steps into that place to occupy it temporarily, until the collective or punk in general can arrive at a better option.

The same invocation and cancellation of the opposed terms of punk advertising recurs in CrimethInc.'s other textual formats. In addition to advertising in its own zine, the collective prints broadsheet advertisements. One such ad carries a *caveat emptor* at the bottom of a full-page poster for CrimethInc. ("What is a CrimethInc.?"). It reads:

> WARNING: Please do not buy our products because this advertisement looks exciting or because all your friends have them. For your sake, don't waste your money on them unless you know what it is you're purchasing and think that they really might be useful or meaningful to you. Please do not think that merely purchasing these products is going to do anything to change the world, or to improve your life or anyone else's. Right now, we can't effectively distribute these ideas and music without selling them, but just selling them is not our goal; it is only a means to an end. We try to sell these products in a way that does not compromise the power of their content—we want to sell them like we would sell any other kind of weapons against the status quo, with the emphasis on their usefulness in making people feel alive and aware, making people *dangerous*. You should buy a CrimethInc. product like you would buy a bomb—to use it, dangerously!

On the front of this poster (the above warning is on the back, at the bottom) appears a list of products similar to page 3 of the May 1999 issue of *Inside Front;* however, the collective has dropped the ironic tone of the heading in their zine ad. The heading on the poster reads: "To finance some of our other projects, to spread revolutionary ideas, and—above all—to help people celebrate life and emotion with music, we sell records and compact discs by some of our favorite bands." In the lengthy *caveat emptor*—or warning—and in the briefer description of CrimethInc.'s reasons for promoting and selling products—or rationale—the collective invokes what it perceives as a contradiction between commodification and punk (as a force that opposes commodification). Only the affect has changed: now the irony of the zine ad has been replaced with the earnest, but contradictory, call to arms of this broadsheet.

The collective's warning denies that punk products can even begin to change the world or improve anyone's life; yet, the warning also imagines that a punk product could be taken up like a weapon and employed against the status quo precisely to change the world qualitatively. On the other side of the sheet, the rationale laying out the reasoning behind CrimethInc.'s promotion and sales abandons the warning's mistrust of the commodity in favor of an idea of the commodity as a bearer of "revolutionary ideas" and a tool for producing pleasure. This latter expression of faith in the punk product along with the warning's vision of the commodity as a weapon for revolution condition the warning's earlier expression of the punk product's essential inutility. In short, this broadsheet sends a mixed and contradictory message. Because it cannot resolve this contradiction, CrimethInc. again presents both of the opposition's terms, thereby negating the possibility of accepting either option by itself, and, again, the collective puts forth the punk product as a material and provisional third term and partial resolution of the opposition that punk mediates.

A third piece of advertising—a double-sided CD insert that accompanies the band Gehenna's compact disc *The War of the Sons of Light and the Suns of Darkness* (1997)—repeats the pattern and reintroduces irony into CrimethInc.'s advertising: one side carries a slogan: "CrimethInc.: Human suffering, reduced to a commodity, now available for your leisure-time listening pleasure," and the other side gives CrimethInc.'s address and suggests that the reader write for a catalog. The form of this ad reinforces the contradictory nature of its pleas to the consumer. One side observes that when "human suffering" is "reduced" to commodities it becomes ironically pleasurable, while the opposing side presents the reader with straightforward information on where and how to purchase more and similar commodities.

In one further medium, the World Wide Web, CrimethInc. reiterates and renegotiates the punk/commodity contradiction. The collective's website used to feature one of its logos, its name coupled with a line drawing of a man rearing back to hurl a Molotov cocktail. Beneath it appeared the slogan "The Opium of a New Generation," and beneath the slogan was a warning. It begins, "Do not misunderstand this webpage as an endorsement of cyberspace as a legitimate medium of communication or experience" and concludes "we'd love for this page to send you back into the world of the living, ready to act rather than to be just another stop in your passive, virtual tour of webspace entertainment." Similarly, CrimethInc.'s newly designed homepage includes a *caveat:*

> WARNING: Do not expect using this website every day, hour, or week will make you feel more liberated, free, excited, or enlightened. This is just a string of code. The only possible relevance comes from the other lost souls

on the other side of this screen—they might just find you, or you might find them. Take caution, however—it's easy to get lost. / Use this as a tool—like you would the rest of CrimethInc.—it can, if used properly, be a portal from imaginary ideas and ridiculous plans to honest, real connections and bettered existence. With that said, try not to stay *too* long . . ."

In both Web examples, CrimethInc. ironically disavows itself and its use of the Web as paralleling what Marx understood as the ideological task, under certain historical conditions, of organized religion—to placate an exploited people—while concurrently expressing the hope that its website might transcend the restrictions that its existence as a commodity imposes upon it. In other words, the collective's website does not resolve the contradiction that runs through the entirety of CrimethInc.'s project but simultaneously holds open and shuts down the possibility that a punk website can have something to do with resisting commodification, that it can fight against what the collective perceives of as the Web's effort to substitute entertainment for communication and experience—in Guy Debord's words, for "all that once was directly lived" (12).

Poststructuralist theory has traditionally resisted the signifier/signified and representation/reality binaries that CrimethInc.'s websites invoke as they seek to connect the material reality of punk practice directly to the virtual world of appearance that a website offers. The collective describes its websites as signifiers capable of directing their audience to the signified "world of the living." However, the collective simultaneously attempts to disabuse its audience of the notion that the websites can transcend their own character as webspace entertainment, as pure representation encountered on a virtual tour. In its combined cancellation of the Web as a legitimate space and use of the Web—a use that suggests a de facto validation of it—CrimethInc. endeavors to reconstruct the relation between signifier and signified and insists upon the possibility of that relation. The collective's attention to the supposed disconnect between the signifier and the signified parallels its concern with the punk/commodity opposition: just as the collective attempts to imagine punk as noncommodified, it also tries to establish a sphere in which punk products connect directly to experience, in which punk's cultural and virtual creations affect registers outside of themselves and more material than language on the web. In this sense, like punk in general, CrimethInc. both acknowledges and disavows the supposed break between representation and reality. It maintains the connection but skeptically.

In addition to fighting commodification through invoking, canceling, and endeavoring to transcend the contradiction that arises within punk between an anticommercial vector and a necessary complicity with the commodity market, CrimethInc. ads also rely upon irony to critique the ineluctability of commodification. Punk irony resembles what Jameson describes as linguistic parody that maintains the "conviction that alongside the abnormal tongue [it has] momentarily borrowed, some healthy linguistic normality still exists" (*Postmodernism*, 17). However, punks do not necessarily believe that such a healthy normality actually exists but that it should and perhaps could exist. CrimethInc.'s ads conjure up that normality by pointing at the place where it does not yet but should exist, which is to say where it exists as a perceived absence. In this sense, CrimethInc.'s irony contains a utopian component, in Bloch's sense, because it is an irony that necessitates the possibility of a healthy world, from the perspective of which the present state of things could appear abnormal and unhealthy.

The collective's ironic attention, in its *Inside Front* ad, to its "attempts to spark world revolution by selling commodities" gestures toward a healthy but imaginary space, within the field of punk, from whence revolution could be envisioned as something other than selling commodities. The same logic governs the new on-line merchandise catalog that features the ironic slogan: "CrimethInc.: Overthrowing capitalism by selling you CD's, books and teeshirts." Similarly, Gehenna's CD insert describing the CD that it accompanies as "[h]uman suffering, reduced to a commodity, now available for your leisure-time listening pleasure" invokes a possible world in which representations of human suffering could not be rendered saleable, where the ability of the commodity to package and sell would not encompass all aspects of lived experience. In this implied world, perhaps the commodity would not serve as the standard form for transmitting news of human suffering either; instead, certain aspects of human experience would escape commodification, and no one would profit from trafficking in them. Lastly, as I have mentioned, CrimethInc.'s early website describes the collective as "The Opium of a New Generation," a description that again points at the empty place where a punk website might exist without capitulating to commodification or ideology.

CrimethInc. incorporates one final stratagem into its war on the commodity: it disabuses consumers of any notions of superiority over or interaction with products. At the end of their essay on the culture industry, Max Horkheimer and Theodor Adorno conclude that "the triumph of advertising in the culture industry is that consumers feel compelled to buy and use its products even though they see through them" (167). CrimethInc.'s advertising can be read as a material effort to close down Horkheimer and Adorno's discovery. The collective sets out to discover what happens when advertising counts on its consumers' ability to see through it and incorporates that ability into its ads. The implied manufacturers of the products referenced in Horkheimer and Adorno's essay assume that consumers exercise some degree of critical thought, enough to see through the products and advertising of capitalism before buying commodities anyway. But CrimethInc. ads, in their underscoring of the poverty of their commodities that will not spark world revolution, change the world, improve peoples' lives, or transmit real communication and genuine experience (although they should and need to be able to perform all of these acts), appropriate the act of seeing-through from their viewers and incorporate it into themselves, in order to sell the consumer's consciousness back to her as, seemingly, an element of the product. In short, CrimethInc. has alienated the thought process of consciously grasping the commodity form as hollow from the potential consumer, thereby reifying and commodifying the last critical mental function available to the consumer as she faces the commodity in the marketplace. But is this truly a loss?

CrimethInc.'s products steal from the consumer her last solace, her perceived superiority over the commodity and interaction with it as a critical consumer. In the collective's obsessive attention to the contradiction from which it cannot extricate itself, the contradiction between the necessity to sell commodities in order to sustain itself as a collective and the desire to establish a cultural sphere that is not commodified, it returns to that contradiction repeatedly, thereby disabusing the consumer of a final comfort. Because punk positions itself against its own commodification, punks' employment of critical thought serves as a strategy that allows them to live with the ubiquitous presence and nonradical nature of the commodity; the fact that they can see through the commodity to the point where they grasp it as an inadequate but ineluctable form mediates between their desire for a noncommodified cultural sphere and their capitulation to the commodification of punk. A punk might think, "I know that what I am purchasing is only a commodity, but my awareness of that fact grants me a superiority of sorts over both the product—as a false promise—and over duped consumers who expect more than I do from their purchases." And it is precisely this awareness that the CrimethInc. ad refuses the consumer by announcing, "This is just a commodity like any other. What will you do with it now?" In short, there might be nothing radical about buying punk products, but punks are usually allowed to arrive at this realization by themselves.[24] CrimethInc., on the other hand, does this work for them, stripping them of the solace that it might offer.

FROM CRASS TO PROFANE EXISTENCE
TO CRIMETHINC. AND BEYOND

Crass interrogated the extent to which the punk song as a commodity could incorporate aesthetic contradictions and still sell, but in their success at selling their own and others' Anarcho-Punk commodities the members of Crass partially if accidentally canceled the potential to negate commodification that they had hoped that their products would offer. Learning from Crass and

English Anarcho-Punk, Profane Existence set out to push the aesthetic shock value of their commodities to the point at which they would negate commodification and enjoyed a limited success in the temporary economic failure of the collective. Mediating between these two options, the CrimethInc. Anarcho-Punk collective turns to the ad as the locus where the contradictions of the punk commodity come to a head within a cultural field already governed by an antipathy toward commodification, although to varying degrees in different scenes.

What seems hopeful about CrimethInc. is that it has not yet succumbed to either term of the contradiction that it renders visible for punks. Commodification eventually canceled out Crass's anti-commodification and thereby resolved the contradiction materially without transcending it; instead, one term dominated the other. PE dissolved for awhile, thereby sublating the contradiction that it faced: the anti-commodity term overthrew commodification in order to negate it, and, in that negation, PE made a utopian gesture beyond itself. CrimethInc., however, keeps the opposition between punk and commodification alive in its ads and has neither resolved nor transcended it. Rather, it thematizes the double bind in which it finds itself: even though it is a punk collective that emerged from and within Anarcho-Punk and crust, and that bears with it those punk subgenres' mistrust of the commodity, it still needs to make money in order to sustain itself, but it has few means of doing so besides selling commodities.[25] Recognizing the contradictions inherent in its position, the "ex-workers" (as they self-identify) of CrimethInc. return repeatedly, in their ads and catalog headings, to the contradiction that they face as punk producers of commodities, because they are intent upon demystifying that contradiction for punks. Furthermore, they do not propose that their situation can be resolved within the conditions of possibility that confront them but, through dialectics and irony, gesture beyond them toward a qualitatively different mode of punk production. It is for this reason that they underscore the temporary and provisional nature of their trafficking in commodities: "*Right now*, we can't effectively distribute these ideas and music without selling them, but just selling them is not our goal; it is only a means to an end" (*What is a "CrimethInc."?*, my emphasis).[26]

At the end of his introduction to the *Grundrisse*, Marx muses upon the art of ancient Greece: "[I]s Achilles possible with powder and lead? Or the *Iliad* with the printing press, not to mention the printing machine? Do not the song and the saga and the muse necessarily come to an end with the printer's bar, hence do not the necessary conditions of epic poetry vanish?" (111). Marx's point is that all forms of cultural production emerge from specific conditions of possibility that arise within necessarily historical modes of production. Consequently, now that capitalism has been established as the dominant mode of production certain forms of cultural expression, such as the epic poem (or the pyramid, which was dependent upon a slave labor economy) are no longer possible.[27] Anarcho-Punk and its legacies evidence a utopian hope for a mode of production in which the commodification of cultural productions as it exists under capitalism would no longer determine the aesthetic of that production. In short, the oppositional aesthetics of the producers of these subgenres of punk are dialectical attempts to transcend the contradiction between economics and aesthetics in order to arrive at a new aesthetic, free from economics. Ultimately, punks refuse to accept commodity culture as either final, necessary, or inevitable.

chapter three

Punk Economics and the Shame of Exchangeability

No bad religion song can make your life complete.
—Bad Religion ("No Direction")

THE PUNK COMMODITY

While the first half-dozen entries in the collection of essays *Punk Rock: So What?* (1999) might be described as affirmative of the punk project in the sense that they constitute punk as a cultural form that produces moments of positive aesthetic resistance, Mark Sinker's essay introduces the profoundly negative into the book, proffering a version of punk that thematizes its own inability to transcend the structures that it opposes. After analyzing several of early English punk's aesthetic codings, he concludes that instead of affirmation punk aesthetics refuse the state of things as they are. For this reason, in "pursuit of ideals so constructed as to be unattainable," "[a]ll punk codes were always intended to fail" (136). To "celebrate a success in the world's eyes" (135), no matter how small, would mean to accept the world as it is, which would amount to a profound betrayal of punk's commitment to aesthetic negation and to a world qualitatively different from this one.

In the previous chapter, I sketched the aesthetic attacks that punk has launched against the commodity market, while foregrounding the importance of grasping punk's aesthetic practices in relation to its economic ones. In concert with Sinker, I paid attention to the failure of punk aesthetic attacks and extended that analysis to consider not only the English Scene but also the institutionalized aesthetic and economic practices of post-1978 punk in order to schematize the ways in which punk's most oppositional and negationist practices of the past twenty-some years have failed to overturn the commodity market. These at least partially failed practices both underscore the limits of the commodity market and the structures in which punk produces itself and in utopian fashion point beyond them.

In the current chapter, I turn again to the opposition between aesthetics and economics that structures, to varying degrees at different times, the entirety of the punk project and that punk attempts to work through, dialectically, in so many of its moments. The topics of the current chapter unfold from the formative opposition between aesthetics and economics that is embodied within punk in the opposition between punk as a would-be wholly aesthetic form and capitalism as an economic one. Believing that these two forms should not interpenetrate but finding that they cannot keep them separated, punks have attempted and continue to attempt to resolve this contradiction, using varying sets of terms in the different registers of punk. Having endeavored to sketch two of those registers, the historical and the aesthetic, in chapters 1 and 2, I will turn to the register of economics here and the punk practices at work within it. I will first detail the types of punk objects, including the commodity-form (in light of its two poles as Marx identifies them), the collection (with Walter Benjamin's work in mind), and the ways in which, for punks, these modes both exacerbate the aesthetics-economics/punk-capitalism contradiction and serve to mediate it. In spite of Sinker's contentions, punk practices do not always fail.

THE TWO POLES OF THE COMMODITY

The commodity occupies a privileged place in punk, because it mediates between aesthetics and economics, between punk and capitalism. It is in the form of the commodity that punks' cultural products must circulate, meaning that the commodity is simultaneously aesthetic and economic in nature. Nevertheless, punks and punk businesses have, at best, a conflicted relationship with commodification and capitalism, and it is around this relationship that aggregates of punks' anxiety over capitulating to capitalism coalesce in material form as punk zines, songs, liner notes, and activism launched against what punks perceive of as an encroaching capitalism-commodification. Punks rarely differentiate between these socioeconomic forms—the commodity and capitalism—instead conflating the two. For Marx, however, commodification marks an early moment in a capitalist mode of production built upon it, and, for this reason, both concepts need to be interrogated separately in relation to punk.

As I have argued earlier, from the majority of the punk project flows an antipathy toward the commodity-form in general. This antipathy does not at first seem related to ideas derived from Marx's writings on the commodity. In the first six chapters of *Capital,* he describes its development and its sphere of circulation in utopian language:

> The sphere of circulation or commodity exchange, within whose boundaries the sale and purchase of labour-power goes on, is in fact a very Eden of the innate rights of man. It is the exclusive realm of Freedom, Equality, Property and Bentham. Freedom, because both buyer and seller of a commodity, let us say of labour-power, are determined only by their own free will. They contract as free persons, who are equal before the law. Their contract is the final result in which their joint will finds a common legal expression. Equality, because each enters into relation with the other, as with a simple owner of commodities, and they exchange equivalent for equivalent. Property, because each disposes only of what is his own. And Bentham, because each looks only to his own advantage. . . . [T]hey all work together to their mutual advantage, for the common weal, and in the common interest. (1:280)

This cheery synopsis occurs in the penultimate paragraph of the conclusion to Part Two, "The Transformation of Money into Capital." Part Three, "The Production of Absolute Surplus Value," demonstrates that the sphere of circulation under capitalism in England during Marx's time is far from Edenic and negates the summary just offered above, because, as Part Two's final paragraph explains, a more complex form—capitalism proper—has emerged out of the form of the commodity, and, in this new form, "[h]e who was previously the money-owner now strides out in front as a capitalist; the possessor of labour-power follows as his worker. The one smirks self-importantly and is intent on business; the other is timid and holds back, like someone who has brought his own hide to market and now has nothing else to expect but—a tanning" (1:280). For Marx, the commodity-form does not necessarily harbor radical inequalities; rather, the capitalist mode of production, as a more complex economic form based on the simpler form of the commodity, springs from inequalities rooted in the ownership of property-capital.[1] The property-owning class enslaves labor to itself and thereby dissolves the possibility of an Edenic realm of circulation. At this point, it would seem as if punks' problems with commodification, as metonymic of capitalism's logic, must be sought outside of Marx's writings, but, despite his utopian language, it is one of the commodity's internal contradictions underscored by Marx that best explains punks' relations with commodities.

In punks' suspicion of commodification can be read an apprehension of one of the oppositions inherent to the commodity-form: its two poles of value, use-value and exchange-value (*Capital* 1:181). For punks, use-value is privileged over exchange-value, because the preconditions of exchange-value diverge from punks' claims for their cultural productions and the manners in which they want to engage with them. Exchange-value only becomes probable when a product no longer has use-value—for whatever reason—for its owner, and while in the realm of subsistence farming it is possible to imagine producing an unwanted and accidental surplus of a particular food item, in the case of recorded punk music such a surplus becomes improbable. In short, producers of punk music find themselves faced with the fact that they are producing music not only for their own use but in order to exchange it. The intent to exchange falls back upon the punk commodity, tainting it with its own complicity with the commodity market, and while the recognition of this intention might not bring punk producers to regard their products as forms of congealed human labor that satisfy certain needs, they probably will realize that their products are produced not for their own sake but in order to be exchanged for the products of other forms of labor, products that satisfy other needs. Al Flipside, the publisher of *Flipside,* an international punk zine that began in 1977, claims that "the DIY [do-it-yourself] indie, usually working as little more than a labor of love, is only directed by some emotional instinct that drives their projects to completion" (2), but this claim is difficult to reconcile with the fact, which the commodity-form represents, that punk "DIY indies" produce punk commodities not within the register of affect (love or emotional instinct) but within that of economics and necessity (exchange). The important point here is that, according to punk reasoning as exemplified by Al, even a love for punk does not fully justify the pressing of thousands of identical LPs or 7"s or the burning of thousands of identical CDs in order to make a living from punk.

Consequently, within the punk community punks employ several strategies that help them mediate between the felt antagonism between use- and exchange-value, an antagonism that unfolds from the conflict that punks locate between the aesthetic and economic spheres. This antagonism might also be thought of as the shame of exchangeability, because it is the act of commodity exchange that denotes, for punks, the overlapping of these two spheres, and punks often regard their capitulations to the commodity market as a disgraceful selling out of punk. One of punk's mediatory strategies is the privileging of nonreproducible commodities and unalienated labor—the punk rock show is the most important example of this category—over mechanically reproducible commodities produced by alienated labor. Whenever possible, punk performers will attempt to sidestep the sphere of exchange by playing for free; Fugazi and other Dischord label bands frequently play shows gratis in their hometown of Washington, D.C., and they are not unusual in this respect among punk bands. As I argued in chapter 2, the gift stands as the preferred punk object that exchange betrays. Most punk shows are not free, though, meaning that relations of exchange prevail at them. Punks' favoring of the show, free or not, over other forms of punk commodities obeys a mediating logic: the show takes precedence over all other forms of punk, because it combines music and community and is an experiential and embodied phenomenon that can never be replicated or fully captured in live recordings, photos, videos, zine accounts, and/or personal narratives. It must be experienced directly, and unlike other commodities cannot be hoarded or accumulated. At best, all nonperformance punk commodities only carry traces of the affect and community that shows attempt to evoke.

As Simon Frith notes in *Sound Effects: Youth, Leisure, and the Politics of Rock 'n' Roll* (1981), punk rock did not initially demand a technically sophisticated recording process, but the often poor sound quality of early punk recordings and the current interest in deliberately cheap-sounding, "lo-fi" recordings (especially on the Estrus, Man's Ruin, Sympathy for the Record Industry, Baloney Shrapnel, and Jettison labels' new wave of Garage Punk bands)[2] also suggest that, formally, recorded music intentionally takes a back seat to performance. Many punk bands, past and present, do not aim to produce technically proficient recordings of their music to correct the mistakes that they make live but endeavor instead to create a representation of the energy of a live show, complete with mistakes but without establishing a substitute for live performance. It is for this reason that zine contributors and reviewers frequently disparage the releases of punk labels such as Lookout!, Fat Wreck Chords, Honest Don's Records, and Dr. Strange Records: the products of these labels tend to sound cleanly produced.

The same logic governs both of the above mediatory practices, the privileging of shows over recordings and raw over clean production: punks valorize modes of punk commodities that they take to represent affect rather than professionalization, because the latter category denotes economics in ways that the former does not. Affect connotes emotion and the body, as the bearer of emotion, both of which punks place at a greater remove from economics than professionalization, a term that suggests the erasure of the body. The body is literally absent in recordings but not during shows, while in cleanly produced music the body's signifiers—such as coughs, the squeak of fingers shifting on strings, stage banter, etc.—disappear. Some punks draw the implication that labels striving for a professional sound direct too much energy and money into recording a marketable sound, instead of acknowledging and accepting that recorded music will never (and should never) replace shows. Consequently, zine column, review, and letter writers devote plenty of space to assessments of whether or not particular punk labels that are technically independent are qualitatively different from the majors. For most punks, independent punk labels stand as the last bastions and protectors of affect, which punks read as proof of authenticity, in opposition to the major labels' myopic attention to profit.

COLLECTING PUNK/PUNK COLLECTING

At first blush, collecting in general might appear to be little more than the simple accumulation of dead or frozen labor and it *is* such an accumulation, but it is also another form of punk's mediation of use- and exchange-value. Although music is far from the only collectible punk commodity, it is the most common. Almost all punks, with few exceptions, collect recorded punk rock, and many punks are famous for gradually acquiring massive collections. As I will explain in more detail below, a particular punk's record collection often serves as a history of that punk's life *as a punk*. The MaximumRockNRoll house in San Francisco maintains the best known and possibly largest collection of punk rock in the world. Technically, Tim Yohannon, the founder of *MaximumRockNRoll (MRR)*, owned it until his death on April 3, 1998, and it is now the property of the MRR collective, but it has always been available to *MRR* writers, their friends, and those who could convince the editors of *MRR* that they deserved access. *MRR*'s current coordinators, Arwen Curry and Mike Thorn, add roughly two hundred new pieces of music to the collection every month. I mention the semipublic MRR collection not because it is the norm in terms of punk collections but because it stands as the model, much as the *MRR* zine operates as the unofficial and often resisted policing force of the punk community. Before entering new 7"s or LPs into the library, Yohannon always reinforced the record sleeves' borders with green electrical tape, thereby partially destroying their exchange-value, emphasizing their use-value, and marking them as MRR's communal property.

Most punk collections are privately owned assemblages of punk commodities, and, as with any commodity that can be collected, limited releases and first pressings (of 7"s, EPs, LPs, and in rare cases CDs) are prized and collectors seek them. However, there are two types of punk collectors: punks refer to the first type as "collector scum" who are willing to pay high prices for rare LPs, EPs, early pressings, and rare zines. The scum earn their appellation through their valorization of punk commodities strictly in terms of exchange: they value records for the money for which they were, and can again be, exchanged. The world of collector scum is the world of the record collector convention, and, although such conventions abound, punk zines ignore them for the most part as zones where the exchangeability of punk takes precedence over its use-value.

A group of collectors also exists whose members are similar to Walter Benjamin's conception of the "true collector." As Benjamin claims for true book collectors, the true punk collector "enjoys a relationship to objects which does not emphasize their functional, utilitarian value—that is, their usefulness—but studies and loves them as the scene, the stage, of their fate," where fate is "[t]he period, the region, the craftsmanship, the former ownership . . . the whole background of an item [that] adds up to a magic encyclopedia" ("Unpacking," 60). Benjamin does not even introduce the possibility of amassing books (the special object of the collector in his case) in order to resell them, presumably because this act would brand a person a bookseller, a concept that suggests an entirely different relation between people and things than the concept of collector as he understands it. The bookseller is a capitalist and invested in exchange, while the collector opposes the seller as a cultural curator. While the seller's only obligation is to her- or himself, the curator's obligation extends beyond the individual: true punk collectors exercise a stewardship—which Benjamin describes as a social process of rescue and renewal—over punk products for the benefit of the punk community at large. I will return below to this social obligation that Benjamin implicitly situates within collecting.

While former ownership rarely figures in a punk's assessment of her record collection, region, period, and craftsmanship might: the LPs and 7"s that constitute a collection bear traces not necessarily of the region in which they were produced (although the regionalization of scenes does suggest a loose connection between punk records and the locales with which their genres of punk are associated) but of the region in which they were purchased. In the current punk scene, these places include a variety of possible affects, ranging from associations with searching the World Wide Web mail order sites and bidding on eBay, to ordering mail order catalogs and subsequently ordering from those catalogs, to searching independently owned record stores and especially used record stores, to purchasing recordings at show venues. At even the smallest shows, tiny distributors often run merchandise tables offering cheap punk LPs and 7"s that the distributors calculate will appeal to the audiences of the performing bands.

Additionally, almost every band, no matter how little known or independent, usually runs a merchandise table of its own, which the band members often operate themselves when they are not on stage and convince friends to watch during their set. Records purchased at these tables serve as material traces—souvenirs—of the show itself, reminders for an individual punk of the music that was performed and the community of punks with which she or he witnessed that performance. For each individual punk, the records serve as material signifiers that invoke shows as memories and the affects that the punk absorbed as experiences. In combination, a collection of records performs a gathering of these experiences/moments, jogged loose of their places in linear time and massed together into an individuated, random access memory machine. Collections become databases that are constantly added to and allow for a punk's specific points of memory to be compressed into or at least linked with objects, suitably enough called records, and frequently accessed and reshuffled without regard for their chronological ordering or their singular occurrences in real time. Records, like memories, can be accessed repeatedly, and each return to a record has the potential of adding a new moment, image, or layer of memory to it. The punk collection as a mass of interrelated affects stands opposed to the randomly gathered products that fill the record bins of stores and carry little to no affect for the store's owners. The collection also bestows upon the individual punk the ability to exercise agency, at the level of the collection, over the construction and manipulation of punk history in ways that she cannot over the logic of the scene as a whole. She becomes an active creator of a material version of punk history, from which she can exclude what she deems unworthy and to which she can add what she feels that other collectors have neglected.

"Period" suggests a double meaning for punk record collecting: it is both the period in an individual punk's collecting life and the period within punk as a historical, cultural movement that the record signifies. Records acquired early in a punk's career as a collector often denote the early period of a punk's life as a punk, bearing with them whatever nostalgia she associates with the possibilities that punk initially suggested to her and subsequently has or has not yet fulfilled. A record is also a moment of punk history, a particular although not necessarily static place in the process that is punk. For example, an early Dead Kennedys album might serve as a node through which a punk cathects the early San Francisco hardcore scene. True punk collections become highly individuated but legible records and open maps of a punk's relationship with punk, "open" because their territories are always shifting, because there is always room for another record; there is always unexplored terrain.

Although records are mass produced, craftsmanship still plays a slight role for punk collectors, most evidently in marbled LPs and 7"s, which are records pressed upon nonblack ("colored") vinyl. During manufacture, while a record's base vinyl has not yet solidified, vinyl of a second color or of several other colors is dripped onto or mixed with the base color to produce a marbled effect. Marbling, which is never precise, both guarantees that no record of a particular pressing is identical to any other record of the same pressing—let alone records from other pressings—and it seems to evidence a human hand at work in the production process. The irregular swirls rarely raise the exchange-value of a record expressed as its price but can be read as markers of human design and input in the production process, as an erosion of the reification of records. Marbling valorizes the process of production and the human role in it by rendering their effects visible, which makes the process envisionable and transfers an affect related to human labor to the marbled album that solid black vinyl cannot invoke. Again, affect squares off against professionalism.

In contrast to true collectors, collector scum miss the point of collecting, because they valorize records in what punks view as the least personal and most vulgar manner possible: scum exchange their congealed and, more importantly, abstract human labor—in the form of money—for punk rarities. True collectors never pay "collector scum prices," and, what is more, to the relatively small amount of abstract human labor, expressed as a price, with which they valorize a particular record when they purchase it, they add the nonabstract human labor of their own ongoing search for punk records. True punk collectors spend less time in new or used record stores catering specifically to punks than in general-interest used record stores, because these two types of stores operate according to different logics. Punk collectors will not always eschew punk stores, because they can purchase new releases there at standard new record prices; however, these new releases, while quite possibly necessary to the collector, would seem to bear the majority of their value in their prices.[3] In general interest used records stores, the prices are smaller and also seem to bear a smaller percentage of the records' value, the majority of which accrues from the labor of the collector's search, of which the record becomes an expression when it is found and purchased. Consequently, while a new punk record selected from the "indie" (independent) bins at Amoeba Records in San Francisco stands in an oppositional relationship with its price—depending on how much the collector earns, it is an expression of a certain number of hours of abstract human labor-time—the punk rock record culled from the used bins of The Whizz (a general interest record store in Columbia, Missouri) does not have the same relation to its price.

The price of the used punk record from The Whizz represents only a small fraction of abstract human labor that the punk collector exchanged for it and does not represent the use-value that accrues from the labor of the search that led to it. Because the labor of the search at Amoeba Records is negligible, it adds little to no use-value to the records purchased there. In contrast, although a punk's ongoing search for used punk records could be divided into discrete and quantifiable units in terms of hours spent searching and even hours per record found, it does not represent itself to the punk collector as such, nor would such an equation between labor-time and records contribute to the exchange-value of the records. Labor-time spent searching does not actually count as labor per se, because it will never be valorized in terms of exchange-value, so even spreading the whole of a search's labor-time across the number of records found does not produce the same equation between price and record that a consideration of the new record and its price, as an expression of the abstract, socially necessary, and surplus labor required to produce it, does. Instead, searching—hence collecting—produces an individual form of use-value that becomes invested in the relation between the record and the collector, rather than standing opposed to them as a price. Additionally, the labor-time of searching never becomes abstract, because it is always labor of a specific and individual quality—the individual's mode of searching. For the above reasons, to the collector scum a collection is worth the sum of the prices of its records and can be exchanged for that sum, while a true collector's records always represent more to the collector than the sum of their prices. The records bespeak not only the abstract human labor that went into them but the collector's individuated labor spent finding them.

Writing in *MaximumRockNRoll* in December 1999, Mark Murrman recounts a narrative exemplary of several elements of the collecting process as I have outlined it above. (In the late '90s, Murrman was the zine's resident expert on late '70s American punk records and, consequently, was continuously searching for early and often out-of-print punk. He is a rabid collector.) He describes his discovery of a particular album:

> While living in Bloomington, I'd go into the little record store almost daily, looking for *anything* new that might have come in the used bins. Usually, it wasn't much. One day, though, I hit pay dirt. Some old punk sold his entire collection of 70s rock 'n' roll. Unfortunately, both my roommates found their way to the record store before I did and cleaned up. Still, I got a lot of good stuff, including the only LP released by the CHORDS. At the time, I'd never heard of 'em. Now, I still love that record.

He admits that "it's not the hardest record in the world to find," which suggests that his search and what it adds to the record matters more to him than an LP's rarity, which often determines its price, especially for collector scum. In fact, he neglects to mention the price of the album at all, instead focusing his observations on his unique labor in a particular place and at a particular time, rather than his final exchange of money, as a representation of abstract human labor, for the album. In his narrative, he neatly eliminates any mention of money, replacing it with his love for the album that grows out of his collecting process.

Murrman's narrative and love illustrate "affective-value," which can serve as an umbrella term for the varieties of use-value that I have derived from collecting as a punk practice. My attention to the specific methods with which punks create affect arises, again, from what many punks understand as an opposition between affect and professionalization: just as raw—as opposed to professional—production values help to guarantee the authenticity of a punk product, punk collecting adds affect to a commodity that a collector scum, who could also be called a professional collector, cannot. This supplementary affective-, or use-, value—which cannot be translated into exchange-value—also springs from the processes of rescue and renewal that Benjamin describes regarding books: "[O]ne of the finest memories of a collector is the moment when he rescued a book . . . and bought it to give it its freedom. . . . To the book collector, you see, the true freedom of all books is somewhere on his shelves" (64). Benjamin's idea transfers easily to the sphere of punk, in which a collector finds a good (for whatever reason) punk record and, as Benjamin implies, plucks it from the realm of exchange-value and inserts it into the realm of use-value, moving it from the economic sphere of commodities and abstract human labor to the more private sphere of the collection and of personal labor of a specific quality.

The record obtains its freedom within the collection, because it is only there that its owner can relate to it as the bearer of the set of unique social relations that make up both the process of its acquisition, its place within its owner's punk history (which the collection represents), and its understood relation to punk as an historical field. These investments take the form of memories around the record's purchase—the talk and interaction with the vendor or vendors and, often, others in the store who share an interest in punk—as well as the sharing of the record with other punks. Although punks often become protective of their collections and refuse to lend out 7"s and LPs, part of the punk ethic of collecting includes an injunction to play and record records for other punks, especially rare records to which most punks do not have access.

Consequently, it is within the collection that the record takes on what might be considered the positive side of commodity fetishism and ceases to exist as an undistinguished and undifferentiated unit in a store's mass of arbitrarily related objects. A record's rescue also constitutes its renewal, the performing of which is "the collector's deepest desire" for Benjamin, because renewal is always a renewal of the old world (61). The collector extends a new lease on life to the record by dislodging it from obscurity and transferring it to a collection. As Jean-Luc Godard claims in *Masculin/Féminin* in one of the phrases that flashes across the screen, "Human labor brings dead things to life." The collector also renews the old world when she or he expends labor to remove the punk commodity, understood as a historical artifact, from obscurity and reinserts it into the new world, thereby revivifying not only the object itself but the historical moment and forces to which it testifies.

Along these lines, Benjamin remarks that the book collection must be transmissible, because "a collector's attitude toward his possessions stems from an owner's feeling of responsibility toward his property. Thus it is, in the highest sense, the attitude of an heir" (66). Within the practice of punk collecting, this injunction assumes material form when the collector feels an obligation to remove objects deemed valuable from the realm of exchange, thereby to maintain the attention to them to which they are entitled and to shift them from the realm of exchange to that of use. As Benjamin's comment suggests, it is not merely the collector's brain—the affects and memories that it attaches to objects—that invests a collection with value; instead, the practice of collecting can be read as the undertaking of a social obligation that extends beyond the individual person to objects and their connections to history. The punk collector regroups and preserves objects that the commodity market has dispersed in order to uphold a social rather than merely individual need to maintain the material archive of punk history. Although the punk record collection can never be transmitted with the individuated memories, images, and labor that went into its creation still attached, it can, (and, for punks, must) be transmitted in order to prevent its dispersal into the ranks of nonindividuated commodities.

VIVA LA VINYL

In the above consideration of collecting, I have emphasized the LP and 7" at the expense of the CD. The main reason for my special interest in vinyl is the attention that true punk collectors bestow upon it, sometimes to the point of excluding all CDs from their collections. There are several reasons for this preference: LPs were introduced in the United States in 1948, CDs in 1983 (Krasilovsky and Shemel, 8); LPs have existed since punk began, while CDs have not; and some punk is only available on LP, so that early punk LPs are older than all CDs. Consequently, and as a general rule, the search for used punk LPs involves more personal labor than the search for CDs, and the value of LPs and not CDs is more likely to be supplemented with the labor of searching. LPs are also more difficult to collect, because they are currently produced in much smaller quantities than CDs are. According to the Recording Industry Association of America's (RIAA's) figures, music manufacturers shipped 3.4 million LPs/EPs in 1998, accounting for 34 million dollars, compared to 847 million CDs, accounting for 11.4 *billion* dollars. Vinyl sales, including LPs, EPs, and 7"s, accounted for roughly .003 percent of the music industry's revenue in 1998 compared with CDs, including CD singles, that accounted for roughly 96 percent (Jeffrey, 76).[4]

Because of the conditions surrounding their production, LPs serve as better bearers of the fate of objects than CDs do: LPs literally have more history as a format. Punks' appreciation of this history echoes Benjamin's description, in "The Work of Art in the Age of Mechanical Reproduction," of the authenticity that works of art held before they were technologically reproducible. He describes the "authenticity of a thing" as "the essence of all that is transmissible from its beginning, ranging from its substantive duration to its testimony to the history which it has experienced" (221). Punks fear the loss of authenticity in CDs and favor LPs, even though LPs are also reproduced through technological means. This punk practice suggests that there are gradations of authenticity: faced with a choice between LPs and CDs, punks choose the format that enjoys the greatest proximity to authenticity, the LP, because of its history and because of the fact that it is not mass-produced to the same degree that the CD format is.

Benjamin subsumes his conceptualization of authenticity beneath another term, aura, that also resonates with punk collecting. He proposes that "that which withers in the age of mechanical reproduction is the aura of the work of art. . . . [T]he technique of reproduction detaches the reproduced object from the domain of tradition. By making many reproductions it substitutes a plurality of copies for a unique existence" (221). However, Benjamin apprehends the disappearance of aura dialectically, locating in the loss of tradition and uniqueness a resultant gain in the mass reception of, and participation in, art. In Benjamin's words, the "technique of reproduction . . . in permitting the reproduction to meet the beholder or listener in his own particular situation . . . reactivates the object reproduced" (221). Although punks want to disseminate their various texts as widely as possible, they embrace the CD's facilitation of that dissemination much more hesitantly than Benjamin welcomes technically reproducible art. While it is a frequently invoked claim in punk zines that potential punks must be exposed to punk somewhere, and exposure to a Rancid CD in a shopping mall chain store might provoke a consumer to trace Rancid's music back to its authentically noncommercial roots and to the realm of noncommercial punk, this is the only manner in which punks valorize the spread of punk through newly available commercial means. The new format must lead back to the older ones.

The rarity of vinyl is not the only reason that punks fetishize it more than CDs. Commenting on 7"s in an interview in 1994, Tim Yohannon remarks,

> I love 7"s. I think they're the best format. To me, listening to music isn't about getting stoned and lying on the floor. It's about playing something, play a track and it's like "Wow! That makes me think of this song" and you go grab it off the shelf and you throw that on, and then your buddy goes "Oh no, listen to this!" and grabs something. To me that's the kind of energy and quickness and continuity that I like. (189)

Interestingly, Yohannon praises the energy, quickness, and continuity of playing 7"s, when these exact descriptors could be turned against them (if manufacturers and sellers of CDs felt even slightly threatened by 7"s) in favor of CDs. But his point is clear: the 7" and the LP to a slightly lesser degree demand a form of at least somewhat active listening—a labor of listening—that CDs do not require. LPs and especially 7"s create a different listening experience, one involving more involvement and participation from the listener, who, at the very least, must turn over the LP every twenty minutes on average or the 7" every three to seven minutes (depending on whether it spins at 45 or 33 rpms). A 7" never serves as background music. Yohannon also implies that the 7" requires the listener to be more conscious of the music in ways that listening to CDs does not; for example, turntables do not allow for the continuous play or shuffling functions that CD players perform. The listener must make frequent decisions based upon her familiarity with specific songs in her collection. She cannot rely upon her general impressions of entire albums or CDs but must constantly choose 7"s based upon criteria that she mentally sorts through after every song or two.

More importantly, the ethic of consumption that Yohannon's attention to vinyl invokes includes the idea that the commodity should serve as a bridge between people; it should aid in establishing groups or collectives. He describes a situation in which people employ punk records in order to further their interactions with one another, and he negates an isolated and complacent consumption of punk in favor of a social and active use that the punk product should initiate and/or facilitate. In short, the consumption of punk should be social and it should engender thought, and the punk commodity should be capable of interacting with thought, which it has the power not only to generate but also to clarify and extend. The addition of qualitative and social forms of labor to the act of listening parallels the addition of a specific type of labor—searching—to collecting: the labor of listening valorizes vinyl not in terms of exchange-value but in terms of use-value. For the collector, vinyl represents the labor of its search and the labor of its use, and, in the vinyl collector's emphasis upon and augmentation of use-value, she mediates the felt conflict between use- and exchange-value.

Within the punk community, collectors proffer various reasons for collecting vinyl: punk sounds better on vinyl than on CD; punk originally appeared on vinyl and was meant to stay there; and the mechanics at work in turntables and vinyl records are more comprehensible and material than those at work in CD players and CDs. For some of the same reasons, in addition to vinyl punks often favor vintage stereo equipment, preferring boxy cabinet speakers, vacuum tube or solid state amplifiers/receivers, and belt-driven turntables to tiny speakers, digital pre-amplifiers, and direct drive turntables (or, more likely, CD or DVD players). Underpinning these preferences runs a nostalgia that acquires material form as collections for the cultural productions of early punk and the contemporaneous machines that provided access to those productions (although vacuum tube amplifiers/receivers technically predate punk). A possible logic behind this nostalgia for not just the commodities but the historical moments of early punk echoes not only the practice of punk collecting that I have described above but the logic that Susan Buck-Morss attributes to Benjamin's conceptualization of nostalgia. She writes that his investigation of mechanically and mass-produced commodities designed to appear "in the fantastic form of the old, organic nature" revealed "the distorted form of the dream 'wish,' which is not to redeem the past, but to redeem the desire for utopia to which humanity has persistently given expression" (145). While, Buck-Morss argues, Benjamin's utopia was "the

communist goal stated by Marx . . . [of] the harmonious reconciliation of subject and object through the humanization of nature and the naturalization of
humanity" (146), in the context of punk the goal is a little less grand.

The punk project is shot through with a nostalgia of which collectors are
only the exemplars; punks' nostalgia for earlier punk scenes and their imita-
tions and repetitions of the music, style, and concerns of those scenes evidence
the same nostalgia. In the act of collecting both vinyl and stereo components
and rescuing them from used record store bins, pawn shops, garage sales, used
electronics stores, and eBay lies the desire to revivify whatever utopian desires
fuelled the first few scenes of the punk project without reaching fruition. In
this claim, I come full circle and return to one of the theses of my first chapter,[5] that punk can be mapped according to the desires that constitute it and
that recur throughout the punk project. Punk has always been nostalgic,
though, even in its earliest scenes. The material expressions of punk nostalgia
that I have located in punk collecting and collections denote an accompanying nostalgia for modes of negation and resistance that have suffered in a
deeply skeptical and ironic age but that punks nevertheless attempt to revivify in the present. In their desires to resist commercialization, seize control
over the means of production, foster collectivity, and enter into History, punks
breathe new life into historical practices of refusal, negation, renewal, and
utopian thought, all in opposition to capitalism as they understand it.

DISPLACED LABOR

Another explanation for punk's attention to the commodity does not rely upon
mediating between use- and exchange-value but upon ideology. Punks displace
an anxiety over their necessary complicity with capitalism as small capitalists
themselves and over the expropriation of surplus labor, their own and others',
onto the form of the commodity. They perform an inverted fetishization of the
commodity, imagining not that its material form betrays an intrinsic form of
value that is not socially determined but imagining, instead, that the material
form of the commodity testifies to a dearth of value, that its existence as a
mass-produced object precludes its valorization. This emptying of the commodity serves an ideological purpose for punk, allowing its producers to obfus-
cate much of the very real labor that, in congealed and abstract forms, constitutes the exchange-value of punk products. This obfuscation functions
according to the division of labor within the production of the punk commodity: while punks recognize and commend the "good labor" of musicians, label
owners, small distributors, recording engineers, and even consumers purchasing punk products, all of which is "punk labor" and highly visible to punks, they
ignore the labor of those who fall outside the punk community but contribute

to the mass production and shipping of punk commodities, including factory and postal workers as well as many of the links in the chain of labor that bring the punk product from conception to mass-produced commodity. For punks, the labor of these workers, whose products and services are not directly produced by or purchased from punks, remains invisible behind its prices.

This ideological understanding of the labor behind punk products also manifests itself in punk's past and continuing promulgation of the supposedly DIY approach to music making. As Doug Henwood, publisher of the politics and economics newsletter the *Left Business Observer*, comments in *Punk Planet*,

> [T]he independent model can only be applied in certain contexts. You can't universalize it. You can't have "independent" computer companies or locomotive manufacturers. . . . You have to think about what kind of arrangements make for large-scale operations, unless you want to give up on industrial civilization. I don't think most people seriously want to do that, even if they might fantasize about it. Once you start trying to conceive of some larger-scale, more cooperative way of doing things, you have to get beyond the fetish of independence. (47)

Punks rarely move beyond this fetish, preferring to imagine that the labor that they exploit is only, at worst, their own visible labor and displacing, in their demonization of the commodity rather than capitalism proper, their sense that they are implicated in the exploitation of the workers who handle punk commodities from the moment that they disappear from the punk realm—the recording studios—until they magically reappear within it—as mass-produced commodities sold by independent punk labels and distributors.

THE GOOD SIDE OF THE COMMODITY

Up to this point in the current chapter, I have concentrated on the "bad side" of the commodity that punk's mediation of the two poles of the commodity-form attests to, but I will now turn to the "good side" of contemporary capitalism and the circulation of commodities as these forms relate to punk. As I have argued, the punk project throws light upon the internal opposition between use- and exchange-value in the commodity as it attempts to mediate and sublate that opposition and endeavors to celebrate punk commodities as use-values and downplay them as exchange-values, as well as de-emphasizing its own complicity with capitalism. It also serves as a placeholder for the possibility of a cultural form that resists its own commodification. In this sense, punk is, again, an answer to and a mediation of the opposition that Horkheimer and Adorno locate between the culture industry and art that correlates with the aesthetics/economics opposition within punk. In other words, punk's skepticism over and mediation of the commodity-form does not develop solely as a set of ideological maneuvers that allow punks to reconcile themselves to the necessity of acting as capitalists, regardless of how small their ventures are. For Horkheimer and Adorno, the culture industry (and the commodity as its dominant form)

> perpetually cheats its consumers of what it perpetually promises. The promissory note, which, with its plots and staging, it draws on pleasure, is endlessly prolonged; the promise, which is all the spectacle really consists of, is illusory: all it actually confirms is that the real point will never be reached; the diner must be satisfied with the menu. (139)

As opposed to art as a process of aesthetic sublimation that constitutes itself over against the commodity market, and in its representation of fulfillment denotes a broken promise, the culture industry, embracing rather than opposing commodification, merely represses the anxieties that emerge concerning its failings, and, consequently, not only is desire never satisfied but the industry does not even implicitly acknowledge, as art does, its inability to satisfy it (140–141). Instead, the culture industry closes off the possibility of ever providing pleasure. Eventually, with the absorption of art into the culture industry, "a change in the nature of the art commodity itself is coming about. What is new is not that it is a commodity, but that today it deliberately admits that it is one; that art renounces its own autonomy and proudly takes its place among consumption goods constitutes the charm of novelty" (157).

What I have tried to indicate thus far is that punk in all of its modes, and especially in its most oppositional forms such as Anarcho-Punk and crust, never assumes its place as a commodity proudly but only with resistance and through mediation, as well as with mistrust and skepticism. I am not trying to argue that punk is art in the sense that Horkheimer and Adorno conceive of it (and the debate over the disappearance of the difference between high and low art is either concluded at this historical moment or too expansive to rehearse here), but I will argue that punk occupies the privileged site that Horkheimer and Adorno reserved for art but could not fill. The stark polarization of art's resistance to the economy and the culture industry's complicity with it do not apply to current U.S. culture, as they might have in 1944, in part because punk mediates that opposition: it is both resistant and a commodity. Consequently, commodification and capitalism have positive potentials that the Frankfurt School ignores but that become evident within the punk project.

While developing the concept of a "relative form of value," Marx comments that relations between objects—and the fact that a commodity's value cannot be grasped in terms of any inherent qualities of the commodity itself but only in its relation to other commodities (*Capital* 1:43)—resemble relations between people. He draws a parallel between his discovery that "the physical body of commodity B becomes a mirror for the value of commodity A" and his observation that "a man only sees and recognizes himself in another man. Peter only relates to himself as a man through his relation to another man, Paul, in whom he recognizes his likeness" (144).[6] Marx's eventual point is that value relations between commodities not only resemble relations between people but are in fact such relations. In this case, of course, it is not literally the commodity that valorizes itself in other commodities but people who valorize commodities—as bearers of value—by exchanging commodities for other commodities because of the congealed and socially necessary labor in the commodities for sale and in the other commodities that serve as their equivalents.

The same logic applies to the formation of groups in general and punk in this particular instance. A punk is valorized not by her individual act of will but by the recognition of other punks, the willingness of other punks to see in her an equivalent of the punk species (rather than Marx's "commodity species"), although each individual punk represents a different type within the species. In the case of people, recognition takes the place of exchangeability; in recognizing and measuring her value as a punk, according to other types of punk, punks are willing to facilitate her circulation within the punk community, be it local, regional, national, or international. In a sense, punks recognize within one another the socially necessary labor of becoming a punk, a labor that includes attaining and displaying knowledge of the textualities of punk, investing in punk clothing, and adopting punk ideas and diction. In addition, the punk of this example recognizes herself as such through social relations that the circulation of commodities both facilitates and doubles. Through already-existing zines, clothing styles, punk rock shows, etc., and her recognition of herself in them, she becomes interpellated—in the Althusserian sense of being positioned within (and subjected to) a social structure—into her local punk scene or the punk community at large. From this perspective, the form of the commodity facilitates the formation of groups that, although not comprised entirely of or by commodities, nevertheless become recognizable as groups, both to themselves and others, through the circulation of punks and the circulation of commodities, both of which obey the same laws of exchange.

MRR in particular fostered the interpellation of individuals into an international punk community via commodities. As Gavin McNett writes, "During *MRR*'s first couple of years [1982–1983], scene reports began coming in from Europe, Asia (mostly Japan), South America (mostly Brazil) and Australia. Later, scattered missives filtered in from places like Iceland,

Micronesia, Saudi Arabia, Israel. . . . Then detailed exegeses from those places—and finally trade routes." McNett might have added to his mapping: as "trade routes" were established, the possibility of an international punk community, bound together by the circulation of commodities and the concomitant interpellation of punks into the scene, became possible and existant. The circulation of commodities, with their use- and exchange-values, also fulfills one of the basic desires that underlies the punk project: transmitting and promulgating punk itself. A messianic impulse invests punks with the need to proselytize.

In this chapter, I have investigated the form of the commodity and the material practices through which punks recuperate it to some degree, for, while they maintain a wariness regarding it, there is a good side to the commodity for punk. Most importantly, the circulation of punk commodities serves as one of the necessary conditions of the formation of punk groups, scenes, and an international community that are recognizable as such to punks. Not only does the commodity represent labor as a set of social relations, but it facilitates extra-labor relations between people critical of the very relations that valorize the commodity as an exchange-value. Aside from the commodity's good side, punks also practice forms of mediation between the use- and exchange-value that oppose one another within the commodity-form. These mediations include privileging use-value over exchange-value—the punk show as a nonreproducible experience stands as the best example—and supplementing the commodity's use-value with qualitative forms of nonproductive, affective labor: the labor of collecting and the labor of listening. Punk collecting also imbues commodities with punk history. However, punk's mediations do not effectually resolve the commodity's contradictions. At best, they attempt to retool them in the undying punk hope of at last escaping from the constraints of the economic sphere, where anything can be measured quantitatively and everything can be exchanged.

chapter four

Market Failure:

Punk Economics, Early and Late

You are not what you own.
—Fugazi, "Merchandise"

IN THE EARLY '90s, a line of T-shirts emerged in both independently owned and chain record stores. The shirts claimed, on their fronts, "This is not a Fugazi T-shirt." The producer of the T-shirts assumed that fans of the punk rock band Fugazi were aware that its record label, Dischord, refused to market its bands. On the backs of the shirts appeared the lyrics, "You are not what you own," from the Fugazi song "Merchandise." Dischord allowed for the possibility of such shirts when it refused to copyright its bands' names, in a conscious attempt to eschew the commercial impulse to create intellectual property. What the shirts represent, however, is Dischord's lack of control over its products within the marketplace: in this instance, a T-shirt manufacturer who might or might not run an independent business successfully mobilized the anticommercial impulses of Dischord to integrate his or her own product into the commodity market.

In the previous chapter, I unraveled punk's central opposition between aesthetics and economics to arrive at new oppositions, expressed in new paired terms. From the opposition between use- and exchange-value, the origins of the punk antipathy toward the commodity-form emerges, as well as punk's strategies for mediating that opposition, and the commodity-form itself comes into play as a mediation between punk and economics, a mediation that achieves some positive effects for punks, who benefit from the constitutive forces of commodity circulation. I now wish to insert the punk commodity back into the broader context of the economics of the U.S. music industry, in order to raise and attempt to answer a question: If punk simultaneously marks an effort to oppose as well as mediate the commodity market, to what degree is this opposition effectual? Assuming that punks set themselves against capitalism in general and the music industry in particular, how have they affected them?

In chapter 2, I mapped the aesthetic and economic practices that the most ardently anticommercial punk institutions employed and continue to employ in opposition to the commodity market and underscored the utopian impulses that emerged from their aesthetic practices in particular. I now want to redraw punk in terms of economics, in order to present the history of "punk economics." This history demands a slightly different periodization of punk than the one that I employed earlier. During the period of "early punk economics," from 1974 to 1977, the aesthetic vector of punk shaped the punk project more than economic concerns. After 1977, in response to the initial sellout of late '70s English punk bands and in order to preserve control over itself as a field of production, Anarcho-Punk began foregrounding punk's economically contestatory practices aimed at resisting capitalism. Penny Rimbaud, Crass, and Anarcho-Punk in their 1978 incarnations marked the break where punk's economic vector began to wield as much influence over punk as its aesthetic vector, the break between "early" and "late punk economics."

Learning from Crass Records and Anarcho-Punk, Greg Ginn of Black Flag, Jello Biafra of the Dead Kennedys, and Ian MacKaye and Jeff Nelson, co-owners of Dischord Records, helped found, between 1979 and 1988, an independent and underground economic punk network across the United States and Western Europe whose purpose was to socialize the means of production—to improve upon them and make them more easily available to a larger number of people—within the international punk scene. The economic work of Ginn et al. was taken up and advanced by the Profane Existence Collective and *MaximumRockNRoll* in the late '80s and early '90s (especially in terms of punk's international scope) and in the early '90s through the present by Larry Livermore and Chris Appelgren at Lookout! Records, Slim Moon at Kill Rock Stars, Fat Mike at Fat Wreck Chords, Ruth Schwartz at Mordam Records, Dr. Strange at Dr. Strange Records, as well as at hundreds of tiny punk labels around the globe.[1] Although punk has not yet succeeded in overturning the dominant mode of economic production proffered it—the commercial practices of the major record labels—it significantly alters the material conditions of existence for thousands of punks across the globe. True, punks are unable to absent themselves wholly from commodification and small-scale capitalism, but in their attempts to resist these economic forms they sometimes fail commercially, which is a sort of punk success after all. And in their continual effort to establish a zone of exchange that is qualitatively different from capitalist commodity exchange, punks both testify to the need and desire for such a zone and refuse to abandon the possibility of creating one.

EARLY PUNK ECONOMICS

The economic history of punk can be divided into two unequal parts: early punk economics, from 1974 to 1977, and late punk economics, from 1978 to the present. Nineteen seventy-eight is a logical year to posit a break, because until that year the economic vector of punk took a back seat to its aesthetic vector, while the selling out of the English scene in 1977 marks the moment at which punk began to move underground economically, and its economic vector subsequently became at least as important as its aesthetic one. The most thorough account of the early economic situation that birthed punk is Simon Frith's *Sound Effects: Youth, Leisure, and the Politics of Rock 'n' Roll* (1981). Having described the birth of pop music in the '20s and traced its history through the moment when it became accessible to white working-class teenagers of the '50s in both England and the United States, Frith finds rock emerging out of folk and blues as an artistic (by which he means thought-provoking and intelligent relative to pop) musical form in the '70s. The baby-boomer generation's capacity to consume began to flower in that decade, Frith writes, and large amounts of capital circulated through the rock music industry, which produced the boomers' music of choice. This increase in capital resulted in a division of labor in the industry and a consequent surge of not only professional musicians but specialized promoters, managers, publicists, distributors, producers, technicians, advertisers, etc. (Frith, *Sound Effects*, 137).

As the expense of producing a rock album grew, the major record labels began to dominate the industry by creating or purchasing the full range of the necessary means of rock production: they obtained their own manufacturing facilities; they established their own distributors that distributed primarily their products; they became major music publishers, purchasing the back catalogs of earlier music producers; and they invested in and gave widespread distribution to the newly available technological processes for producing home sound systems as well as electrical instruments (141). By becoming vertically integrated and thereby expanding their control over the full range of the various branches of production, the major record labels could, through competition, drive smaller producers out of business or envelop them, which is exactly what they did. Frith found that "by the end of the 1970s . . . the majors in the USA (CBS, RCA, WEA, MCA, PolyGram, Capitol) accounted for more than 90 percent of the record market in terms of both volume and sales; the 'independents' had a smaller share than at any time since the beginning of the 1950s" (138).

However, the majors' domination of the music market came at a price. According to Frith's argument, the Big Six never successfully manipulated— that is, rendered entirely predictable—rock consumers' tastes, and, consequently, they gradually developed an extremely expensive system of overproduction and promotion, whereby only about 10 percent of the records that they released earned any profit. That 10 percent, however, in addition to the money made from investments in other areas of the music industry, could sustain the labels between hit records, because the massive promotion and distribution budgets paid off in the form of immense sales when albums succeeded. However, the high costs of overproduction and promotion ensured that only the majors controlled enough capital to be able to afford to lose money on 90 percent of the records that they released (148).

Frith argues that in reaction to the prohibitive costs of producing commercial music in England in the late '70s frustrated musicians who felt shut out of record producing rebelled and were responsible for an "explosion of independent rock music-making production," (155) the production of "punk rock."[2] For Frith, punk rock became possible as the most basic instruments of music production became cheaper and access to them became more widely available. While the majors' costs of recording and promoting technologically sophisticated albums were rising, musicians who reverted to "front-room studios" and recorded using four-track tape recorders could create music relatively cheaply (156). Independent record labels, such as Stiff Records and Chiswick, emerged to release punk rock, and soon "independents sold enough to establish a viable 'alternative' record business [in England], with its own network of studios, shops, clubs, [and] charts" (156). An independent label, for Frith, is one that does not have a distribution deal with the majors (156). The early economic history of punk in England is not the same as that of the United States, where, Frith writes, there were "punks whose only way onto record was to do it themselves, but their labels did not have the same impact in America as in England. To reach the national market (and so make the majors take notice) required a much greater outlay, and radio access was more limited" (157). Frith also claims that the U.S. branches of the majors effectively absorbed punk, rendering it fairly ineffective ideologically except in localized cases.

Considering both English and U.S. punk again, Frith summarizes the potential for economic resistance that he finds inherent in punk as a whole:

> [P]unk opposed commercial music in two ways. First, it denounced multinational record companies with a version of the assertion that "small is beautiful"—punk music was, authentically, the product of small-scale, independent record and distribution companies. Second, punk demystified the production process itself—its message was that *anyone* could do it. One effect of this was an astonishing expansion of local music-making. (159)

However, for Frith, punk must be understood, ultimately, as an "unsuccessful musicians' revolt" (84), because the "new sounds, disco and then punk, came from independents, and were, in their turn, standardized and co-opted into new record company divisions" (155). Here Frith invokes the familiar incorporativist, "escape and capture" model often applied to popular culture. He notes that in England independent punk labels turned to the majors for distribution, and the United States' sheer size and consequent distribution costs and complexities worked against punk's chances of penetrating the "national market," until the major labels signed punk bands.

A contradiction arises here that is not unique to Frith: he locates punk rock's potential power in the moment when it seems capable of establishing an "independent, economic alternative" to "multinational record companies," yet its failure, he argues, lies both in its absorption into the Big Six and in its inability to maintain in England, or attain in the United States, national but independent financial viability. However, he also notes that the U.S. majors did not "take notice" of U.S. punk to any significant degree. He reads punk's economic failure—independent and commercial—as its broader cultural failure. I intend to argue just the opposite. Mark Sinker comments upon punk aesthetics: "All punk codes were always intended to fail" (136), and, although he is referring specifically to aesthetic codes, the same logic applies to certain economic ones. For punk to succeed, especially economically, would mean succeeding in the very realm—as Frith acknowledges—that it positions itself against. Such a success would amount to a profound betrayal of punk's commitment to economic resistance.

In Julie Burchill and Tony Parsons's *The Boy Looked At Johnny* (1978), the co-authors, writing three years before Frith, invoke the same contradiction that Frith does. They comment upon the irony of punk rock beginning to obtain "Capitalist Corporate Structure Commercial Viability" (35) in England in 1977, and they bitterly observe that "[a]s soon as any ostensibly dangerous new musical phenomena appear in the sweaty clubs giving a righteous finger to the status quo, it [*sic*] is enticed in from the cold by the same old dangled carrots of sex/drugs/cash/fame and run through the mill of commercial assimilation. What were once sharp, angry fangs are rendered soft, ineffective gums" (88). Yet, they also harangue the Ramones for failing to achieve chart success in England or the United States in the late '70s and the Damned for "failing to make the Top Twenty in 1976" (50). Similar arguments appear in both Gina Arnold's *Route 666: On the Road with Nirvana* (1993) and in the majority of the articles/chapters in *Punk Rock: So What?* (1999), edited by Roger Sabin.

LATE PUNK ECONOMICS

Frith, Arnold, Burchill and Parsons, and Sabin et al. declare punk dead at the moment that it slips beneath the radar of corporately controlled media outlets, but punk's success in its own terms lies precisely in its commercial failure, especially when it is willfully induced, as is the case with the contemporary band Fugazi, whose situation I will turn to below. Punk for itself is never commercially successful, by definition. According to the logic of late punk economics, the moment that a punk band succeeds commercially, which for punks means working with a major label, it ceases to be punk. For example, in 1994 when the consummate Pop-Punk band Green Day signed with Reprise Records, which is owned by Time Warner, the band ceased to be punk; however, Green Day's early albums on Lookout! Records, which is independent of the majors, maintain their punk credibility, although they have been tainted retroactively by the band's sellout, resulting in the dilemma for punks of deciding whether or not to purchase music that hovers in an indeterminate zone between commercial viability and punk.

For punks, the moment of purchase, of commodified consumption, holds a special charge, because it is in that moment that the process of exchange approaches transparency. Money or credit of a certain amount becomes the equivalent of the punk commodity and vice versa: the "punk object" that punks want to situate outside of exchange and apart from money comes to serve as an equivalent for money. In short, it is the moment of exchange that gives the lie most explicitly to any desire to absent punk from the realm of capitalism. Furthermore, punks' valorization of DIY enterprises when producing or purchasing punk commodities and their strict avoidance of corporate products attest to an underlying conceptualization of the dollar as a vote in the commodity marketplace. Most punks understand the purchase of corporate products as an act that materially supports not only a specific corporation but corporate capitalism in general and, correlatively, imagine that purchasing goods from DIY enterprises supports not only a specific enterprise but all DIY enterprises.

Consequently, after 1977, what remains punk to punks is the network of bands, stores, labels, distributors, and venues that consciously align themselves with punk and that continue to operate outside the reach of the major labels, outside of commercial music. It was in 1977, by which point the Sex Pistols seemed to have succeeded commercially[3] and numerous other English Scene punk bands such as The Clash and X-Ray Spex had signed recording deals with major labels[4]—deals granting the labels large degrees of control over the bands—that punks began to redefine themselves in economic terms. Beginning in '78, a rapid shift in method and emphasis occurred within punk attempts to engage in economic resistance. For early punks, economic concerns were secondary to aesthetic ones and accompanied punk's early aesthetics almost as a byproduct. Resisting the commercial market largely meant producing music, often out of necessity, independently of the major record labels, then the Big Six. What the English and New York scenes' subsumption into the music industry demonstrated, though, was that aesthetic forms of divergence from the popular rock sounds of the late '70s would no longer guarantee that bands were economically resistant.

DISCHORD RECORDS AND FUGAZI

Frith notes that in the mid-'70s U.S. punks were adopting do-it-yourself tactics out of necessity but were quickly driven out of business or absorbed by the majors, but he writes in 1981, shortly before a new wave of U.S. do-it-yourself punk institutions emerged in the late '70s and early '80s, bearing with them new economic strategies for avoiding commercialization. The most prominent of these—and one that has attracted the major label interest that Frith cites as simultaneously the hallmark and death knell of punk success—is embodied in Dischord Records, based in Washington, D.C., and Fugazi, a band that releases its albums on the Dischord label. In 1980, before going on to found Fugazi in 1988, Ian MacKaye established Dischord with Jeff Nelson in order to release eight songs by the Teen Idles, a hardcore punk band in which they both played at the time. Dischord and Fugazi, in which MacKaye plays guitar and sings, became the paragons of an important strand of punk economics in the early '80s and have maintained that status up to the present.

In 2003, Dischord and Fugazi remain the most celebrated examples, for punks, of a punk record label and band that have attempted to free themselves from the commercial economy by wresting control of the means of production from the music industry in its multinational guises. Fugazi's conscious and public promotion of its own and Dischord's business practices accounts for part of this celebrity, while the business practices themselves explain the rest.[5] One strategy that Dischord began to employ in 1980 and continues to employ today, in direct contrast with the majors, centers on eschewing the division of labor—what Frith terms the "professionalization"—that overtook the music industry in the '70s. Frith explains that as the majors entered the world market, they discovered a newly global demand for U.S. rock products (*Sound Effects*, 150), and to meet it they required a web of interlocking professionals in "order to produce records, mount shows, manage careers, and orchestrate sales appeal" (137). He blames the "routinization" of rock's sounds on this division of labor. In contrast to the majors, Dischord, which MacKaye continues to co-own and co-manage, distributes and sells its recordings via mail order or direct sales to record stores whenever possible, although Southern Records, an independently owned distribution company,[6] handles the majority of Dischord's distributing needs that mail order and direct sales cannot meet. The band also controls all of its own touring, recording, production, and engineering (Fairchild, 28).

Forgoing the usual commercial division of labor, Dischord avoids the vertical integration of the majors that would establish ownership of the instruments of production for the label. Rather than investing in its own recording, production, and distribution facilities and processing the bands on Dischord through them, MacKaye and Nelson do not place bands under contract and, consequently, cannot dictate where they record their albums. The *Washington Post* quotes Guy Picciotto, one of the singers and guitar players for Fugazi:

> A major-label contract, by definition, makes you an employee of the record company. No matter how good a contract you negotiate, you do not have complete creative control. This is a fact of the record business. This is a fact about Dischord: It does not sign contracts with bands whose recordings it releases, and it allows them total artistic control. (Brace, 24)

Frith's understanding of the recording industry concurs with and expands upon Picciotto's synopsis. He explains that

> the record company does not just act as the record publisher. The standard recording contract makes it clear that record companies, who are the legal owners of the finished product, the physical recording, expect to exercise the right of their ownership, controlling what music is issued, how it is produced, when it is released. Companies may decide what songs will be on a record, in what order, with what packaging; they are at liberty "to determine arrangements, accompaniments, etc."; they can organize an act's performing schedule, as an aspect of record promotion. Companies have the final power to decide whether a song or sound is of sufficient quality to meet the artists' contractual obligations—they are thus able to prevent them from recording elsewhere. (*Sound Effects*, 109)

Dischord forgoes all of the above "privileges" by refusing to claim possession of its bands' products. It does not even reserve the right to cancel a record or CD release if a band does not record the sort of sound in the studio that initially garnered the label's interest in the band.

In addition to avoiding divisions of labor wherever possible, Dischord refuses to develop the "multimedia sales techniques" (150) that Frith finds the majors advancing in the mid- to late '70s. The label never nationally publicizes record releases or concerts for Dischord bands through corporate media outlets, preferring to advertise in independent zines, through word of mouth, and over the World Wide Web. Although label employees initially silkscreened Dischord T-shirts and hung them on clotheslines to dry behind the company's headquarters (MacKaye's mother's house) in D.C. (Connelly et al., 165), they quickly discontinued this form of promotion and have not engaged in T-shirt or sticker promotions since the early '80s. At most contemporary punk rock shows, the merchandise table—at which audience members can purchase records, CDs, stickers, patches, shirts, and zines—remains a ubiquitous fixture, but Fugazi never operates one, although Dischord does not prevent bands on its label from operating their own tables.

Many Dischord bands, and Fugazi in particular, attempt to disengage themselves from what they conceive as a system of commercially motivated cross-marketing. Believing that music, and especially its performance, should not be marketed in conjunction with alcohol, Fugazi, for example, plays shows only in all-ages venues, thereby preventing bars or arenas from exploiting the bands and audiences for alcohol sales. A December 1999 show in Nashville took place in an old warehouse that had been converted into a club; the club did not sell any alcoholic beverages the evening of the show, although it usually does (it did sell bottled water, cigarettes, and soda). In an effort to avoid exploiting their audiences, Fugazi tickets never cost more than seven dollars, and in D.C. Fugazi and several other Dischord bands often play for free, unless they are playing benefit concerts designed to raise money for specific causes.

Fugazi's success at consistently filling large venues and selling records and CDs over the past twelve years has led to multiple offers from the Big Six, and it is precisely the majors' interest in Fugazi and the band's dismissal of their offers that have cemented its position as the standard bearer of late punk economics. In short, Fugazi and Dischord stand as exemplars of a band and a record label that could sell out and become commercial but choose not to, and therein lies a component of what punks recognize as economic resistance. Implicit in the logic at work here is the familiar tension between punk and the commercial music industry and the ineluctable interpenetration of the two that structures so much of punk as a field, in spite of punks' best efforts to combat commercial influences. Ironically, the value of Fugazi and Dischord hinges, in part, upon their value in the commercial music market, which manages to exert its ability to determine value even in the case of punk's most celebrated anticommercial enterprise. Nevertheless, it is in the refusal of the major labels that Fugazi and Dischord's punk value lies, because in refusing commercialization they prove that they are not independent enterprises by default (because they could not garner major label interest) but are consciously independent, a fact that grants their independence greater validity for punks.

LOOKOUT! RECORDS

Following Dischord's example to some degree, Larry Livermore founded the Lookout! Records label in 1987 in Laytonville, California, before moving it

to Berkeley in 1989. As in Dischord's case, Lookout! initially attempted to
avoid the commercial practices of the Big Six: the label was not vertically
integrated; it endeavored to allow its bands some autonomy; and, in its early
years, the label did not sign contracts with its bands. John Goshert, guitarist
for the now defunct punk band Monsula, comments that when Monsula
agreed to release music on Lookout!, the label did not demand that the band
members sign a contract and did not dictate the terms of the band's recording or touring. In addition, the label did not have sales quotas that bands had
to meet in order to remain on the label; consequently, the release of Monsula's second album, *Sanitized*, on Lookout! in 1992 did not depend upon the
sales of the first album, *Structure*, which was released in 1991. Although the
members of Monsula chose to do so, the band was not required to tour in
support of either album.

According to Goshert, the band's members have received 60 percent of
the price of each copy of *Structure* and *Sanitized* that Lookout! has sold since
the records recouped the amounts that the label initially invested in them.
This initial investment included the money the label paid the recording studios that the band members (not the label) chose to employ,[7] as well as production and distribution costs. (Until 2000, Lookout! had a distribution deal
with Mordam Records, an independent record distributor that handles the
products of thirty-four independent labels.)[8] Sixty percent is a remarkably
high royalty rate. Frith estimates the average rate in the '70s at between 12 and
15 percent for commercial acts, with incredibly lucrative performers earning
as much as 22 percent (*Sound Effects*, 83). In the mid-'90s, the rate fell to an
average of 7 to 12 percent (Krasilovsky and Shemel, 4) and has not changed
significantly since then. What was punk about the early business practices of
Lookout! was that the label not only paid a high royalty rate, and therefore did
not seem to be out to fleece the bands, but it also invested capital in punk
bands, such as Monsula, without using its investments as the tool that would
render bands beholden to the label as the owner of the means of production.

Current Lookout! business practices differ from the label's original ones,
most notably in that the label now signs bands to contracts. In 1998, Livermore sold the company to Chris Appelgren, who continues to own and operate it today. Even before the sale, George Tabb, the singer for the Pop-Punk
band Furious George and a columnist for *MaximumRockNRoll (MRR)*,[9] published an account of his business dealings with Lookout! in the February 1997
issue of *MRR*. He and the other members of Furious George signed a contract with Lookout! to do an EP,[10] and Tabb claims that he had a verbal agreement with Lookout! that the label would follow the EP with an LP[11] and give
the band a merchandise agreement as well as tour support. The label reneged
on everything but the EP. Lookout!'s changing policies, Tabb's public attack
on the label, and the public support that Tim Yohannon, the founder and pub-

lisher of *MRR*, granted to Tabb's claims against Lookout! have combined to place the label in the median zone between indie and major labels that two other large and supposedly independent record labels now occupy.

Along with Lookout!, Fat Wreck Chords and Dr. Strange Records engender copious debate in punk zines over whether or not there is any difference between them and the current "Big Five" major labels.[12] Additionally, some of what were formerly the largest indie punk labels have forfeited their punk status within the last few years, when their connections to major labels became public knowledge (which usually means that their status was published in *MRR*). Epitaph Records, Revelation Records, and Nitro Records, all of which were founded as indies by people in the U.S. punk scene, currently benefit from financial support and/or distribution deals with the majors, and their albums are eschewed by punks or purchased when the labels re-release classic punk that cannot be obtained without paying collector scum prices for early pressings.[13]

THE FAILURE/SUCCESS OF DISCHORD, FUGAZI, AND LOOKOUT!

My attention to Dischord, Fugazi, and Lookout! Records should not be understood as a testimonial to the radical, subversive, or messianic nature of independent punk bands and labels. Doug Henwood comments in a *Punk Planet* interview:

> In a practical sense, a lot of independent operations screw their employees and customers over as much as anybody else does. You could say that there's often something other than the logic of profit maximization at work in independent operations, but you can't be sure of that. There are lots of scum bags and frauds everywhere, including independent music labels and publishers. (47)

Although Dischord, Fugazi, and Lookout! do not (or did not initially, in the case of Lookout!) seem to be composed of scumbags—in Henwood's sense of the word—it is the labels' and the band's failings by commercial standards and by DIY standards that constitute punk's highlighting of the problem of establishing an independently run sphere of exchange qualitatively different from the commercial sphere.

Punks' attempts at economic oppositionality exhibit three interrelated, partial failures, but all three, when inverted, can be turned into punk successes of a sort. First, Dischord and Lookout! fail in the broad terms of the commercial commodity market and its apologists, such as Gina Arnold, Julie

Burchill and Tony Parsons, and several of the authors in *Punk Rock, So What?*
The DIY approach to production mobilized within punk fails to pose any
sizeable material threat to the majors in terms of market share (I will return
to specific percentages of market share below). Even if DIY production is
assumed to be qualitatively different and, hence, a viable alternative to commercial production (a point that I will contest below), it has had little economic effect on the music industry, failing as it has to carve out more than a
tiny slice of the indie market. This failure to become competitive with the
major labels serves as a measure of punk success, though, because punks
understand their lack of market dominance, and the conscious avoidance of it
in Fugazi's case, as a guarantee that an economic logic ("profit maximizing,"
for Henwood) does not govern their production.

Second, in terms of individual punks, few of Dischord or Lookout!'s
musicians derive a living from their music. This fact is true not only of these
specific labels but of punk bands generally: few generate enough revenue to
meet the band members' means of subsistence, and most punks work at non-
music, or at least nonperformance (such as record store), day jobs in which
they are exploited to a greater or lesser degree than they are when they work
as musicians. Here, the failure lies in the DIY punk community's inability to
absent its members from the commercial sphere, especially that portion of it
not overseen by the logic of late punk economics. However, it is this exact failure to make a living from punk that punks read as a success of sorts. Punk
should create neither profit nor careers for its practitioners, and the inability
of punks and their businesses to make profits is often read as a badge of
authenticity and an inverted form of success, where "making a living" denotes
a form of economic and capitalist success, a form—however small—of selling
out. Punks often consciously divorce themselves from punk as a career, where
the word suggests the manner in which a person is willing to exchange his or
her labor in order to survive economically. This intentional distancing of
punks from profit marks a failure in commercial terms and a success in punk
terms. Writing under his given name (Craig O'Hara), Jim Filth, the lead guitarist for the Lookout! band Filth explains in exemplary fashion that "the idea
of making large sums of money off punk (without exploiting it) is not a very
popular or feasible idea" (160). And across the top of page three in almost
every issue of *MRR* appears the zine's stance on profit: "MaximumRockNRoll
is a monthly publication. All work is donated and no one receives any salary.
All proceeds are either invested in technological improvements or go to other
similarly not-for-profit projects. Anyone is welcome to reprint anything from
MRR, but only if it's not-for-profit."

Although Dischord and Lookout!, as well as other DIY punk labels, have
also failed to establish a mode of producing rock music radically different from
the majors' mode, it is not insignificant that these institutions have turned

back the clock on capitalism. Dischord and Lookout! (and *MRR*) represent
sustainable *C-M-C'* enterprises instead of *M-C-M'* corporations like the
major labels,[14] even if the difference between the two is one of size rather than
of kind. Furthermore, it is this third partial failure that renders visible the
problem inherent in punk's attempt to free itself from the sphere of commodity exchange. As Frith claims, independence for punks seems "to refer primarily to the question of artistic control" (*Sound Effects*, 159), and he might
have added, "for a small group of producers, composed primarily of musicians
and label owners." Despite his attention to who benefits from punk production, Frith privileges the recording and distribution of rock music at the
expense of the material means, outside of the field of punk, by which music is
mass-produced and distributed. Regardless of how independent a punk record
label endeavors to be, it still makes capital available to bands that allows them
to rent recording studio time and engineers and employ factories and printing
facilities to produce their compact discs, records, CD liner notes, jewel box
cases (for CDs), record sleeves, etc. However, Dischord and Lookout! employees do not work in those factories, in which the workers exchange their labor
for wages as they would when producing any non-punk, commercial commodity. In the sphere of manufacturing, the difference between producing
punk products as opposed to others is a difference in the sheer number of people exploited in relation to the number that could be exploited. Dischord and
Lookout! refrain from accumulating as much capital, hence surplus labor, as
the Big Five and do not exploit the labor power of as many workers as the
majors. These punk labels also avoid exploitation in terms of numbers of
workers by eliminating some of the branches of labor that have sprung up in
commercial music making between bands, labels, factories, and stores.

The labor of the band members must not be neglected, either. Although
they do not have to sign away their creative control as they would with major
labels, bands on Dischord and early Lookout! bands are and were still
expected to tour the United States and sometimes Europe in order to promote
their records. Touring means playing the same songs repeatedly in city after
city. In short, the musicians' labor becomes repetitive, the songs become units
of exchange-value rather than use-values, and, as Marx writes, "[a]s use-values, commodities differ above all in quality, while as exchange-values they can
only differ in quantity, and therefore do not contain an atom of use-value"
(*Capital* 1:128). In the sphere of touring, the bands' music loses much of its
use-value to its creators as they play it less and less for reasons other than its
exchangeability, and it enters the market as a punk rock show more and more
as a commodity facing all other commodities as a price, or quantity of abstract
human labor, rather than as a unique form of labor with a nonquantitative
value of its own. I do not mean to suggest that shows do not differ significantly from one another; the context in which a punk band performs usually

changes with each performance, because bands rarely play more than one show in the same town. Nevertheless, in band interview after band interview in zines and books, musicians treat the actual performance of their music as a constant that does not warrant any commentary and focus, instead, upon what they remember changing from venue to venue—the places, the crowds, the travel between venues, the people with whom they interacted before and after shows, etc.[15]

Summarizing punk's complicity with commercialization, Frith writes: "'[I]ndependent records,' made by do-it-yourself companies [remain] commodities" and notes that "the most enterprising punk company [in England]—Rough Trade—was . . . based on a shop" (*Sound Effects*, 159). Today, Lookout! Records runs its own label store, as do several other punk labels, including Dr. Strange. Frith reads Rough Trade's shop- (consumerism-) based business practices as symptomatic of an "'alternative' production system that both paralleled the established industry (alternative shops sell records made by alternative record companies and featured in the Alternative Charts) and was integrated into it" (159). This integration continues in 2003 and is especially apparent in chain record stores, where Dischord and Lookout! products appear alongside the products of the Big Five. The distributors that the chains most frequently employ—often "one-stops," such as Alliance Entertainment Corporation (AEC), that carry the products of myriad corporate labels—might not carry Dischord and Lookout! products, but stores can still order directly from even the tiniest labels and bands or establish relationships with independent distributors, such as Southern or Mordam, that carry exclusively independent bands.

Dischord and Fugazi's attempted independence from and resistance to commercialism also suggests less a move toward a different mode of production than a nostalgia for an earlier one. MacKaye, especially, combines the role of musician with that of label owner and manager, embodying an idea of entrepreneurialism that hearkens back to what Jean-Luc Godard, playing a version of himself in *Prénom Carmen* (1983), refers to as the "classic capitalism" of a perhaps nonexistent but certainly bygone period that attempted to satisfy real needs with the best possible commodities.[16] MacKaye seems to have entered the music industry for a noncommercial reason: he is wholly invested in it as a performer and artisan and wants to level the playing field for other musicians. In short, he did not help found Dischord because he saw an economic opportunity in it; nevertheless, he operates within punk as a small-scale capitalist.

As I have implied above, throughout the '90s and up to the present punks have witnessed what appears to be the financial success of several of the largest independent punk labels, including Dischord, Lookout!, Fat Wreck Chords, and Dr. Strange. Debates rage in contemporary punk zines over whether or not specific bands, labels, zines, and people have sold out, and the criteria by which to judge punks, their bands, and punk texts seem increasingly more difficult to formulate when large independent labels seem poised to compete with the major labels. It seems that punk's noncommercial, independent, economic resistance to the Big Five is starting to resemble commercial success too closely: in short, this financial success is beginning to look like punk failure. But, in actuality, do any of these punk labels threaten the major labels in the market? Are any independent labels within shooting range of major-label size? How economically underground is the punk underground?

According to a special issue of *The Nation* (Aug. 25/Sept. 1, 1997) devoted to the music industry and appearing twenty years after the period that Frith addresses, a new Big Six (Time Warner, Sony, Philips Electronics, Seagram, Bertelsmann AG, and EMI) control 79 percent of the music market in terms of sales, leaving 21 percent for the "indies," (*Project*, 25–28). *The Nation* breaks that 21 percent down into eight genres (rap, rock/punk/alternative, gospel, folk/alternative, blues/R&B, country, jazz, and classical) and lists some of the more prominent labels constituting those genres. The magazine's researchers note, however, that they define "indie" as music "[d]istributed independently of the major music companies. However, some independent distributors (ADA, RED) are owned in whole or in part by one of the Big Six; the Big Six use indie distributors for some releases, and some indies use the Big Six to distribute a particular label or artist" (28).

For punks, these acknowledged connections with the majors disqualify labels and bands from "indie" status, and punks make a point of keeping track of the music industry and who owns it. In 1994, *MRR* published a diagram that charted the major corporate record companies (entitled "Some of Your Friends Are Already This Fucked: Everything You've Wanted to Know About Major Labels"). *Flipside*, also an international zine, released its own set of updated diagrams (for the Big Five) in their May/June 1999 issue. It is worth revisiting *MaximumRocknRoll*'s advertising criteria here, because the U.S. and international punk community, even when individuals or factions within it disagree with the zine, reluctantly acknowledge *MRR* as the arbiter of what can and cannot be considered punk in economic terms. *MRR*'s policy reads, "We will not accept major label or related ads, or ads for comps [compilations] or EPs that include major label bands" (1). "Related ads" include those for bands that appear on indie labels but are distributed by major labels or their affiliates. This policy does not apply exclusively to ads; *MRR* also refuses to publish reviews of, interviews with, or articles on major label–connected bands. In short, the amount of indie, and punk as a subdivision of indie in this case, control over the music market seems to have grown over the past twenty years, from 10 percent to 21 percent, but only if indie is defined fairly loosely, which is not the case in punk.

Janine Jaquet, a senior researcher for the Project on Media Ownership at Johns Hopkins University, argues that the above percentages and "numbers suggest a proliferation of indie labels and a surge in innovative music across musical genres. Too bad that's not what's happening" (10). Instead, she finds that

> rather than indicating healthy growth in all genres, most of the indie sales these days seem to be coming from just one genre, rap. No one tracks these figures, but many observers agree with Tom Silverman, chairman of rap label Tommy Boy Records (50 percent owned by Time Warner), that while rap probably makes up only 5 percent of indie labels, it accounts for the majority of indie sales. (10)

Rather than considering what was occurring among indie music producers in 1997 exceptional or exciting, Jaquet explains that a "true boom in independent music would involve acts making and selling their music to a broad audience—not just in mom-and-pop stores to die-hard fans—without relying on one of the Big Six" (10). If Jaquet's estimates are roughly accurate, then rap accounted for over half of the 21 percent of the market that "indies" constituted in 1997, leaving roughly 10 percent or less, as was true in the late '70s, for all other indies (even if indie is loosely defined).

Developments in the music industry over the last few years suggest that in 2003 the percentage of indie control of the market has fallen below 1997 levels. The Big Six no longer exists, having been consolidated into the Big Five: in 1998, Seagram (which is the parent company of the Universal Music Group but also a subsidiary of Vivendi Universal) purchased PolyGram Music from Philips Electronics. John Seabrook, writing for the *New Yorker* in 2003, estimates that currently "[f]ive global music companies control more than eighty-five percent of the record business," adding that the "remaining fifteen percent is divided among some ten thousand independent labels" (45). He lists the new Big Five as Universal (Seagram), Warner Music (AOL Time Warner), Sony Music Entertainment, BMG (the Bertelsmann Music Group), and the EMI Group, noting that in 2002 Universal alone controlled 29 percent of the market. The above numbers from *The Nation* and the subsequent developments in the music industry indicate that punk, as it defines itself, has not attained commercial success and does not occupy a position from which it can compete with the majors. Of the "important labels" that *The Nation* categorizes into eight genres under its "Indies" heading, only two are punk labels: Crypt Records and Dischord Records. For Crypt, the Oblivians and the Raunch Hands are listed as the largest sellers, while for Dischord, Fugazi is. Given the estimate that rap accounts for 50 percent of indie sales and the fact that most of the indie labels that *The Nation* lists have major-label connections, it is likely that punk accounts for only a very small slice of the indie pie and an even tinier slice of the world music market, probably less than 1 percent. Dischord is an important label to punks not because it poses a threat to the majors or rivals any of them in size but because of its twenty-year-old reputation for refusing the advances of the Big Six and the Big Five and its ongoing attempt to operate according to business standards somewhat different from those of the major labels. Currently, it is the only large (by strictly indie standards) independent label that maintains its punk status for the punk community.

In the *Grundrisse*, Marx writes that workers confront capitalists as both laborers and consumers. In the workers' moments of leisure, the capitalist "searches for means to spur them on to consumption, to give his wares new charms, to inspire them with new needs by constant chatter, etc." (287). Against the background of the commercial forces of the music industry, punk figures strangely as the cultural form that does not attempt to "inspire new needs" that can, supposedly, be met by the commodity. Instead, punk repeatedly plays to the old needs because they have not yet been met. If the relation between capitalist and consumer is the relation upon which, for Marx, "the contemporary power of capital rests" (287), then punks' refusal to "chatter" in the commercial tongue and their distancing of themselves from music producers who do, guarantee that punk will never succeed commercially. Punk, for itself, relegates itself to the margins of the music business; it is composed of punk producers who do not sign with the majors, regardless of whether or not they are asked.

For the above reasons, Al Flipside complains about the ever-present potential insolvency of punk rock, when in fact that liminal status is punk's real strength. Al writes:

> [Y]ou know the story. A new label starts up with all the good intentions that have been dissected in the pages of Flipside for the past 20 years. The label sells a few here and there through the usual underground distro [distribution] channels and then, as happens sometimes, the band starts to take off. And they sign to a major. Every time. Immediately the financial support the DIY indies (the label, the distributors, promoters, bookers, artists, clubs, fanzines . . .) need to get the new system off the ground is ripped out and plugged into supporting the same old thing. (2)

But punk cannot function otherwise. Mark Sinker finds early English punks aesthetically negating the ideas about community that their historical moment proffered them, in order to preserve the possibility of a potential social organization that did not yet exist. For him, the aesthetics of punk behavior attempted but conspicuously failed to overturn the dominant "economy of desire" but thereby rendered its logic visible and suspect. In this chapter, I propose that punk economic strategies attempt a similar overturning of the literal "economy of music."

Jon Savage writes that, in 1979, "[p]unk was beaten, but it had also won. If it had been the project of the Sex Pistols to destroy the music industry, then they had failed; but as they gave it new life, they allowed a myriad of new forms to become possible" (541). A similar statement can be made for the punk project's thirty years. Although punk has still not destroyed the music industry, it continues to explore the margins of commercial music production and thereby throws its logic into relief and opens it up for scrutiny. Punk has also established and continues to establish itself as a set of economic strategies within capitalism that allow literally thousands of punks worldwide to live lives significantly different from those that the commercial music industry could offer them as its workers. True, punks never wholly escape or transcend the economic conditions in which they are mired: they cannot fully eschew commodification or small-scale capitalism. But in their attempts to resist them they fail in commercial terms, which is a sort of punk success after all. And in their continual effort and failure to establish a zone free from commodification, punks attest to a continuing cultural desire for something else.

In this chapter, I have outlined an economic history of punk and argued that, for early punks, economic resistance was secondary to aesthetic concerns and largely meant producing music, often out of necessity, independently of the six major record labels. Economic resistance to the Big Six accompanied punk's early aesthetics almost as a byproduct, because the bands' divergence from the popular rock music of their day marked them as commercially unsaleable. By the late '70s, aesthetic resistance no longer necessarily produced economic resistance alongside itself, and, consequently, punk's First Wave of selling out precipitated a shift of focus within punk from aesthetics to economics. Although aesthetic attempts at negation were not completely abandoned, and chapter 2 describes their most negationist forms, it is at this historical moment that many of punk's cultural commentators declare that it is dead or, at the very least, that it reached its peak between 1976 and 1978. In terms of a new aesthetic, they might be correct, but in economic terms they are not. Concerning its relationship to and alignment with the capitalist mode of production, punk was most commercially successful between '76 and '78, and again in the early '90s when Green Day and Pop-Punk began to amass capital for Lookout!, but punk for itself has never been allied with commercial success. Something did happen to punk in 1978, but it did not die; it went back underground; it refused success on commercial terms.

While it is true that, in terms of its relationship to the major labels, punk has not sold out to the extent that punks imagine and fear that it has, what I have stressed in this chapter is that punk fails twice, according to the criteria of cultural theorists and according to its own criteria. Not only does punk not pose any substantial threat to the major labels (as Frith, Burchill and Parsons, Arnold, and Sabin et al. hoped that it would) but punks have also failed to establish a zone of exchange that is radically different from commodity exchange as it exists under capitalism. In their continued refusal, in most cases, to exchange their "punk labor" for enough money to meet their means of subsistence and their inability to resolve for themselves the contradiction inherent to the commodity-form between use- and exchange-value, punks fail both as good capitalists and as perfect anticapitalists. They are poor business-people and unable to negate business itself as the element in which they must stake out their survival. However, through its double failure, which is really an ongoing process of failing and never a final failure, the punk project testifies to the need for something beyond itself, for some sort of resolution to the commodity-form that allows labor to be experienced as qualitative rather than quantitative, for some social structure that does not yet exist. Punks refuse to abandon the possibility of creating such a structure.

chapter five

Screening Punk

PUNK CINEMA?

Thus far, I have privileged music and zines over other genres of punk textuality, but I want to broaden my working definition of punk in this chapter to allow for the possibility of punk cinema. The only requirement that needs to be relaxed from the provisional definition of punk that I proffer in chapter 1 is the insistence upon punks doing the producing. What I want to propose is that punk might not belong wholly to self-identified punks. Perhaps punk denotes not just a scene or series of scenes or the people that constitute them but an aesthetic and material methodology or set of practices for cultural production in general. If this is the case, then non-punks could produce punk products. It is with this proposition in mind that I turn to punk cinema.

Currently, "punk cinema" signifies, in loose talk, films that obey a particular aesthetic, that are composed of certain formal properties, that mimic punk's speed, frenetic energy, anger, antiauthoritarian stance, irony, style, anomie, or disillusionment. It is in this sense that I understand Darren Aronofsky's recent characterization of his latest film, *Requiem for a Dream* (2000), as "a punk movie" (Stark, 2). I wish to advance a more dialectical approach here, one that grasps punk cinema's aesthetic as emerging from and informed by punk economics as I have detailed them in earlier chapters. In short, as with other punk commodities, I aim to demonstrate the necessary interdependence of punk film's aesthetics and economics; as usual, punks' concern with economics becomes the obverse of punk's aesthetic. Any attempt to articulate the logic of a punk cinema aesthetics must therefore attend to the assumptions about and commitments to particular means of production that it bears along with it and reflects.

Punk's DIY approach figures as one of the constitutive and liberatory elements of punk cinema just as it is for punk rock and punk zines. Within the field of punk, in order for the term *punk cinema* to carry some weight, to describe something more than a consumable aesthetic, it must bear, aesthetically and economically, a filmic version of the old punk democratizing dictum, "This is a chord. This is another. This is a third. Now form a band."[1] Just as anyone can produce punk—and should—anyone can produce punk cinema—and should. In its best moments, musically and filmically, aesthetically and economically, punk reminds us that rather than one giant, linear feed-pipe with Time-Warner-AOL-Verizon-Microsoft-Disney-McGraw-Hill-Martha Stewart at the production end providing us with all of our consumables, we need to become producers ourselves, to lay out our own rhizomes of converging and diverging pipes. We need more little pipes, not a single, monstrous one.

As I have claimed throughout this book, for music to be punk a band must be capable of producing, distributing, and performing it with little or no specialized training, without prohibitive financial investments, and without ties to corporate investors, which means producing music outside of the Big Five major labels that are responsible for roughly 85 percent of the global music market. Attending strictly to economic or production concerns does not produce a satisfactory definition of punk rock, however, because any number of bands and even whole subgenres of rock—the early '90s "lo-fi" music of Sebadoh, Guided by Voices, and Daniel Johnston to name just one—have practiced DIY economics without obtaining or even desiring punk status. Excluding aesthetics might lead to the potentially awkward position of heralding the Grateful Dead as one of the most financially successful punk bands ever, following their formation of an independent record label, Ice Nine, for publishing their music and books. For this reason, I want to return to the interrelatedness of aesthetics and economics within punk to propose that part of what punk cinema inherits from punk rock is the mandate to express that aesthetics-economics relation as an element of its aesthetic. When punk passes into film, it demands of film that it offer up traces of its production, that it open itself out to its audience as an open text by pointing up how it came to be rather than reifying its means of production and thereby folding in on itself as a closed text.

Turning back to film, a cognate of this aesthetic and economic model for punk rock could only embrace films not only made without any support—in terms of production, distribution, or exhibition—from the eight major studios that dominate the film industry today (Columbia/Tri-Star, Warner Brothers, Paramount, Universal, MGM, Twentieth Century Fox, New Line Cinema, and Disney) (Monaco, 254) but also demonstrative of that lack of support. Additionally, punk filmmakers, like punk musicians, must be capable of producing their work with little or no specialized training and without prohibitive financial investments, and their work must aesthetically reflect these material concerns. This combinatory of elements is meant to democratize access to the means of producing film. The filmic version of the *Sideburns* zine maxim might run: "This is a camera. This is film stock. This is a subject. Now shoot a movie." This push for democratization and the economic prerequisites that it demands disqualify numerous films that might otherwise be considered punk cinema according to the conventional definition of this term that I am trying to supplant. The pace, violence, and irony of *Natural Born Killers* (1994) correlates with hundreds of punk songs—The Eyes' "Kill Your Parents" for example, with which the film shares a similar theme—but Warner Brothers produced the film, owns it, and exercised control over its creation. The film also employs a panoply of technically sophisticated practices that potentially stand between spectators and their desire to make their own movies. Similarly, Alex Cox's *Sid and Nancy* (1986) takes the Sex Pistols and Nancy Spungen (Sid Vicious's girlfriend) as its subjects but was bankrolled by MGM and maintains the high gloss of a Hollywood product, while Julien Temple's *The Filth and the Fury* (2000), a documentary on the Sex Pistols, is a New Line Cinema production with the veneer of a big-budget film. Within the parameters of the definition for punk cinema that I am proposing, the major Hollywood studios stand in as the filmic analog for the major labels of the recording industry, because both perform gatekeeping functions in terms of economics and aesthetics: both define a dominant economic and aesthetic model. Consequently, the Hollywood studios' usual product signifies the antithesis of punk cinema.

THE PUNK MARQUEE: WHAT'S SHOWING?

Up to this point, I have been arguing that punk economics inflect a film's aesthetics in identifiable ways; in fact, the two poles converge in order to buttress and extend one another. But what does this process produce? What do the results look like? Early punk cinema efforts take punk itself as their subject, such as Amos Poe's *Blank Generation* (1976), a documentary in which Poe shoots punk bands performing at Max's Kansas City and CBGBs, two of the pivotal nightclub venues for the New York Scene of '74–'76. Gina Marchetti notes that in two of Poe's films, *Blank Generation* and *Night Lunch* (1975), the audiences at the shows appear in the films as characters of a sort. She adds that *Blank Generation* "is actively engaged, through point-of-view camera positioning and hand-held, dance-like camera movement, in the punk performance. The filmmaker becomes part of the punk crowd, part of the punk event" (60). The barrier between producer and consumer becomes permeable, and the audience become not punk musicians but performers nevertheless, and the camera and its operator become part of the audience to the point of dancing with the other fans. The film is also a low-budget enterprise made independently of the Hollywood studios.

In *Blank Generation,* the filmmaker becomes a fan, but in *The Punk Rock Movie* (1978) the fan becomes a filmmaker. Don Letts, a Rastafarian DJ at the Roxy club in London, shot the film. Jon Savage writes: "[C]aught up in the general sense of empowerment, the DJ picked up a Super-8 camera" (328). The film is composed almost entirely of footage of punk bands rehearsing and performing at the Roxy in London and is similar to Poe's formally: Letts shoots most of it from the audience's point of view; the camera is hand-held and is not a Steadicam; available light is used almost exclusively; and the camera movement seems to follow Letts's shifting attention as he focuses on a lead singer, pans to a guitarist, zooms in on the guitarist's hands or face, zooms out, pans left to take in part of the audience, etc. The sound is not professionally mixed but corresponds with the place in the club from which Letts is shooting, so that in one instance, while he is shooting singer Wayne County from a point close to one of the speakers, the sound of the bass guitar drowns out the other instruments, and, although he focuses on County for much of the song, County's vocals are barely audible.

Letts also almost completely eschews narrative. There is no voice-over, and no sub- or intertitles inform the viewer of when or where each scene was shot or who is performing. Instead, the film's organizing principle is the punk song and the English Scene of '76–'78: each scene begins with one of the scene's bands beginning to play a song at the Roxy. When the song is over the scene is over, and the film makes a direct cut to the next band and song. If the viewer lacks a context in which to place the music or bands at the beginning of the film, then it could easily appear to be a conglomerate of crudely filmed pieces of concert footage, which, in one sense, it is. This open formal structure does not foreclose on possible readings or meanings to the extent that commercial, hence non-punk, narrative films do, whether they are documentaries or not. Consequently, *The Punk Rock Movie* disrupts the division of labor that other films establish.[2] Letts's film militates against the aesthetic conventions of narrative Hollywood films that attempt to guide readings along carefully described channels, pushing the labor of reading toward the pole of pure absorption and away from an active construction of the text. In the case of Letts, the filmmaker ceases to be the creator of a univocal meaning, and much of the labor of interpretation falls to the viewer. The film opens itself out, encouraging and prodding the spectator to shift from the position of a passive (to a greater or lesser degree) recipient to that of an active producer of the film's possible significations. The viewer controls the instruments for producing meaning, instruments that Hollywood filmmakers usually reserve as their own property, for their own use. Letts's film is "writerly" rather than "readerly" in Roland Barthes's sense, and it functions as

Barthes imagines that the literary work does that makes "the reader no longer a consumer, but a producer of the text" (S/Z, 4).

Walter Benjamin theorizes this shift from consumption to production through his concept of the "mimetic faculty." If punk initiates movement over that divide, it is in part because of a process similar to what Benjamin describes when he proposes that the means by which certain cultural artifacts are produced bear with them the power to "stimulate" and "awaken" the "mimetic faculty" that lies dormant in a group of potential producers, of not-yet-producing producers ("On the Mimetic," 333–36). As the example of Letts demonstrates, it seems entirely possible that the means of producing mid- to late-'70s English and American punk generated a social and cultural charge that emerged from the domains of rock music and fashion to infuse a group of filmmakers who translated, and are still translating, punk's noncorporate, DIY logic into their own medium. In terms of aesthetics, Letts's film also bears material traces of its low budget as well as his inattention to professional production values. These traces combine and contribute toward an aesthetic that communicates a version of Benjamin's mimetic function, an implicit message that not only can anyone interpret this film and become a producer of thought, interpretation, critique, but anyone can become a producer, make a film, pick up a camera and start shooting without concern for Hollywood editing, lighting, *mise-en-scène*, narrative structure, directing, producing, etc. The film stands as material proof that a fan need not remain wholly bound to consumption but can partake actively in the scene; in Letts's words: "their [The Clash's] DIY ethic inspired me to pick up a Super 8mm camera and record what was going on at that time" ("The Clash—Live"). Letts's example also indicates that the mimetic function is not limited to a particular medium but jumps between media. Inspired by a shift in the means of representation in one medium, punk rock, Letts translates that shift into another medium, film.

Thus far, I have drawn examples of punk cinema solely from documentary-style films that take punk rock or punks as their subject, but for the purposes of the definition that I am proposing here punk cinema need not concern itself with punk per se. A question immediately arises: If punk cinema does not take punk as its subject, then should, for example, California Newsreel or Andy Warhol films be included beneath the punk cinema umbrella? What about the French New Wave? Are *Dutchman* (1966), *Sleep* (1963), *Paris Belongs to Us* (1960), and other avant-garde films examples of punk cinema? To grant this term greater efficacy as a descriptor, it is necessary to articulate further the aesthetic to which it refers. Lawrence Grossberg's categorization of a subsection of punk as "critical-alternative" serves as an opening gambit, although both halves of his category might be productively tightened. Punk cinema's aesthetic can be understood as critical not only in Grossberg's sense of affirming "its own negativity" but also in terms of what it negates or critiques—the capitalization

of film through commodification. This critique assumes an "alternative" form
that "mounts an implicit attack on dominant culture" (46) if I sharpen Grossberg's "dominant culture" and read it as the dominant Hollywood aesthetic—
the closed form or readerly text.[3] Before turning to an example of this aesthetic,
I will examine a film—*Rude Boy* (1980)—that, by resisting Hollywood's aesthetic as well as its dominant economic model, resists its own circulation as a
commodity. So that punk cinema might figure more clearly against the background of the major production companies that it opposes, I will subsequently
interrogate a film—*Fight Club* (1999)—that initially seems to resist the Hollywood aesthetic before violently capitulating to it.

AT THE BIJOUX: *RUDE BOY*

Running alongside the first several years of punk rock's history there emerged
a series of documentary-style films addressing it, and this form prevailed in
films about punk for several years, although fictional films as well as hybrid
documentary-fictional films soon arrived on the scene. In fact, the hybrid
form knows an odd popularity in that subgenre of punk cinema that takes
punk as its object of study. A fairly early example is producers Jack Hazan and
David Mingay's *Rude Boy*, which was released by Buzzy Enterprises Limited.
The film was produced independently of the major production companies,
without any financial assistance from either the Clash (its nominal subject) or
CBS (the Clash's record company), although Hazan admits that the film cost
around five hundred thousand pounds to produce. The amount is cheap by
Hollywood standards but still prohibitive to many would-be independent
filmmakers. In addition to the producers' DIY economic approach, Hazan and
Mingay also cleave to an aesthetic that suggests that anyone can make a
movie. Shot between 1977 and 1979 and released in the spring of 1980, the
film employs many of the formal elements of Letts's *Punk Rock Movie*. The
producers devote a significant portion of the film to concert footage of the
Clash, some of which is shot from the point of view of the audience with a
hand-held camera (but not a Steadicam), although, as the main character, Ray
Gange, begins working for the Clash as a roadie, the film incorporates shots
from behind the stage. All of the nonconcert footage is shot using a station-
ary camera that never tracks, often waiting for the actors to enter the scene
before panning or tilting to follow their movements. Like Letts's film, no
voice-over or text orients the audience by establishing the film's time period
or location. The sound has been professionally mixed but was recorded on
location rather than foleyed in subsequently.

   For two years, the film sporadically documents the life of Ray Gange
(who plays himself), a twenty-year-old London punk and Clash fan who

cheats the dole by moonlighting at a pornography bookstore in London. Gange's friends include Joe Strummer—the Clash's lead singer—as well as the Clash's road manager, who offers Gange a job as a roadie. The film shifts back and forth between the fictional life of Ray Gange and concert and studio footage of the Clash, although it also combines the two: Gange appears in the crowd at several actual Clash shows, chats with Joe Strummer about politics on two occasions when Strummer, as himself, explains his political stance (and Gange expresses either his own, a fictional one, or some hybrid of the two), and speaks to the crowd at a Rock Against Racism (RAR) concert (historical, not fictional) in an effort to support the Clash and to quell angry National Front supporters.

The film blurs the line between documentary and fiction, which makes it reminiscent of *The Great Rock 'n' Roll Swindle* (1979), in which Julien Temple splices documentary footage of Sex Pistols concerts together with a fictional detective story in which Steve Jones, the lead guitarist for the Pistols (playing himself), searches for the band's manager, Malcolm McLaren, in order to solve the mystery of what happened to the money that the Pistols supposedly accrued for McLaren. This blurring in *Rude Boy* serves two purposes. First, the film places punk within the context of "official History" (History, capital *H*); in the first few minutes of the movie, Gange watches a parade in honor of Queen Elizabeth's Silver Jubilee pass beneath the housing project in which he lives and spits upon it. The film also includes newsreel footage of Margaret Thatcher "making inflammatory calls for law and order" (Savage, 519), as well as documentary coverage of Socialist Workers' Party clashes with the National Front. As Guy Debord claims, history before capitalism expressed "nothing more than the activity of individual members of the ruling class" (105) and, under capitalism, expresses the history of the economy, while Fredric Jameson characterizes postmodernism as "an age that has forgotten how to think historically" (*Postmodernism*, ix). It is against such seemingly limited possibilities, and in the hope of retaining the notion of a history that can be participated in, that *Rude Boy* foregrounds, on one end of the political continuum, royalty marching past with pomp and circumstance and, on the other, a left wing political party agitating against fascism. Together, these events constitute a history that becomes both the royal backdrop against which the history of punk plays itself out and the socialist history into which the Clash attempts to intervene during an RAR concert.

The film endeavors to construct a piece of punk history and to underscore punks' effects upon official, bourgeois History and vice versa by imagining punks as capable of producing history. This desire might explain the predominance of the documentary in both early and contemporary punk cinema, which includes numerous documentary or semidocumentary films[4] that record punk as such and thereby establish a space for it. Through the conflation of fiction and history, *Rude Boy* also opens up the possibility that anyone can become involved in history. For the first third of the film, the camera follows Gange around London as he works in a pornography bookstore, tangles with the police, and passes time with friends, including Strummer. Although nothing distinguishes Gange from his working-class friends, he finds himself working for the Clash after he publicly supports them at the RAR concert. Gange's spontaneous, literal entrance onto the stage corresponds with his entrance into the larger political issues in which the Clash is embroiled. The film constructs punk history as a gateway into official History, an entrance that can open at particular, rarified moments, and allow punks to pass through.

If this historical trajectory is part of a positive agenda for punk cinema, then *Rude Boy*, at least, also negatively forecloses on some of the same options that it proffers. Gange takes to drinking heavily and the Clash's road manager, Johnny Green, fires him, partly for his alcohol use and partly, as Green explains, because the band is becoming more "professional," which seems to mean that it is downsizing its crew and cutting loose all hangers-on. Gange drinks more heavily yet and metamorphoses into a leech, coming to Clash shows when he can and, in one scene, watching young roadies setting up equipment and bemoaning how old they make him feel. In one of Gange's final scenes, Strummer asks him, "What are you going to do with yourself, anyway?" to which he replies, "I don't know." Rather than providing any sense of closure, the film leaves Gange at this point. Presumably, the Clash will continue touring, but for all of the film's attempts to link the band with the ongoing racial and political clashes and violence occurring in London in the late '70s, it stops well short of ever suggesting that any identifiable effects resulted from this particular intersection of punk, race, and politics. It is equally indeterminate about Gange's fate; if anything, he seems slightly worse off at the end of the film than at the beginning, and there is no reason to believe that he has learned anything much from his experiences with the Clash, except, perhaps, that even punks expect their employees to work and that heavy drinking makes that expectation difficult to fulfill.

As with *Punk Rock Movie*, *Rude Boy*'s writerly narrative adheres to an aesthetic that situates the spectator as an active interpreter of the text by forgoing the narrative expectations—for closure, especially—that the major Hollywood studio films have fostered in their viewers for decades. Additionally, the narrative moves slowly and meanderingly, without the linear structure and clear teleology that Hollywood cinema compulsively repeats. Over the course of the film's two hours and ten minutes, little actually happens in commercial film terms: Gange works in a bookstore and talks to Clash members; he works for the Clash for a time; and the Clash fire him. It is difficult to imagine this story being successfully pitched to a Warner Brothers agent. Jon Savage describes it as "not much of a story, and the device [the pseudo-documentary format] is often laboured" (520), while *Melody Maker* comments that "the lack of dramatic climaxes makes for odd viewing in a film with a rock background" (Watt, 9–10) and adds that the Clash allegedly found the film boring upon first viewing it. What *Melody Maker* and the Clash are responding to with surprise and boredom is what could be considered *Rude Boy's* negative success at refusing to proffer the usual pacing and narrative structure of the dominant Hollywood aesthetic.

It might seem logical to assume that when punk filmmakers translate punk's aesthetic into their own medium, they will produce movies paced like punk rock, which is frequently frenetic, raw, and repetitious. But this assumption discounts punks' concern with the economic conditions of possibility for producing music or film. Punk cinema's producers adopt an aesthetic that resists the easy commercialization and corporatization of their products, because these forces wrest ownership over the process of production away from the producers themselves. Furthermore, the major labels and major Hollywood studios serve as industry gatekeepers, deciding which bands and films to invest in and which to relegate to obscurity. Accepting the industry in such a role would foreclose on punk's constitutive drive to democratize access to production. A new slogan would have to be coined: "This is a chord. This is another. This is a third. Now make a demo and send it to the major labels." The point is that much punk cinema, including *Blank Generation, The Punk Rock Movie,* and *Rude Boy,* militates against the Hollywood aesthetic and, consequently, its own commercial success. Not only is *Rude Boy* lengthy and not telos-driven, but Mingay and Hazan devote considerable time to concert footage and to filming songs in their entirety. In terms of narrative structure, this device grinds the plot to a halt at steady intervals. In some cases, the Clash songs comment upon the film's events—Gange is especially taken with Mick Jones's "Stay Free" and its parallels with Gange's life—but other songs—"Garageland" and "I Fought the Law"—seem to have been included for their own sake.

Several scenes and shots not driven or necessitated by the plot also slow the film's tempo. In one of the final scenes, Johnny Green and one of his roadies enjoy a relaxed discussion of past roadies with whom they have worked. Perhaps their talk could serve as a cautionary tale for Gange, but Green has already fired him at this point, so he is not in the room when the discussion occurs. The film also follows Gange as he sets up the Clash's equipment, walks around London, and pursues two women with whom he has brief sexual encounters. Rather than advancing the plot or mimicking the pace of punk rock, these scenes do the opposite and thereby fail to fulfill the expectations of Hollywood cinema, which usually eschews any scene that does not move the narrative forward. No doubt there are economic reasons. Gilles Deleuze writes that "cinema . . . lives in a direct relation with a permanent plot, an international conspiracy." "This conspiracy is that of money; what defines industrial art is not mechanical reproduction but the internalized relation with money." He adds that money "is the obverse of all the images that the cinema shows and sets in place" and concludes that "[t]his is the old curse which undermines the cinema: time is money" (77). Hollywood cinema seems ever more intent on packing more bona fide occurrences into the time (money) that it has available, while punk cinema, in opposition to this money-event ratio, stretches its events and thereby demonstrates that money is not imperative, that it can be "wasted," that it does not drive the film. Resisting the dominant aesthetic of the major labels, punk rock sped up rock's pace, but punk's shift from music to celluloid demanded an inverse logic: the Hollywood aesthetic—linear, teleological, and fast-paced—had to be diverted, rendered open-ended, and slowed down. In punk cinema, scenes that do not advance a film's narrative signify an unconcern with money and therefore with the commercial market, but this unconcern also means that punk cinema will continue to be made despite that market, from which it refuses to take its cues.

IN THE MALL CINEPLEX: *FIGHT CLUB*

Numerous films could be understood as exhibiting an aesthetic that more approximates if not the speed and rawness of punk rock then its ideological commitments and, in particular, its anticommercial, anticommodification edge. David Fincher's *Fight Club* (1999) stands as an interesting example of such films, featuring neither punks nor punk rock but espousing a nominally anticommercial ideology while also invoking anarchism. One of the film's two protagonists, Tyler Derden (Brad Pitt), offers denouncements, manifesto-style, that correlate closely with some of punk rock and punk cinema's commitments. In 1990, Ian MacKaye hoarsely and repeatedly screams, "You are not what you own," the final lyric of "Merchandise," MacKaye's punk band, Fugazi's, paean to anticommercialism. Tyler comments to *Fight Club*'s narrator, Jack (Edward Norton), "The things you own end up owning you," and later speaks directly to the camera: "You are not your job. You're not how much money you have in the bank. Not the car you drive. Not the contents of your wallet." Not dissimilarly, in *Rude Boy*, Joe Strummer tells Ray Gange that he has spent a lot of time thinking about the differences between the political Left and Right, and that there's "nothing in" the Right's desire for plenty of disposable income and luxury goods. If you succeed as a member of the Right, he tells Gange, one day "some guy is gonna come to your country mansion and blow your head off," and his implication is that the guy will be right to do so. An entire army of these shooters springs to life in *Fight Club* as the soldiers of Project Mayhem, Tyler Derden's anarchist army, intent upon freeing the world, or at least the United States, from corporate control.

Fight Club was released on October 15, 1999, before the November 30 demonstrations in Seattle; nevertheless, Project Mayhem's activities seem to foreshadow the anarchist Black Blocs' violent resistance to the State in Seattle, Washington, Quebec, Prague, Genoa, etc., over the past four years. Near the film's conclusion, Jack discovers that the army is divided into autonomous cells capable of acting without direct orders from above. As viewers, we watch Project Mayhem soldiers perform acts of vandalism directed against corporate America: the side of a skyscraper is set ablaze, a window displaying computer hardware for sale explodes, a piece of "industrial art"—a metal globe, invoking globalization—is blown free of its base and subsequently rolls through the front window of a "franchise coffee bar," presumably a Starbuck's—a target of the Black Bloc in Seattle and elsewhere—and, in the film's final scene, skyscrapers housing the United States' major credit card companies are demolished. The members of Project Mayhem, the movie suggests, are American men, primarily urban whites in their twenties and thirties, who, exhausted with working as "white collar slaves" and estranged from their natural, violent, masculine, hunter-gatherer, and warrior impulses, turn first to Fight Clubs that host bare-knuckle, no-holds-barred fights between consenting adult males and then to organized anarchy in order to reestablish their masculinity and ground their lives epistemologically, two projects that the film conflates. A symbiotic relationship obtains here: regaining a traditionally phallic masculinity becomes synonymous with situating oneself as an agent capable of acting violently upon one's environment. Directly opposed to this sought-after agency is a corporate America that emasculates the men who serve it, rendering them impotent, passive consumers, as exemplified early in the film by Jack and Tyler's knowledge of creature comforts, including duvets, a knowledge that Tyler reads as symptomatic of their loss of masculinity and meaningful existence. The anarchic cells of Project Mayhem multiply rapidly and spread across the United States, suggesting that millions of potential members are working at boring, emasculating, unethical corporate jobs such as Jack's: he investigates accidents for one of the "major" car companies and applies "the formula" to his findings to determine whether or not the company should recall faulty parts (it only does so when it will cost less to issue a recall than it will to pay for the probable lawsuits that would otherwise ensue). Apparently, beneath the starched shirt of corporate America lies the force that will explode it—violent, anarchic, hypermasculine desires waiting for a spark, in the form of a charismatic leader, to set them off. Tyler Derden embodies that spark, despite the corporate drudge persona—Jack's—efforts to disavow those desires.

Fight Club's anticorporate, anticommercial stance correlates nicely with punk's, even down to the film's invocation of anarchism, a political stance with which numerous punk bands have aligned themselves, beginning with Crass in the late '70s and continuing through contemporary Anarcho-Punk bands such as those on Profane Existence's record label. Anarcho-Punks have also participated—sometimes in the Black Bloc groups—in the protests in Seattle, Washington, Quebec, Prague, and Genoa. In short, punks share two things with the anti-WTO mobilizations that are invoked *avant la lettre* in *Fight Club:* constituents and a fundamental desire to alter qualitatively the management of global economics.

The film's conclusion, however, radically forecloses upon the anarchist, social, and punk possibilities that its ideological positioning has forced open. Jack and we, the viewers, gradually apprehend the extent of Project Mayhem, and this apprehension parallels our discovery of the split nature of Jack/Tyler's subjectivity—the fact that Jack and Tyler embody the superego and id of a single person—so that just when the film is poised to unleash Tyler's anarchistic project along a narrative axis concerned with social aims—the destruction of the material foundations of credit for millions of people—this narrative line grinds to a halt and, in an ingenious but violent twist, the film redeploys its narrative along the axis of the individual, the personal, that of the Jack/Tyler conflict. Just before the first building collapses, Jack confronts and kills Tyler, the externalized element of his psyche invested in leveling the economic playing field in the United States, after which Project Mayhem soldiers present Marla (Helena Bonham Carter), their captive, to him. The film's concern with world-historical issues, with the split between corporate America and the employees-turned-anarchists that would destroy it, is suddenly displaced onto the split within Jack between the warring halves of his psychical apparatus, and, after this conflict is resolved, onto the Jack-Marla relationship. From the moment of Tyler's death, the social considerations that the film has raised serve, literally and figuratively, as a backdrop against which Jack reaffirms the primacy of conventional, heterosexual romance. The first building falls and Jack turns to Marla, takes her hand, and says, "I'm sorry . . . you met me at a very strange time in my life," an apology that removes the event that is occurring before them from the realm of the world-historical and recasts it as merely part of a transitional stage, albeit an odd one, in Jack's life. The film seems to be acting out some sort of compulsion—the Hollywood film market's, I suspect—to reject all of the more radical ideological options that it has unleashed, but the accumulated force and the social imaginary's desire to see these options expressed demands the drastic plot contrivance of splitting Jack into two partial subjects, one committed to a social plan and one (suddenly and inexplicably) committed to a heterosexual romance, so that the romantic can kill off the revolutionary.[5]

This move is all the more surprising considering the explicit homoerotic charge that the film carries. Midway through the film, with Jack as his audience, Tyler bathes and waxes poetic about absent fathers, explicitly verbalizing the film's underlying logic: "We're a generation of men raised by women; I'm not sure another woman is what we need." The fight clubs enact a simple and familiar substitution demanded by this logic and its clash with the opposing force of Hollywood's usual prohibition on gay sexuality: for that sexuality, the film substitutes violence framed as a form of intimacy, with each fight cathected by its participants and concluding with an embrace. In a conventional Hollywood homophobic staging of homosocial and homoerotic desire, men can touch one another intimately only with their fists.[6] It is not difficult to imagine a homoerotic subtext to the particularly savage beating that Jack inflicts upon Angel Face (Jared Leto), after which Jack mutters, "I just wanted to destroy something beautiful." What was beautiful? There are at least three possibilities. Angel Face himself could be the object of Jack's desire. Sexual relations between Jack and Angel Face might also figure as beautiful for Jack but vanish as an option as Jack mutilates Angel Face's beauty, thereby removing its temptation and the likelihood of Angel Face ever reciprocating Jack's feelings after such physical abuse. The scene preceding the Jack–Angel Face fight establishes a connection between Tyler and Angel Face that invokes Jack's jealousy, so the beautiful thing that he must destroy might also be a suspected burgeoning intimacy between Tyler and Angel Face. Again, the film substitutes male-male violence for, or as, male-male intimacy.

Although intensely homoerotic collectives of men do not necessitate misogyny, *Fight Club* pairs the two, rendering the final dismissal of homosex in favor of the creation of a heterosexual couple all the more peculiar. After Marla first spends the night with Tyler, he assures Jack that he does not love her and that she's just a "sport fuck," a comment that does little to dispel the overt homoerotic bond between Tyler and Jack. In fact, it is difficult not to read the film's portrayal of heterosex as parodic and patently ridiculous, forced into the film to satisfy an audience or a film industry assumed to harbor heterosexist expectations.[7] Fincher presents us with a surplus of filmic clichés during Tyler and Marla's sexual encounters: the bed, walls, ceilings, and floors shake rhythmically; plaster falls from the ceiling; lights flicker on and off; Marla shrieks and moans incessantly; sounds of thrashing and heavy objects hitting the floor and walls emanate from Tyler's bedroom; and, as an added touch, Tyler pauses once to appear at the door of his bedroom wearing only a yellow dishwashing glove. Apparently, he and Marla engage in heterosex so voracious that any household implement might become cathected through it. The film's surplus of clichéd signs connoting sexual pleasure serve to suggest the exact opposite—a lack of genuine eroticism or gratification. Tyler clearly treats heterosex as a fight but one that pales in comparison to fight club meetings, where much more is at stake. And Marla, the only female character with any significant screen time, is less a character than a plot device for satisfying

a narrative necessity for the Hollywood aesthetic: the creation of a heterosexual couple, Tyler-Marla and then Jack-Marla. The film's radical reinscription
within one male of the dominant homoerotic relations that seemed to obtain
between two males serves to dissolve the force of those relations and combines
with the closing down of the film's political tendencies to proffer the viewer a
tightly bound readerly text, bereft of its writerly potential.

I do not mean to argue that the film successfully or completely shuts
down the destructive or homoerotic impulses that it has fostered throughout
but that the production of the Jack-Marla couple in the final frames serves to
rob the demolition of the major credit card company skyscrapers and the film's
explicit homoeroticism of their power. As the final skyscraper tumbles, while
Jack and Marla hold hands, a few frames of film depicting a penis—the same
penis, it would seem, that Tyler was splicing into Disney films earlier in the
movie—intervene before the credits roll. The film has prepared us to understand these images through Tyler's earlier explanation that they leave their
mark upon an audience even though they pass so quickly that they cannot
enter consciousness, and the same logic now seems to apply to Tyler himself.
He has been killed off and thereby sublimated, driven into the unconscious
where he belongs but from whence he will haunt Jack. The film thereby
reasserts the dominance of the conscious mind and superego over the unconscious and the id, while simultaneously demanding that viewers cathect
through the Marla-Jack heterosexual relationship all the desires that they were
formerly encouraged to invest in the film's overt homoeroticism and its investment in an anticorporate, anticommercial, anticonsumption problematic.
Apparently, these sublimated desires cannot be definitively banished (with
Tyler's death) but will rear up occasionally like so many flickering images of a
penis, seen but not acted upon. Nevertheless, through proper repression, they
can be kept from impinging upon normative, individuated concerns. The film
becomes a cautionary tale about the danger that ensues when the superego
fails to keep the id in check, where the id functions as the political unconscious (to use Jameson's term), a set of social, collective desires that are radically homoerotic, anticorporate, and anticapitalist in nature. Interestingly, only
a psychotic break—Jack's internal bifurcation—can free non-individuated
desires from the repression necessary to keep them dormant. This logic further demonizes homosexuality and social aims in favor of individuated, personal ones by situating the former in the domain of psychosis.

The film, in fact, prepares us to reject our earlier investments in its homoerotic and anarchic trajectories well before its concluding scene. Early depic-
tions of fight club meetings suggest a growing collective of disenchanted male
corporate drudges, together with members of the working class (the manager
of a bar provides the original fight club's first venue), whose physical acting
out of homoerotic desires establishes a community and collectivity that their

corporate lives have been lacking. This is the community that Jack sought in healing groups during the film's first half hour, groups that often fostered physical and emotional intimacy between men ("Remaining Men Together" is the testicular cancer support group's motto). Similarly, *Fight Club*'s early acts of vandalism and property destruction take place to the approving tones of Jack's voice-over and the Dust Brothers' mid-tempo, upbeat soundtrack, featuring their trademark hybrid of hip-hop and rock. But by the time that a member of the Project Mayhem army, Robert Paulsen (Meat Loaf Aday) is killed while destroying a piece of "corporate art," Project Mayhem has grown into a proto-military, crypto-fascist operation whose members shave their heads, dress identically, give up their names, and follow Jack/Tyler's commands unquestioningly and unthinkingly ("The first rule of Project Mayhem is you don't ask questions about Project Mayhem"). In a disturbingly uncanny scene, Jack discovers members of a chapter of Project Mayhem in a city far from the first fight club's origins chanting words that he spoke to the original group a few days earlier ("He has a name. His name is Robert Paulsen."). The group has adopted them as pure dogma without any concern for or even comprehension of the context from which they emerged, and the scene prepares the ground for the film's coming shift from the social project that has clearly become fascistic to Jack's individuated concerns.

After September 11, it has also become difficult to view the film's final scene without associating Project Mayhem's "controlled demolition" with terrorism. *Fight Club*'s images of imploding and collapsing skyscrapers eerily presages the terrorist attacks upon the World Trade Center and the Pentagon. More forcefully than the film ever could, this world-historical event encourages the viewer to link the film's social aims with terror, despite the real differences between the New York and Washington, D.C., terrorist strikes and Project Mayhem's operation, which occurs at night against empty buildings and destroys not people but the computers and buildings that house the United States' system of credit.

There is one further compromise in *Fight Club*'s ideological commitments that stands as a limit case for the Hollywood film aesthetic in general: the film refuses to critique film itself. After moving into a house without a steady supply of electricity, Jack admits that, "by the end of the first month, I didn't miss TV," but this is as close to an interrogation of visual media as the film can come. *Fight Club* can never propose that Hollywood film, or *Fight Club* itself as a commodity, cannot resolve or fulfill the desires that it sets in motion. The film's material means of production prohibit it from making a series of statements, including: "don't watch this movie; don't buy this movie; don't pay for this movie; don't go to movies"; or even, "don't go to Hollywood movies," and this prohibition serves as one of the limits to its anti-commercial bent.

Perhaps it is no surprise, then, that the film has managed to wed cult status with commercial success, despite the fact that it did not recoup its costs at the box office. Katherine Nilles argues that the film flopped at the box office but "has found renewed life among college students." According to VidTrac, a trade association that tracks VHS and DVD rentals in the United States, *Fight Club* was the seventy-fifth most popular video in December 2000, out of one thousand videos (Nilles). Elita Bernardo, a VidTrac employee, notes, "That's pretty good since it came out in April (2000)" (qtd. in Nilles). She adds that most videos disappear from the top one thousand rentals by the eighth month after their release. Nilles interviews several undergraduates from various universities about the popularity of the film, one of whom, David Meldman, comments, "[I]t's very relevant to my life growing up in suburbia. . . . Society tells us that the idea is making as much money as possible, not to do something you're moved to do. It's refreshing to see something that says there is something more out there." Meldman has seen the film six times so far. He explains why: "I don't see capitalism and materialism changing, so its issues will stay with us" (qtd. in Nilles). What interests me about Meldman's comments is that, read symptomatically, they suggest that whatever desires *Fight Club* might awaken quickly become channeled into repeated viewings of the film. Rather than moving consumers to become producers, like punk products, the film's material effect seems to be not just consumption but repeated consumption of the same Hollywood commodity, a decidedly non–punk cinema activity. The question is not why the film has not inspired the creation of anarchist cells, for, as Benjamin makes clear regarding the "mimetic faculty," the cultural production does not represent a method for resistance or revolution but contains within itself a different sort of possibility, that of producing production. What is it, then, about the film's logic that prevents it from invoking the mimetic faculty common to Benjamin's writings and to punk?

This logic lies not in the film's aesthetic and ideological aims, regardless of whether or not their anticommercial, anticonsumption elements can be recuperated, but in the material conditions of its production. First, the film was produced by Twentieth Century Fox and cost sixty-three million dollars to make, a prohibitive amount of money for any DIY enterprise. Such a film requires corporate backers and major studio production that leave its DIY and punk cinema status questionable. The film also bears legible signs of its expense in its aesthetic, particularly in its computer-generated graphics and animation. The French company BUF Compagnie created six three-dimensional computer-generated special effects for the film. For five of the effects, BUF created images that seem to have been shot by a microscopic virtual camera that enjoys an amazing freedom of movement. In scenes interspersed throughout the film, the virtual camera follows the train of Jack's thoughts as he narrates them: it tilts down through the interior of an office building, granting the spectator a cross-section of the building while passing through the ceiling of story after story before stopping in the parking garage beneath the building and zooming in on a van; it pulls up and back from the bottom of Jack's wastepaper basket, snaking around pieces of trash as it does so; it zooms in for a seemingly impossible close-up on a gas stove's burner that it tracks a complete circle around; it tracks across the top of the stove and behind the refrigerator, before tracking down the wall in the one-inch gap behind the refrigerator and zooming in on the compressor spark just as it ignites; and, finally, it zooms in upon a home-made bomb and tracks along individual wires in the bomb's network of fuses. The BUF website notes that, surprisingly, the wastepaper basket sequence was one of the most expensive to render into 3–D images, requiring as much as thirteen hours of work for a single frame in some instances (BUF Compagnie). Taken as a group or individually, these special effects serve to signify to the film's viewers that the production of this film lies beyond not only their financial means but probably their understanding. Rather than suggesting that the viewer can enter into the critique of commodity culture that the film launches, the special effects and the aesthetic that they produce deny that possibility by obfuscating and mystifying their means of production. They thereby reify the film's production and the film as a product from viewers and shut them out as participants in the expensive economy of signs in which the film trafficks. This logic also evidences itself in the film's early pairing of special effects with its ostensibly critical ideological stance: as the viewer watches Jack moving about his condominium, he comments dryly, in a voice-over, on how his life's desires have become identical with those suggested to him by the Ikea catalog of home furnishings ("I'd flip through catalogs and wonder, 'What kind of dining set defines me as a person?'"). As he speaks, his apartment assumes the look of a life-sized Ikea catalog page, with the catalog's descriptions of the items that Jack owns floating in bubbles beside them. Oblivious to these descriptions, Jack walks about the apartment. In this case, the special effects both bear the film's ideological critique—Jack's life has become an Ikea catalog page, a glossy ad for something other than itself—and stand as a signifier of the material prohibition of engaging in that critique. How is such an effect accomplished? Who has enough money to create such effects?

It is also worth noting that the film begins with its lengthiest special effect: the virtual camera traces a pathway literally through Jack's brain, dodging between dendrites before eventually emerging out of his mouth and traveling up the barrel of a pistol. The film is front-weighted with effects: the "brain trip" and Ikea effects (which BUF did not produce) as well as three of the BUF effects occur within the film's first half hour, which is also the most critical of "corporate culture." BUF's final effect—Tyler's death by gunshot—

occurs in the film's last scene, and a non-BUF special effect—five skyscrapers implode and collapse while Jack and Marla watch—concludes the film. This structuring of effects creates an early impression for viewers that the film's economy of signs will be doubly out of their reach—in terms of money and intelligibility—and leaves them with this sense as the film's credits begin to scroll. In sum, *Fight Club* critiques for its viewers, providing them with consumable criticism and a readerly text as it forecloses on the option that they could mount their own analyses. The film produces a reified system of signs with which to interrogate corporate and consumerist America, but the very production of this economy of technologically sophisticated, expensive signs bars the viewer from engaging in the conversation.

DÉNOUEMENT

Despite the casual use to which the term *punk cinema* has been put since the inception of punk rock, the concept, as I have reimagined it here, denotes an identifiable aesthetic for cinema production, bolstered with a correlative economics. Adherents to this model of filmmaking demand of cinema what punks demand of punk productions—it should encourage production, in any medium, through both aesthetic and economic means. Punk cinema employs an open, writerly aesthetic, it engages with history, and it critiques its own commodification. It can be negatively defined as non-Hollywoodized, where a Hollywood aesthetic demands a closed, readerly text unconcerned with history and obfuscating its position within the relations of production. Unlike *Fight Club,* punk cinema is independently produced and renders its means of production—the material conditions of its possibility—intelligible and accessible through its aesthetic. Punk films, such as *The Punk Rock Movie* and *Rude Boy,* foreground their conditions of production, which stand as material signifiers of the possibility of making music or a film, participating in critique, or doing both at once.

Beyond Punk

If punk is dead, what the hell is this?
—Album Cover, Various Artists,
Not So Quiet on the Western Front

You can't kill what's already dead.
—Anonymous

PUNK'S NOT DEAD

In the March 1999 issue of the *Baffler,* Mike O'Flaherty writes—as so many commentators have written before him—that punk is, at last, dead. What is most interesting about O'Flaherty's account is that punk does not die in the usual place. Habitually, critics of punk assert that it died in England in the flurry of major label signings of 1977, although some critics maintain that it lasted a little longer, until the Sex Pistols' last show on January 14, 1978. For O'Flaherty, though, punk endures as hardcore in Southern California and Washington, D.C., but in 1984 it becomes "indie rock." As such, it sheds its punk rock skin but maintains its independence from the major labels until the late '80s, when it becomes "alternative rock" and achieves commercial success, because it is "so compatible with the values of the entertainment industry. Planned obsolescence, the promise of the new and improved, the sneer of willful cultural amnesia" (109). Although O'Flaherty grants punk a slightly longer lease on life than most critics, he follows his forbears in eliding all of the punk that followed 1984. There is a rich tradition of declaring punk dead, from Dick Hebdige's 1979 proclamation that it died in 1978 to O'Flaherty's 1999 claim that it died in 1984, but the hundreds of contemporary independent punk scenes and the thousands of self-identified punks spanning the globe fly in the face of punk's would-be executioners.

In place of the now hackneyed death sentence for punk, I have proposed something else in this book. I have striven to uncover the utopian and ideological impulses in the aesthetic and economic spheres of punk, where ideological impulses are understood as those that advance the capitalist agenda of rendering aesthetics and economics coterminous and commodifying all desires, and utopian impulses are understood as those that advance a cultural project based upon freely "associated producers" who own the means of production and are organized into collectives for the purpose of satisfying their needs and bringing forth a "true realm of freedom" (*Capital* 3:959).

Within the punk project, the conflict between ideology and utopia parallels the opposition between economics and aesthetics. Punk's governing ideological impulse is the impulse to produce punk commodities and to reproduce the means for producing them, while its governing utopian impulse is to have done with economics altogether. As Herbert Marcuse notes, "economic freedom" can mean "freedom from the economy—from being controlled by economic forces and relationships" (4). Upon this "economic freedom" punks would build an aesthetic sphere that economic contingencies neither condition nor determine, an aesthetics for itself.

In the introduction to her book on the proletarian fiction of 1929–1941, Barbara Foley claims that "[i]f Marxism is to arise like a phoenix from the ashes of state capitalism, it is useful to study texts inspired by this phoenix in an earlier incarnation—for their cautionary lessons as well as their testaments to possibility" (ix). As I have described them, punk's aims are slightly less grand than those of the authors that Foley considers. Nevertheless, it is necessary within the context of a critical cultural studies to produce and circulate knowledge about how actually existing projects for resisting capitalism and commodification are faring, in order, as Foley suggests, to avoid their mistakes and to maintain and recuperate what is useful in them. The punk project's failures and successes are intimately and dialectically bound together and often emerge from one another. Punk's aesthetic negation peaked with the English Scene and, specifically, with the Sex Pistols. In the band's hyper-spectacle, in its self-conscious highlighting of the commercial music industry's ability to absorb and commodify all attacks upon its dominant aesthetic, the Sex Pistols highlighted, dialectically, both the continuing need for an aesthetics that escapes commodification and the impossibility of arriving at such an aesthetic realm within the constraints of capitalism. Some of punk's scenes have taken up this aesthetic project and continue to advance it, continually revivifying a perceived need for new aesthetic options.

Economically, punk did not peak with the Dischord or Lookout! record labels; rather, the owners of these labels, and of labels like them, cling to an antipathy for the commodity that allows them to displace their complicity with the social relation upon which capitalism is based (the relation between

owners of capital and workers) onto the objects that that social relation produces. Nevertheless, the adherence of punk record labels to DIY policies constitutes these labels as enterprises rather than corporations. Additionally, one
form of punk's economic success emerges from the impulse encoded within its
failures, especially the bankruptcy, temporary or long-term, of the Anarcho-
Punk collectives. Repeatedly, these collectives—including Crass, Profane
Existence, the Epicenter Zone, and CrimethInc.—testify to punk's underlying need to establish an economic base that does not rely upon a form of
exchange dependent upon exploitation and profit for its existence. Such an
economy could not be capitalist. Punks' struggles establish an aesthetic sphere
that is not saturated with the logic of the commodity market to the degree
that the commercial music industry is, and punks keep alive—and keep collective—a desire to supplant the capitalist commodity market with a more
socialized and collectivized system of production and exchange.

In 2003, punk continues to mount its two-pronged attack upon capitalism, employing both aesthetic and economic practices. As avant-garde artists
have done before them in the realm of modern art, punks apply pressure to the
cultural commodity, pushing at the form of the mass-produced punk rock
song and forcing it to contain multiplicities. Sometimes, by turning the logic
of the commodity on its head and producing commodities explicitly aimed at
creating rather than satisfying needs, punks also inadvertently demonstrate
that the eternal deferral of satisfaction is in fact the very purpose of the commodity. However, punks' attention to this aspect of their products underscores
both the commodity's power to subordinate to its form and render saleable the
most disparate components as well as the poverty of the commodity—its
inability ever wholly to satisfy a need, because each commodity advertises
another commodity.

Punks link their aesthetics to their economics to stake out, locally and
temporarily, social and material spaces in which a limited number of people
can, for the most part, own their own means of production, which is precisely
what DIY entails. In order to do-it-yourself, you must own the means for
doing it. Punks have not separated themselves wholly from capitalism—try as
they might to replace the commodity with other objects, including the gift—
but they do demonstrate that, even in the increasingly global economy of the
early twenty-first century, an earlier form of capitalism can flourish—the
enterprise instead of the corporation. If abolishing capitalism through punk
rock is the ultimate aim of punk, and it is, then punk has so far failed, but as
a process and a project committed to transforming consumers into producers,
it succeeds on a daily basis.

Finally, and most importantly, punks—including those who protested
the World Trade Organization, World Bank, and International Monetary
Fund meetings in Seattle, in Washington, D.C., in Quebec City, in Prague,

and in Genoa, among other places, and those who protested the wars against Iraq in 1991 and in 2003—counter the assumptions of our cynical-ironic historical moment as well as postmodern theory, both of which find the surface of contemporary commodity culture a sheer face that offers few handholds to those who would grasp and change it. In fact, there are fissures everywhere, but they are not mapped in the Arts and Leisure section of *The New York Times*. Instead, their topography is described in the zines that punks distribute, for free, at the local, independently owned record store or information shop just down the street.

Notes

CHAPTER ONE. LET'S MAKE A SCENE

1. For a material demonstration of this claim, refer to any issue from the past seven years of the punk zines with the largest circulations: *MaximumRockNRoll, Punk Planet,* and *The Big Take-Over.* The writers of most smaller punk zines understand the same succession of scenes as "punk history."

2. For much more thorough descriptions of the New York scene's principal people and events than I can provide here, refer to Clinton Heylin's *From the Velvets to the Voidoids: A Pre-Punk History for a Post-Punk World* (1992), Lester Bangs's *Psychotic Reactions and Carburetor Dung* (1987), Legs McNeil and Gillian McCain's *Please Kill Me: The Uncensored Oral History of Punk* (1996), chapters 2 and 3 of Tricia Henry's *Break All the Rules! Punk Rock and the Making of a Style* (1989), the seventeen published issues of the zine *Punk,* edited by John Holmstrom, and Holmstrom's reissue of selected pieces from the zine, *Punk: The Original* (1996).

3. Tricia Henry explains that between 1972 and 1974 there were three clubs that booked underground rock bands occasionally: Max's Kansas City, The Mercer Arts Center, and Club 82. In 1973, the building housing the Mercer Arts Center was condemned and the Center closed, leaving Max's Kansas City and Club 82 (50–51). According to Steven Hager, author of *Art After Midnight* (1986), Club 82 was more "a hangout for transvestites and glitter bands" than a place for underground music (2).

4. For a grueling account of the deaths in the New York Scene, refer to parts five and six of Legs McNeil and Gillian McCain's *Please Kill Me: The Uncensored Oral History of Punk Rock* (1996), 299–407.

5. For a more detailed description of the economic conditions that birthed punk, refer to chapter 4.

6. Simon Frith defines "progressive rock" (or "prog rock") as a term that the major labels coined in the late '60s. For Frith, the term marks the labels' attempt to "differentiate their stars from the mass of pop performers [in order] to service the student market: increasing promotional emphasis was placed on musicians' technical skills, on their instrumental artistry, their willingness to experiment, their unwillingness to be bound by formulas or conventions." Prog rock's "new musical values"

included "improvisation, virtuosity, stamina, [and] originality" (*Sound Effects*, 74). In terms of English bands, Led Zeppelin and Pink Floyd typify prog rock, while in the United States the Grateful Dead, the Allman Brothers, and Yes exemplify the sub-genre, as do Can and Hawkwind in Germany. Prog rock bands tend to incorporate more musicians and instruments than previous rock bands did, including keyboards and a variety of wind and percussion instruments, while songs include lengthy solos, often for several of the band's musicians, and last for significantly longer than rock or pop songs. In 2004, prog rock continues but has been renamed "jam rock" and includes Phish, Blues Traveler, and bands that emerged from the Grateful Dead after Jerry Garcia died.

7. John signed a recording deal with MCA for eight million dollars in 1974, "the largest amount ever given to a record artist at that time" (Theroux and Gilbert, 223).

8. Numerous institutions track, and have tracked, music sales and radio play. Relying upon different approaches, these institutions have compiled differing charts. I have chosen to draw from Gary Theroux and Bob Gilbert's text, *The Top Ten: 1956–Present* (1982), which compiles listings from an "analysis of national trade chart activity, major market radio air play, industry sales figures, and music licensing tally reports" (ix).

9. Marcus has written three books on punk (so far), including *Lipstick Traces: A Secret History of the Twentieth Century* (1989), *Ranters and Crowd Pleasers: Punk in Pop Music, 1977–92* (1993), and *Inside the Fascist Bathroom* (1999). I will concentrate upon the first of these books, which is the only extended argument that Marcus mounts. The other two books compile his numerous and brief reviews, interviews, and articles related to punk.

10. For a detailed account of the Sex Pistols' interactions with the media, see John Savage's *England's Dreaming: Anarchy, Sex Pistols, Punk Rock, and Beyond* (1992), 254–89. More completely than any other text, Savage's book describes the history of the Sex Pistols and their place within the English Scene.

11. For a reprint of the diagrams and text, refer to Savage's *England's Dreaming*, 280.

12. Greil Marcus's *Lipstick Traces: A Secret History of the Twentieth Century* (1989) offers a fuller explanation of what he considers the "avant-gardist" strategies that informed punk rock than I can provide here. For a further account of the avant-garde and punk, see chapter 6, "The Seventies: The Fusion of Avant-Gardism and Youth Subculture," of Neil Nehring's *Flowers in the Dustbin: Culture, Anarchy, and Postwar England* (1993).

13. Refer to chapter 4 for a more thorough description of the control that the major labels exercised over their acts.

14. For a more complete consideration of punk aesthetics, refer to chapter 2.

15. I do not wish to close down the possibility that collective desires were at work in Frampton's audiences; rather, I want to stress that the forms that A&M's intense capitalization of Frampton assumed served to discourage the expression and realiza-

tion of such desires. For an investigation of how rock and roll makes possible active and resistant audiences as it "inscribes and cathects a boundary within social reality . . . outside of the affective possibilities of the ruling culture (the hegemony)," see pages 29–63 of Lawrence Grossberg's *Dancing in Spite of Myself* (1997).

16. A&M, although technically not one of the Big Six, was distributed by CBS in 1977. However, A&M beat out CBS in a bidding war for the Pistols. A&M was eventually swallowed by PolyGram.

17. McLaren's reference is probably an appropriation of the first hippies' slogan, as documented in Tom Wolfe's *Electric Kool-Aid Acid Test* (1982), "Never trust a prankster." The term *prankster* referred to the Merry Pranksters, the original group of proto-hippies that converged around Ken Kesey and his ranch in La Honda, California, in the '60s. Their slogan is probably an appropriation of drug culture doxa: "Never trust a junkie."

18. For a full account of the tour, refer to Jon Savage's *England's Dreaming* (1992), 444–60.

19. *Get in the Van: On the Road with Black Flag* (1994), by Henry Rollins, is a collection of journal entries that Rollins wrote, while singing for the band between 1983 and 1986. It is an extremely detailed account of the band's history during that time period. Marian Kester and F-Stop Fitzgerald's *Dead Kennedys: The Unauthorized Version* (1983) serves as a decent introduction to the DKs, leaning more on Fitzgerald's photos than on Kester's narrative.

20. For an informative account of the first Los Angeles and San Francisco scenes, see *Hardcore California: A History of Punk and New Wave* (1983), edited by Peter Belsito and Bob Davis; *Make the Music Go Bang: The Early L.A. Punk Scene* (1997), edited by Don Snowden; *Forming: The Early Days of L.A. Punk* (1999), by Claude Bessy et al.; *We Got the Neutron Bomb: The Untold Story of L.A. Punk* (2001), by Marc Spitz and Brendan Mullen; and Steven Blush's *American Hardcore: A Tribal History* (2001).

21. The 1982 double LP, "Not So Quiet on the Western Front," which was re-released in 1999, provides an excellent index of songs from the most prominent early-'80s, San Francisco hardcore bands. The compilation includes a Dead Kennedys song and provides some insight into the musical context from which the DKs emerged.

22. For a discussion of the aesthetics of punk, refer to chapter 2.

23. It is worth noting that Greg Ginn, the principal songwriter and lead guitar player for Black Flag, eventually expands upon the formal ways in which the first hardcore scene expresses itself. He reclaims the guitar solo and technical mastery of the guitar for punk.

24. Greg Ginn's and Jello Biafra's decisions to found independent record labels can easily (too easily, I would argue) be understood as pragmatic and entrepreneurial moves within the logic of capital. I pick up and address this specific problem in chapter 4.

25. For a response to the newly masculine, aggressive, and physically dangerous elements of L.A. punk shows, refer to Exene Cervenka's comments in *Volume 9: Punk* from the made-for-television series, *The History of Rock 'N Roll*.

26. In 2000, Biafra campaigned to become the Green Party's nominee for president.

27. The "pogo" was a punk dance. Dancers kept their arms at their sides and their legs as stiff as possible, while energetically jumping up and down and often colliding with one another.

28. The most complete and compelling books addressing this scene are, in 2003, *Banned in D.C.: Photos and Anecdotes from the D.C. Punk Underground (79–85)* (1988), edited by Cynthia Connolly, Leslie Clague, and Sharon Cheslow and *Dance of Days: Two Decades of Punk in the Nation's Capital* (2001), by Mark Andersen and Mark Jenkins.

29. For a more complete account of the founding and the economics of the Dischord Records label, refer to chapter 4.

30. Again, see chapter 4 for the details of Dischord's business practices.

31. For a theorization of the opposition between homosocial and homosexual male behavior, refer to the introduction, pages 1–20, of Eve Kosofsky Sedgwick's *Between Men: English Literature and Male Homosocial Desire* (1985).

32. The current definitive book on NYHC is a set of interviews done by Beth Lahickey and compiled as *All Ages: Reflections on Straight Edge* (1997).

33. In addition to the media that I've already listed, *USA Today* was interested in doing a longer piece on Riot Grrrls, and ABC News, Maury Povich, and Maria Shriver all contacted members of the group about possible interviews.

34. EPs are longer than singles (or 7"s) but not as long as full-length LPs.

35. For a more thorough account of Lookout!, as well as Dischord's, business practices, see chapter 4.

36. John Doe, rhythm guitarist and lead singer for the late '70s and early '80s L.A. band X, gives a friend a homemade tattoo with a pen and a bottle of ink in *The Decline of Western Civilization, Part 1,* Penelope Spheeris's documentary film on the early L.A. portion of the California Hardcore Scene.

CHAPTER TWO. PUNK AESTHETICS
AND THE POVERTY OF THE COMMODITY

1. For a microeconomic assessment of the form of the commodity as it relates to punk, refer to chapter 4.

2. Refer to chapter 1 for a working through of DIY and its application to punk.

3. *Shibboleth: My Revolting Life* (1998), Penny Rimbaud's autobiography, provides the most complete account available of the history of Crass. "... In Which Crass Voluntarily Blow Their Own," the liner notes to the Crass double LP, *Best Before . . . ,* is an abridged version of *Shibboleth,* and "A Series of Shock Slogans and Mindless Token Tantrums," a booklet included with Crass's double LP, *Christ—The Album,*

includes pieces that were later incorporated into *Shibboleth* as well as, in Rimbaud's words, his attempt "to explain how the large-scale atrocities of this century have contributed towards the stupification, paralysis and apathy that exist in the face of genocide and annihilation" and his hopes for future modes of resistance to authority.

4. Fingers Tarbuck played piano on one album, on which Honey Bane sang, and Paul Ellis played "strings" on a single album.

5. For Louis Althusser's famous description of Ideological State Apparatuses (ISAs) and Repressive State Apparatuses (RSAs), refer to the chapter, "Ideology and Ideological State Apparatuses (Notes Towards an Investigation)," from his collection of essays, *Lenin and Philosophy* (1971).

6. For examples of the political positioning of the Riot Grrrls and the Dead Kennedys, see the Riot Grrrl and California Hardcore sections of chapter 1.

7. As I will explain later in this chapter, not only ads but commodities as well aim to create needs.

8. For an account of how much control the major labels exercised, and exercise, over the bands on their labels, see chapter 4.

9. A "flexi" is a 7" pressed on cheap and extremely thin (hence flexible) plastic or cardboard.

10. For a description of the desires that structured English punk in the late '70s, refer to chapter 1's section on the English Scene.

11. Chumbawumba still exists, in 2003, but signed to a major label, EMI, in 1997 and has subsequently been disavowed by Anarcho-Punks.

12. For my earlier examination of zines, refer to the Riot Grrrl section of chapter 1. A history of the zine would require much more space than I can devote to zines here. Several texts have undertaken that project, though. For a good introduction to zines, consult *Zines: Volume 1* (1996) and *Zines: Volume 2* (1997), both edited by Vic Vale and published by V/Search. Additional worthwhile accounts include *The World of Zines: A Guide to the Independent Magazine Revolution* (1992), edited by Mike Gunderloy and Cari Janice; *The Book of Zines: Readings from the Fringe* (1997), edited by Chip Rowe; Trina Robbins's *From Girls to Grrrlz: A History of Women's Comics from Teens to Zines* (1999); Tom Trusky's *Some Zines: American Alternative and Underground Magazines, Newsletters & APAs;* Stephen Duncombe's *Notes from Underground Zines and the Politics of Alternative Culture* (1997); and *The Factsheet Five Zine Reader: The Best Writing from the Underground World of Zines* (1997), edited by Seth Friedman. None of these publications offers a good sense of the number of zines that exist or the breadth of the material that zines cover, though. For both of these considerations, an excellent source is *Zine Guide & Index,* now in its sixth issue (Fall/Winter 2003). The current issue provides short descriptions of more than 1,500 zines, an international list of zine distributors, and five indexes, one organized by band/musician, one by person, one by subject, one by place, and one by record label.

13. The "power violence" subgenre of punk produces slightly less aurally comprehensible lyrics. Chris Dodge's Slap a Ham Records label is the largest producer and

proponent of this subgenre, while the band that Dodge fronts, Spazz, is the most popular and influential in power violence.

14. Refer to chapter 1 for a consideration of the English Scene and spectacle.

15. I have included Jameson's translation of the passage from Bloch. Neville Plaice, Stephen Plaice, and Paul Knight render the same passage, on page 127 of their translation of *The Principle of Hope, Volume 1* (1995), as "Every great work of art thus still remains, except for its manifest character, impelled towards the latency of the other side, i.e. towards the contents of a future which had not yet appeared in its own time, if not towards the contents of an as yet unknown final state."

16. Various punk collectives have published *BYOFL*, always in conjunction with MRR. On the web, it is available at <www.byofl.org>.

17. Unfortunately, no one tracks the number of people who make use of *(BYOFL)*. In 1997, the Profane Existence Collective comments, in a compilation of their zine articles, *Profane Existence: Making Punk a Threat Again, The Best Cuts, 1989–1993,* "It has become such a successful resource that we have resorted to not listing ourselves because the massive response is too much for us to keep up with! Although by no means complete, it is still a valuable gateway to the underground DIY punk rock movement today" (57).

18. Blackened Distribution was PE's distribution arm and all that remained of PE in 1999. Now that PE has returned, Blackened Distribution has been renamed the Profane Existence Distro.

19. For a more complete account of the dissolution of the PE Collective, reference *Profane Existence, Issue #37.*

20. For an account of Epicenter's termination, consult the San Francisco *Guardian,* Vol. 33, No. 39, 52–55 and *MaximumRockNRoll,* September 1999, No. 196.

21. For an explanation of "abstract human labor," see Marx, *Capital,* 1:142, 150.

22. I have chosen to concentrate upon Profane Existence as the largest and most influential Anarcho-Punk collective and on CrimethInc. as one of the inheritors of PE's mantle and as a more sophisticated and nuanced form of the contemporary Anarcho-Punk collective than PE is. However, there are numerous other punk collectives (not all of them devoted to Anarcho-Punk), including the ten member collectives of the Anarcho Punk Federation (APF), the MaximumRockNRoll House in San Francisco, the ABC No Rio Collective in New York City, the 924 Gilman Street Project in Berkeley, the Manifest Destiny Anarchist Punk Collective in Chico, Cal., and Extreme Noise in Minneapolis, as well as many branches of the activist group, Food Not Bombs, which, although not explicitly a set of punk collectives, is staffed at least partly by punks in many locations.

23. The PE Collective advertised in almost every issue of *MRR* between 1989 and 1999 and began advertising again after the zine's rebirth in 2000. For specific examples of PE ads from the last few years, refer to the following issues of *MRR:* #137 (October 1994), #146 (July 1995), #163 (December 1996), #169 (June 1997), #185

(October 1998), #190 (March 1999), and #242 (July 2003). Page numbers are unavailable, because the editors of *MRR* do not number the zine's pages.

24. Refer to chapter 4 for an explanation of how punks reconcile their antipathy to commodification with their entrepreneurial and enterprising drives. Most frequently, they ignore the products that they produce during their manufacturing stages, when they are removed from the realm of "punk producers," and seize upon them again when they reappear, as if by magic, within the realm of punk distribution and sales. Punks cultivate a strategic blindness regarding the manufacturing of their products.

25. In addition to the act of selling commodities, CrimethInc. members engage in a variety of illegal practices, such as petty theft, freight train hopping, and dumpster diving (for a more complete list and a definition of "dumpster diving," see the following note). CrimethInc.'s early activities outside the law were aimed primarily at keeping the collective's members alive. For an example, refer to CrimethInc.'s broadsheet, "Why I Love Shoplifting from Big Corporations," whose author enthuses over the material and representational meanings of theft: "Nothing compares to the feeling of elation, of burdens being lifted and constraints escaped, that I feel when walking out of a store with their products in my pockets. In a world where everything already belongs to someone else, where I am expected to sell away my life at work in order to survive, where I am surrounded by forces beyond my control or comprehension that obviously are not concerned about my needs or welfare, it is a way to carve out a little piece of the world for myself—to act back upon a world that acts so much upon me." However, CrimethInc.'s methods for resisting capitalism have expanded recently. An issue of one of the collective's free tabloids, *Harbinger*, includes suggestions such as "YOU CAN mix styrofoam into gasoline to make it stick—this recipe has been used for the filling [of] Molotov cocktails" (6). But, because the collective posits theft and other illegal activities as means of survival and disruption rather than as means of amassing wealth, it must accrue more money than its current illegal practices bring in, if its members wish to promulgate information through commodified means of communication and distribution, including the mail, the telephone, professionally printed zines, etc.

26. For Crass, PE, and CrimethInc., a collective's work involves more than its institutional economic and aesthetic practices. These collectives also did, or do, encourage, distribute information on, and participate in various forms of collective and personal political activism. Because a consideration of this activism would occupy more space than I can grant it here—entailing, as it would, punk's relation to new social movements in Europe and the United States, such as squatting, eco-anarchism, eco-terrorism, etc.—I have chosen to bracket off that material for future consideration. But I want to note here that Crass promulgated political life choices such as vegetarianism and participated in collective political acts such as the mid-'80s Stop the City demonstrations in London that attempted to prevent the city's major economic institutions from transacting business for as long as possible. PE engaged in similar political acts, such as encouraging readers to adopt ascetic lifestyles, avoid consumption, refuse to work at jobs that held little meaning for them, and form anarchist collectives. (For PE and CrimethInc.'s writings on work, refer to any of the forty-two issues of the Profane Existence zine, as well as the first issue of CrimethInc.'s free propaganda newspaper,

Harbinger #1, which returns to the problem of work repeatedly, especially in the final article, "What's So Bad About Capitalism," as do the seven issues of *Inside Front* that are still available [numbers 8–13 and number ∞].) The members of CrimethInc. also promote stealing from corporations, veganism, train-hopping, "dumpster diving," and vandalism, among many other activities. ("Dumpster diving" refers to the practice of retrieving food from dumpsters located behind restaurants and supermarkets. On a daily basis, numerous businesses in any U.S. town discard significant amounts of food for a variety of reasons, including because it has not been purchased before its expiration date [regardless of whether or not it is still edible] or because it was not used over the course of the day [in the case of restaurants] and is deemed unfit to serve the next day [again, regardless of whether or not someone could eat it.]) Recently, as Johnny Temple, the ex-bass guitar player for Washington, D.C., and Dischord Records band Soulside and the current bass guitar player in Girls Against Boys (Girls Versus Boys) notes in the October 18, 1999, issue of *The Nation,* all of the various subgenres of punk that position themselves politically seem to have found common ground in Mumia Abu-Jamal's case. However, he adds that the "mobilization to save Mumia Abu-Jamal is one of the few grassroots movements to unite punks with other artists and activists" (18). After 9/11 and the U.S. invasions of Afghanistan and Iraq, there are myriad imbrications between what might be termed "punk politics" and non–music oriented "grassroots movements," including pro-peace and antiwar groups.

27. I owe this particular idea to a discussion of the introduction to the *Grundrisse* moderated by Michael Sprinker at the 1999 meeting of the Marxist Literary Group.

CHAPTER THREE. PUNK ECONOMICS
AND THE SHAME OF EXCHANGEABILITY

1. I owe this conclusion to a Marx reading group discussion and Timothy Martel.

2. For an introduction to one of the contemporary Garage Punk scenes (there are several), refer to Jeff Skipski's article, "Confederacy of Scum: One Percenters of Rock N' Roll," in the April/May 1999 issue of *Hit List* (Volume 1, Number 2).

3. I use the word *seem* deliberately to express the logic of "true collecting," because the comparison between use- and exchange-value implicit in this logic is technically impossible. The amount of exchange-value cannot be directly compared to the amount of use-value, because use-value, by definition, cannot be measured in terms of quantity. Use-value and exchange-value exist in mutually exclusive registers, like the signifier and the signified. Any literal comparison of the two is a categorical mistake, yet the comparison, understood figuratively, sheds light on punk collecting.

4. The remaining 4 percent includes sales of cassettes, cassette singles, music videos, and DVDs. All of these formats outsold vinyl in 1998 except for DVD, which was available for the first time that year.

5. See chapter 1 for a mapping of the desires that constitute the New York, English, California Hardcore, D.C. Straight Edge, New York Hardcore, Riot Grrrl, and Pop-Punk Scenes.

6. A similar formulation of equivalent value that parallels interpellation as Althusser imagines it occurs on p. 143: "An individual, A, for instance, cannot be 'your majesty' to another individual, B, unless majesty in B's eyes assumes the physical shape of A, and, moreover, changes facial features, hair and many other things, with every new 'father of the people.'"

CHAPTER FOUR. MARKET FAILURE

1. For an account of Anarcho-Punk economic practices, including those of Crass, Profane Existence, and CrimethInc., see chapter 2. In chapter 1, I describe the anticommercial desires behind the Dead Kennedys and Black Flag in the section on the California Hardcore Scene.

2. Frith seems to assume that there is a direct link between the technical means available to punks and the aesthetic forms that their productions assume. In contrast, in chapters 1 and 2, I have indicated that nonindividuated desires condition aesthetic forms along with the technical means available to punks. It is not difficult to find situations in which punks adopt crude means of production that are no less costly than more "technically advanced" forms in order to express specific desires and achieve certain aesthetics. For example, punks still opt to have their music pressed on 7"s, even though the cost of mastering and replicating a full-length CD is roughly equivalent to that of mastering and pressing a 7". Erika Records, in Downey, California, will master a CD and replicate (from the master copy) one thousand 72–minute CDs for $730.00 or produce a master 7" and then press one thousand black vinyl 7"s (that hold much less than 72 minutes of music each) for $684.00.

3. Although Malcolm McLaren, the manager of the Sex Pistols, brags, in *The Great Rock 'N' Roll Swindle* (1980), a semidocumentary account of the Sex Pistols' rise to fame, about how much money the Sex Pistols made, both Jon Savage and David Huxley's accounts of the complicated financial wrangling around the film's production suggest that most of what the Pistols earned disappeared into the film's production. Savage claims that the film cost £343,000 and left the Pistols with £30,000 in total assets (533). For a detailed account of the film's production, refer to Savage's *England's Dreaming: Anarchy, Sex Pistols, Punk Rock, and Beyond* (1992), and Huxley's chapter, "'Ever Get the Feeling You've Been Cheated?' Anarchy and Control in *The Great Rock 'N' Roll Swindle*," in *Punk Rock: So What? The Cultural Legacy of Punk* (1999). Despite how little the Sex Pistols and McLaren made, no doubt Warner Brothers, currently a subsidiary of AOL-Time-Warner, has consistently earned money from its release of the Sex Pistols' only official full-length album, *Never Mind the Bollocks, Here's the Sex Pistols,* which was produced in 1977.

4. For a more complete listing of English Scene bands that signed with major labels, refer to the section in chapter 1 that addresses that scene or Dave Laing's *One Chord Wonders* (1985), 32.

5. In almost every zine interview that they grant, the members of Fugazi comment upon the band's and Dischord's business practices. For an example, refer to the

Ian MacKaye interview in *Punk Planet* (May-June, 1999). A documentary on the band, *Instrument* (1999), that Fugazi co-produced with the film's director, Jem Cohen, also dwells on the economics of Fugazi.

6. According to Mark Powell, of Southern Records, Southern is unconnected to and not underwritten by any of the major labels.

7. The band chose Sound and Vision, in San Francisco, for *Structure* and Olde West Recording Studios, also in San Francisco, for *Sanitized*.

8. According to Ruth Schwartz, who founded Mordam Records in 1983 and remains the sole proprietor, Mordam has no corporate backing and does not sell or represent any labels that have any financial support from the current five major labels. However, Mordam does sell to many stores, chains, and distributors with all types of backing, corporate and otherwise. Lookout! currently distributes through RED Distribution, which also handles thirty-four labels some of which—LOUD, for example—are at least partially financed by major labels.

9. *MRR* is consistently the most widely read and influential internationally distributed punk zine since its inception in 1982, with a current circulation of roughly twenty-five thousand.

10. An EP can appear in either a vinyl or a CD format. It is longer than a 7" but not as long as an LP (see the following note). EPs can spin at 45 or 33 rpms (rotations per minute), and one side plays for roughly seven to fifteen minutes. The term 7" has replaced 45 as a description of the vinyl single format in punk, because 7"s no longer spin exclusively at 45 rpm; many now spin at 33 rpms. One side of a 7" plays for roughly three to seven minutes.

11. The "LP" is a long-playing, or full-length, record album. One side, spinning at 33-1/3 rpms, will usually play for twenty to twenty-five minutes. Although other labels had attempted to bring out LPs that spun more slowly than 78 rpms earlier, Columbia Records introduced an LP in June 1948 that spun at 33-1/3 rpms, which became the industry's standard speed (Fink, 11).

12. In 1998, Seagram purchased PolyGram Music, reducing the Bix Six to the Big Five. Dr. Strange offers these comments on his website: "Let me start off by saying what we are NOT. We are not a 'company' or 'corporation' making money off punk rock. I've been into punk since 1980 and it is truly a way of life for me. It is who I am and what I will be until I die. I started Dr. Strange Records in 1988 in an effort for like minded people to get rare punk records for FAIR prices. My 'hobby' has not only turned into the biggest mail-order for punk in all the world, but also a record label (in 1989) and a store in California (opened in 1997). We're small . . . there's myself, my wife and my three friends: Chaddie, Hot Dog Boy and Thom-Ass doing the best we can to get you the best 'stuff' for the best prices. So please keep that in mind."

13. For example, Epitaph now owns a stake in Frontier Records, whose founder—Lisa Fancher—sold it in the '90s and has reissued the best-selling titles from its back catalog, such as the Suicidal Tendencies' first (self-titled) album as well as most of the mid-eighties Circle Jerks' albums (Arnold, 41). Nitro Records has bought up several

backlists as well and reissued two early T.S.O.L (True Sounds of Liberty) albums, as well as a double LP collection of the late-'70s band, The Lewd's, various singles and LPs.

14. Refer to chapter 2 for an account of how punks establish enterprises (that obey a *C-M-C'* logic) in opposition to the major labels, which function as corporations (and obey an *M-C-M'* logic).

15. Although Black Flag was not part of the D.C. Scene, *Get in the Van: On the Road With Black Flag* (1994), Henry Rollins's journalistic account of his five years of touring with and singing for Black Flag, is an excellent example of a musician's erasure of the music as a constant in favor of recounting details about the shifting contexts of performance. Under a picture of the band members pushing a van, Rollins writes, "Glen [Friedman, the photographer] didn't know it but he captured the essence of Black Flag right here—endlessly pushing on one of our broken vans" (38).

16. Godard's character adds that contemporary capitalism produces commodities that no one needs, such as atom bombs and plastic cups.

CHAPTER FIVE. SCREENING PUNK

1. For a reprint of the diagrams and text, refer to Jon Savage's *England's Dreaming* (1992), 280.

2. What is happening in punk cinema echoes Tony Bennett's commentary upon *The Voyeur* (1958) by Alain Robbe-Grillet, which Bennett finds calling "into question the fixed division of labour between writer and reader which the traditional novel proposes" and exposing "the conventions whereby the relationship between the roles of writer (the issuing source of meaning) and the reader (the passive recipient of the offered meaning) is constructed" (52). I disagree, though, with Bennett's positing of a "passive recipient," a move that forecloses on the possibilities for resistant readings that occur in spite of a book or film's proffered meanings.

3. The film as an easily consumed commodity might metonymically stand in for capitalism's logic of commodification. The closed form of Hollywood films encourages passive reception and an almost simultaneous reaching for the next commodified text. An open form invites lingering over the commodity and re-reading it. Where time equals money, time that the audience spends thinking about a text is time and money wasted, time that could be valorized through the consumption of further commodities. The less time the audience "wastes" engaged with a commodity, the better, as far as corporatized Hollywood is concerned.

4. A partial list of documentaries on punk includes Amos Poe's *Night Lunch* (1975) and *Blank Generation* (1976), Julien Temple's *Sex Pistols Number One* (1977), *Sex Pistols Number Two* (1977), and *The Great Rock 'n' Roll Swindle* (1979), Maggi Carson, Juliusz Kossakowski, and Frederic Shore's *Punking Out* (1977), Virginia Boston's *Raw Energy* (1977) and *Kids With Yellow Hair* (1977), Don Letts's *The Punk Rock Movie* (1978), Colin Burton's *The Last Pogo* (1978), Dana Lobell's *Anarchy at La Mere*

(1978), John T. Davis's *Shellshock Rock* (1979), Wolfgang Büld's *Punk in London* (1979) and *British Rock: Ready for the '80's* (1980), Stephanie Beroes's *Debt Begins at 20* (1980), Lech Kowalski's *D.O.A.* (1981), Hasan Shah and Don Shaw's *Rough Cut and Ready Dubbed* (1982), Penelope Spheeris's *The Decline of Western Civilization 1* (1981) and *The Decline of Western Civilization 3* (1998), Adam Small and Peter Stuart's *Another State of Mind* (1984), Charles Pinion's *Twisted Issues* (1988), Richard White's *Bad Religion—The Riot* (1990), Scott Treleaven's *Queercore: A Punk-U-Mentary* (1996), Martin Sorrondeguy's *Beyond the Screams: A U.S. Latino/Chicano Hardcore/Punk Documentary* (1999), and Jem Cohen and Fugazi's *Instrument* (1999).

5. Chuck Palahniuk's novel, *Fight Club* (1996), refrains from shutting down the anarchistic forces to the same extent that the film does. In the book's final chapter, after Project Mayhem has failed to bring down the "world's tallest building," the narrator finds himself confined to a psychiatric ward. But, while the film's concluding concern with Jack and Marla seals off the anarchy plotline, the narrator of the novel discovers that even after he has been hospitalized for some time Project Mayhem's plans for "break[ing] up civilization so we can make something better" (208) continue outside the hospital, without his guidance.

6. Martin Scorsese's recent *Gangs of New York* (2002) hypostatizes this particular logic. Bill the Butcher (Daniel Day-Lewis) clearly cathects his killing of Priest Vallon (Liam Neeson). The murder and its memory stand as the single most affectively charged moment in "The Butcher's" life.

7. An interesting change occurs between the novel and film that is symptomatic of this representation of heterosex. The narrator of the novel finds one condom in the toilet after Marla spends the night with Tyler; in the film, he finds three condoms. Even this detail must be exaggerated.

References

924 Gilman Street Project. Gilman Street. 4 May 2000 <http://www.gilman.org/>.

924 Gilman Street Project. Gilman Street. 3 June 2003 <http://www.924gilman.org/>.

Adorno, Theodor W. *Minima Moralia*. Trans. E. F. N. Jephcott. London: Verso, 1951.

Alexei. "Catharsis." Interview. *MaximumRockNRoll*. (Sept. 1999).

American Beauty. Dir. Sam Mendes. Perf. Kevin Spacey, Annette Benning, Mena Suvari. DreamWork SKG, 1999.

Amoeba Collective, ed. *Book Your Own Fuckin' Life #8: A Do-It-Yourself Resource Guide*. San Francisco: MaximumRockNRoll, 2000.

Anarcho-Punk Federation. Advertisement. *Profane Existence* (Summer 1998): 17.

Andersen, Mark, and Mark Jenkins. *Dance of Days: Two Decades of Punk in the Nation's Capital*. New York: Soft Skull, 2001.

Anderson, Perry. *The Origins of Postmodernity*. New York: Verso, 1998.

Arnold, Gina. *Route 666: On the Road to Nirvana*. New York: St. Martin's, 1993.

Attali, Jacques. *Noise: The Political Economy of Music*. Trans. Brian Massumi. Minneapolis: U of Minnesota P, 1992.

Bad Religion. "No Direction." *Generator*. Epitaph Records, 1992.

Bale, Jeff. "The 'Battle of Seattle'? Don't Make Me Laugh!" *Hit List* (April–May 2000): 5–7.

Barthes, Roland. *Mythologies*. Trans. Annette Lavers. New York: Hill and Wang, 1972.

———. *S/Z*. Trans. Richard Miller. New York: Hill and Wang, 1974.

Belsito, Peter, and Bob Davis, eds. *Hardcore California: A History of Punk and New Wave*. Berkeley: The Last Gasp of San Francisco, 1983.

Benjamin, Walter. "The Author as Producer." *Reflections: Essays, Aphorisms, Autobiographical Writings*. Trans. Edmund Jephcott. New York: Schocken, 1978. 220–38.

———. "On the Mimetic Faculty." *Reflections: Essays, Aphorisms, Autobiographical Writings*. Trans. Edmund Jephcott. New York: Schocken, 1978. 333–36.

———. "Theses on the Philosophy of History." *Illuminations: Essays and Reflections.* Trans. Harry Zohn. New York: Schocken, 1969. 253–64.

———. "Unpacking My Library." *Illuminations: Essays and Reflections.* Trans. Harry Zohn. New York: Schocken, 1969. 59–67.

———. "The Work of Art in the Age of Mechanical Reproduction." *Illuminations: Essays and Reflections.* Trans. Harry Zohn. New York: Schocken, 1969. 217–51.

Bennett, Tony. *Formalism and Marxism.* New York: Methuen, 1979.

Biafra, Jello. Interview with David Grad. "Interview with Jello Biafra." *Bad Subjects* 30 (Feb. 1997). (18 Aug. 1998). <http://eserver.org/bs/30/grad.html>.

———. Interview with V. Vale. "Introduction." *Search & Destroy, #1–6, The Complete Reprint.* Ed. V. Vale. San Francisco: V/Search Publications, 1996. iii–vi.

Biddle, Wayne, and Margot Slade. "A Possible Clue in AIDS Disease?" *New York Times,* 27 Feb. 1983, city final ed., sec. 4: 7.

Bikini Kill. Album cover photo. *The C.D. Version of the First Two Records.* Kill Rock Stars, 1992.

———. "Alien She." *Pussy Whipped.* Kill Rock Stars, 1992.

———. "New Radio Lyrics." *The Singles.* Kill Rock Stars, 1998.

———. "Reject All American." *Reject All American.* Kill Rock Stars, 1996.

Bloch, Ernst. *The Principle of Hope.* 2 vols. Trans. Neville Plaice, Stephen Plaice, and Paul Knight. Cambridge: MIT Press, 1986.

———. *The Utopian Function of Art and Literature: Selected Essays.* Trans. Jack Zipes and Frank Mecklenburg. Cambridge: MIT Press, 1993.

Blush, Steven. *American Hardcore: A Tribal History.* Los Angeles: Feral House, 2001.

Brace, Eric. "Punk Lives!" *Washington Post,* 1 Aug. 1993: G1+.

Bratmobile. "The Bitch Theme." *Pottymouth.* Kill Rock Stars, 1992.

———. "Flavor of the Month Club." *Ladies, Women and Girls.* Lookout!, 2000.

Buck-Morss, Susan. *The Dialectics of Seeing: Walter Benjamin and the Arcades Project.* Cambridge: MIT Press, 1989.

BUF Compagnie. *Feature Films: Trashcan* (31 Dec. 2002). <http://www.buf.fr/ FILM_INDEX/>.

Burchill, Julie, and Tony Parsons. *"The Boy Looked at Johnny": The Obituary of Rock and Roll.* London: Pluto, 1980.

Bürger, Peter. *Theory of the Avant-Garde.* Trans. Michael Shaw. Minneapolis: U of Minnesota P, 1984.

Busico, Michalene. "Riot Grrrls; Angry Punk Rock Sisterhood Leaving Boys' Rules Behind for 'Revolution Girl Style Now'." *The Houston Chronicle,* 4 Oct. 1992, 2 Star Edition, Lifestyle sec.: 3.

Carmody, John. "Now Here's the News." *Washington Post,* 13 Oct. 1983, final ed.: D9.

Chedeya, Farai. "Revolution, Girl Style." *Newsweek* (23 Nov. 1992). *Academic Search Elite*. Ebsco Host. McIntyre Library. Eau Claire, WI. 9 June 2003. <http://search.epnet.com/direct.asp?jid=NWK&db=afh>.

"The Clash—Live." *Sony Music* (10 Aug. 2002). <http://www.sonymusic.om/artists/TheClash/bio.html>.

Cometbus, Aaron. *Cometbus #42: Double Duce: A Novel*. Berkeley.

Connolly, Cynthia, Leslie Clague, Sharon Cheslow, and Lydia Ely, eds. *Banned in D.C.: Photos and Anecdotes from the D.C. Punk Underground (79–85)*. Washington, D.C.: Sundog Propaganda, 1988.

Crass. ". . . In Which Crass Voluntarily Blow Their Own." *Best Before . . .* Crass Records, 1984.

———. "Nineteen Eighty Bore." *Christ—The Album*. Crass Records, 1982.

———. "A Series of Shock Slogans and Mindless Token Tantrums." *Christ: The Album*. Crass Records, 1982.

CrimethInc. Advertisement. *Inside Front* (May 1999): 3.

———. Advertisement. *What is a "CrimethInc."?* Atlanta: CrimethInc.

———. *CrimethInc. Catalog* (25 June 2003). <http://www.crimethinc.net/modules.php?op=modload&name=Sections&file=index&req=viewarticle&artid=2&page=1>.

———. *CrimethInc.: The Opium of a New Generation* (1 Oct. 1999). <http://www.crimethinc.cjb.net/>.

———. *WARNING* (25 June 2003). <http://www.crimethinc.net/>.

———. *Why I Love Shoplifting From Big Corporations*. Atlanta: CrimethInc.

Davies, Jude. "The Future of 'No Future': Punk Rock and Postmodern Theory." *Journal of Popular Culture* 29:4 (1996): 3–25.

Dead Kennedys. *Fresh Fruit For Rotting Vegetables*. Alternative Tentacles, 1980.

———. "Well Paid Scientist." *Plastic Surgery Disasters*. Alternative Tentacles Records, 1982.

Debord, Guy. *The Society of the Spectacle*. Trans. Donald Nicholson-Smith. New York: Zone, 1995.

Deleuze, Gilles. *Cinema 2: The Time Image*. Trans. Hugh Tomlinson and Robert Galeta. Minneapolis: U of Minneapolis P, 1989.

Devosby, Jen, Suzanne, Allie, Jenna, Sara, Margaret, Jessica, Colette, and Jong. "Letter From the Editors." *Riot Grrrl #3* (May 1992).

Doherty, Philip H. "Drug Drive Outlined to First Lady." *New York Times*, 12 Oct. 1983, city final ed.: D22.

Dr. Strange. "Who and What is Dr. Strange?" (26 June 2003). <http://www.dr.strange.com/about_us/>.

Duncombe, Stephen. "Let's All be Alienated Together: Zines and the Making of Underground Community." *Generations of Youth: Youth Cultures and History in Twentieth-Century America.* Ed. Joe Austin and Michael Nevin Willard. New York: New York UP, 1998. 427–451.

Erika Records. *Erika Records, Inc.* (7 July 2003). <http://www.erikarecords.com>.

Experience Music Project. *Riot Grrrl* (10 June 2003). <http://www.emplive.com/ explore/riot grrrl/index.asp>.

Fairchild, Charles. "'Alternative' Music and the Politics of Cultural Autonomy: The Case of Fugazi and the D.C. Scene." *Popular Music and Society* 19 (1995): 17–35.

Fear. "Let's Have a War." *The Record.* Slash Records, 1982.

"Fewer High School Students Reported Using Illicit Drugs." *New York Times,* 7 Feb. 1984, city final ed.: C9.

Fight Club. Dir. David Fincher. Perf. Edward Norton, Brad Pitt, Helena Bonham Carter. Warner, 1999.

Fink, Michael. *Inside the Music Industry: Creativity, Process, and Business.* New York: Simon & Schuster Macmillan, 1996.

Fleas and Lice. *Global Destruction.* Profane Existence, 1995.

Flipside, Al. "Indie?" *Flipside* (May-June 1999).

Floyd, Jonathan. Rev. of "Stories for the Big Screen," by Lanemeyer. *MaximumRockNRoll* (May 2000).

Flynn, Tom, and Karen Lound. *AIDS: Examining the Crisis.* Minneapolis: Lerner, 1995.

Foley, Barbara. *Radical Representations: Politics and Form in U.S. Proletarian Fiction, 1929–1941.* Durham: Duke UP, 1993.

Frame, Pete. *Pete Frame's Rock Family Trees.* London: Omnibus Press, 1980.

Frith, Simon. *Sound Effects: Youth, Leisure, and the Politics of Rock 'n' Roll.* New York: Pantheon, 1981.

———. "Art Ideology and Pop Practice." *Marxism and the Interpretation of Culture.* Ed. Cary Nelson and Lawrence Grossberg. Chicago: U of Illinois P, 1988.

Fugazi. "Merchandise." *Repeater + 3 Songs.* Dischord Records, 1990.

Gartland, Greg. Rev. of *Walker,* by Walker. *Punk Planet* (Jan.-Feb. 1996): 83.

Gehenna "The War of the Sons of Light and the Suns of Darkness" Compact Disc. Advertisement. Atlanta: CrimethInc.

Ginn, Greg. Interview. "Everything Went Black: A Complete Oral History." *Punk Planet* (Sept.-Oct. 1997): 36–44.

Goshert, John. Personal interview. 10 Jan. 2000.

Grad, David. "Everything Went Black: A Complete Oral History." *Punk Planet* (Sept.-Oct. 1997) 36–44.

The Great Rock 'n' Roll Swindle. Dir. Julien Temple. Perf. Malcolm McLaren, Steve Jones, Johnny Rotten, Sid Vicious, Paul Cook, Helen of Troy. Warner Bros., 1980.

Green Day. *Kerplunk!* Lookout! Records, 1992.

Grossberg, Lawrence. *Dancing in Spite of Myself: Essays on Popular Culture.* Durham: Duke UP, 1997.

GTE Caller ID. Advertisement. Direct Mail. San Angelo: GTE Network Services.

Hall, Stuart, Tony Jefferson, John Clarke, and Brian Roberts. "Subcultures, Cultures, and Class." *Resistance Through Rituals: Youth Subcultures in Post-War Britain.* Ed. Stuart Hall and Tony Jefferson. London: Harper Collins, 1976: 9–74.

Hanna, Kathleen. Interview. *Punk Planet* (Sept.-Oct. 1998): 36–44.

———. Interview. "Kathleen Hanna: Bikini Kill." *Angry Women in Rock, Vol. One.* Ed. Andrea Juno. New York: Juno Books, 1996. 82–103.

Hebdige, Dick. *Subculture: The Meaning of Style.* London: Routledge, 1979.

Henry, Patricia. *Break All the Rules! Punk Rock and the Making of a Style.* Ann Arbor: UMI Research, 1989.

Henwood, Doug. Interview. *Punk Planet* (Jan.-Feb. 2000): 44–47.

Heylin, Clinton. *From the Velvets to the Voidoids: A Pre-Punk History for a Post-Punk World.* New York: Penguin, 1992.

Hinnant, Kate. "Superstore." Unpublished poem.

Horkheimer, Max, and Theodor W. Adorno. *Dialectic of Enlightenment.* Trans. John Cumming. New York: Continuum, 1994.

"How Much Shock and Awe Can You Take?" *Profane Existence* (Spring-Summer 2003): 8–9.

Jameson, Fredric. *Brecht and Method.* New York: Verso, 1998.

———. *Marxism and Form.* Princeton: Princeton UP, 1971.

———. *The Political Unconscious: Narrative as a Socially Symbolic Act.* Ithaca: Cornell UP, 1981.

———. *Postmodernism, or, The Cultural Logic of Late Capitalism.* Durham: Duke UP, 1991.

Jaquet, Janine. "Indies' Reservations." *The Nation,* 25 Aug.-1 Sept. 1997: 10.

Jeffrey, Don. "Strong '98 Results Rung Up in U.S., U.K.: Multiple Formats Boost U.S." *Billboard,* 27 Feb. 1999: 1+.

Jenkins, Henry. *Textual Poachers: Television Fans and Participatory Culture.* New York: Routledge, 1992.

Kester, Marian, and F-Stop Fitzgerald. *Dead Kennedys: The Unauthorized Version.* San Francisco: Last Gap, 1983.

Kill Rock Stars. *Kill Rock Stars.* 6 June 2003 <http://www.killrockstars.com/>.

Krasilovsky, M. William, and Sidney Shemel. *This Business of Music*. New York: Billboard, 1995.

Lahickey, Beth, Ed. *All Ages: Reflections on Straight Edge*. Huntington Beach, CA: Revelation, 1997.

Laing, Dave. *One Chord Wonders: Power and Meaning in Punk Rock*. Milton Keynes: Open UP, 1985.

MacKaye, Ian. Interview. *All Ages: Reflections on Straight Edge*. Huntington Beach, CA: Revelation, 1997: 95–110.

———. Interview. *Punk Planet* (May-June 1999): 34–43.

Maffeo, Lois. Interview. "Lois Maffeo." *Angry Women in Rock, Vol. One*. Ed. Andrea Juno. New York: Juno Books, 1996. 120–33.

Marchetti, Gina F. "Film and Subculture: The Relationship of Film to the Punk and Glitter Youth Subcultures." Diss. Northwestern U, 1982. Ann Arbor: UMI, 1984. 8305502.

Marcus, Greil. *Lipstick Traces: A Secret History of the Twentieth Century*. Cambridge: Harvard UP, 1989.

———. "Raising the Stakes in Punk Rock." *The New York Times*, 18 June 2000, sec. 2: 1+.

Marcuse, Herbert. *One-Dimensional Man*. Boston: Beacon, 1964.

Martinez, Susan. Interview. *All Ages: Reflections on Straight Edge*. Huntington Beach, CA: Revelation, 1997: 111–114.

Marx, Karl. *Capital, Vol. 1*. Trans. Ben Fowkes. New York: Penguin, 1990.

———. *Capital, Vol. 3*. Trans. David Fernbach. New York: Penguin, 1981.

———. "Critique of the Gotha Program." Trans. Joris de Bres. *The First International and After*. London: Penguin Classics, 1992. 339–59.

———. *Grundrisse*. Trans. Martin Nicolaus. New York: Penguin, 1993.

Marx, Karl, and Friedrich Engels. *The Communist Manifesto*. Trans. Samuel Moore. Oxford: Oxford UP, 1998.

———. *The German Ideology*. New York: International, 1970.

Masculin/Féminin. Dir. Jean-Luc Godard. Perf. Jean-Pierre Léaud, Chantal Goya, Marlene Jobert. Anouchka Films/Argos Films/Svensk Filmindustri/Sandrews, 1966.

MaximumRockNRoll, Feb. 1997: front cover.

———, July 2003: 1.

———, July 2003: 3.

McClary, Susan. "Afterword." *Noise: The Political Economy of Music* by Jaques Attali. Trans. Brian Massumi. Minneapolis: U of Minnesota P, 1992.

McNeil, Legs, and Gillian McCain. *Please Kill Me: The Uncensored Oral History of Punk*. New York: Grove, 1996.

McNett, Gavin. "The Day Punk Died." *Salon* (3 April 1998) (16 Feb. 2000). <http://www.salon.com/music/feature/1998/04/17feature.html>.

Miller, Mark Crispin. "The National Entertainment State III: Who Controls the Music?" *The Nation*, 25 Aug.-1 Sept. 1997: 11.

Minor Threat. *Minor Threat.* Dischord Records, 1989.

Monaco, James. *How to Read a Film: Movies, Media, Multimedia.* Oxford: Oxford UP, 2000.

Morris, Chris. "L.A. Punk." *Forming: The Early Days of L.A. Punk.* Santa Monica: Smart Art, 1999.

Murrman, Mark. "If You Die and Go to Hell, Who Cares?" *MaximumRockNRoll*, Dec. 1999.

Nehring, Neil. *Flowers in the Dustbin: Culture, Anarchy, and Postwar England.* Ann Arbor: U of Michigan P, 1993.

Nilles, Katherine. "'Fight Club' Packs a Wallop With Young Fans." *Milwaukee Journal Sentinel*, Jan. 22, 2001. (10 Aug. 2002). <http://www.jsonline.com/Enter/movies/jan01/fclub22011901.asp>.

O'Flaherty, Mike. "Cordon Sanitaire." *The Baffler*, Mar. 1999: 98–109.

O'Hara, Craig. *The Philosophy of Punk: More Than Noise!* San Francisco: AK, 1999.

Palahniuk, Chuck. *Fight Club.* New York: Henry Holt, 1996.

Powell, Mark. E-mail to the author. 31 Jan. 2000.

Prénom: Carmen. Dir. Jean-Luc Godard. Perf. Maruschka Detmers, Jacques Bonnaffé, Myriem Roussel. Sara Films/Jean-Luc Godard Films, 1983.

Profane Existence Collective. *At Present: What is Profane Existence?* Minneapolis: Loin Cloth, 1997.

——— . *Blackened Distribution Mail-order Catalog #3.* Minneapolis: Profane Existence, 1999.

——— . "Distribution Information." *Profane Existence* (Spring-Summer 2003): 2.

——— . "Fucking Alternative—Fucking Punk Rock." *Profane Existence* (Spring-Summer 2003): 2.

——— . *Making Punk a Threat Again!: The Best Cuts 1989–1993.* Minneapolis: Loin Cloth, 1997.

——— . "Profane Existence Collective Dissolves: Politicians, Cops, and Fascists Rejoice!" *Profane Existence* (Summer 1998): 4–5.

——— . "Submit to PE!" *Profane Existence* (Winter 1998): 2.

——— . *Why a No Pig Zone?* Minneapolis: Profane Existence, 1991.

Project on Media Ownership at Johns Hopkins Univ. "The Media Nation: Music." *The Nation*, 25 Aug.-1 Sept. 1997: 25–28.

Rangonese, Marisa. "Riot Grrrls Castrate 'Cock Rock' in New York." *Off Our Backs* (May-June 2002): 27–31.

Raphael, Amy. *Grrrls: Viva Rock Divas*. New York: St. Martin's Griffin, 1995.

Reagan Youth. "Jesus Was a Communist." *Reagan Youth Vol. Two*. New Red Archives, 1990.

Reinhold, Robert. "Leveling Off of Drug Use Found Among Students." *New York Times*, 19 Feb. 1981, city final ed.: A1.

Requiem for a Dream. Dir. Darren Aronofsky. Perf. Ellen Burstyn, Jared Leto, Jennifer Conolley. Artisan, 2000.

Retodd. "INmajorDIE?" *Flipside* (May-June 1999).

Rimbaud, Penny. *Shibboleth: My Revolting Life*. San Francisco: AK Press, 1998.

"Riot Grrrl is . . ." *Riot Grrrl #6 1/2* (Dec. 1991).

Riot Grrrl NYC! 10 June 2003 <http://rgny.8m.com/index.html>.

Risk, Will. Rev. of *Disconstructed*, by Jack Fluster. *MaximumRockNRoll* (June 2003).

Ritzel, Brent, Ed. *Zine Guide #6*. 2003.

Roessler, Kira. "Everything Went Black: A Complete Oral History." *Punk Planet* (Sept.-Oct. 1997): 36–44.

Rollins, Henry. "Everything Went Black: A Complete Oral History." *Punk Planet* (Sept.-Oct. 1997): 36–44.

——— . *Get in the Van: On the Road with Black Flag*. Los Angeles: 2.13.61: 1994.

Rosenberg, Jessica, and Gitana Garofalo. "Riot Grrrl: Revolutions From Within." *Signs: Journal of Women in Culture and Society* 23 (1998): 809–41.

Rude Boy. Dir. Jack Hazan and David Mingay. Perf. Ray Gange, Joe Strummer, Mick Jones, Paul Simonon, Topper Headon. Buzzy Enterprises, 1980.

Ruscin, Ailecia. E-mail to the author. 17 June 2003.

Sabin, Roger, ed. *Punk Rock: So What? The Cultural Legacy of Punk*. London: Routledge, 1999.

Savage, Jon. *England's Dreaming: Anarchy, Sex Pistols, Punk Rock, and Beyond*. New York: St. Martin's, 1992.

Schwartz, Ruth. E-mail to the author. 1 Feb. 2000.

Seabrook, John. "The Money Note: Can the Record Business Survive?" *The New Yorker*, 7 July 2003: 42–55.

Sedgwick, Eve Kosofsky. *Between Men: English Literature and Male Homosocial Desire*. New York: Columbia UP, 1985.

Sex Pistols. "Anarchy in the U.K." *Never Mind the Bollocks*. Warner Bros., 1978.

Sinker, Mark. "Concrete so as to Self-Destruct: The Etiquette of Punk, its Habits, Rules, Values and Dilemmas." *Punk Rock: So What? The Cultural Legacy of Punk*. Ed. Roger Sabin. London: Routledge, 1999.

"Some of Your Friends Are Already This Fucked. Everything You've Wanted to Know About Major Labels." *MaximumRockNRoll* (June 1994).

Stark, Jeff. "It's a Punk Movie." *Salon.com* (13 Oct. 2000): 2. (10 Aug. 2002). <http://www.dir.salon.com/ent/movies/int/2000/10/13/aronofsky/index.html?pn=2>.

Stevenson, Bill. "Everything Went Black: A Complete Oral History." *Punk Planet* (Sept.-Oct. 1997): 36–44.

Sweeney, Louise. "Reversing Children's Attitudes About Drugs." *Christian Science Monitor,* 25 Apr. 1983, Midwestern ed.: 9.

Tabb, George. "Take My Life, Please." *MaximumRockNRoll* (Feb. 1997).

Temple, Johnny. "Noise From Underground." *The Nation,* 18 Oct. 1999: 17+.

Theroux, Gary, and Bob Gilbert. *The Top Ten: 1956–Present.* New York: Simon and Schuster, 1982.

Timebomb. "The Full Wrath of the Slave" CD/LP. Advertisement. *What Is a CrimethInc.?* Atlanta: CrimethInc.

Turner, Chérie. *Everything You Need to Know About The Riot Grrrl Movement: The Feminism of a New Generation.* New York: Rosen Publishing Group, 2001.

Turner, Wallace. "AIDS Impact Wide in San Francisco." *New York Times,* 28 May 1985, final ed.: B7.

Vale, V. *Search & Destroy, #1–6, The Complete Reprint.* Ed. V. Vale. San Francisco: V/Search Publications, 1996.

Various Artists. *Not So Quiet on the Western Front.* Alternative Tentacle Records, 1982.

Watt, Michael. "Rude Boy—The Movie." *Melody Maker,* 1 Dec. 1979: 9–10.

Weisbard, Eric. "Pop in the 90's: Everything for Everyone." *New York Times,* 30 April 2000, sec. 2: 1+.

Williams, Raymond. *Keywords: A Vocabulary of Culture and Society,* rev. ed. Oxford: Oxford UP, 1983.

———. *Marxism and Literature.* Oxford: Oxford UP, 1977.

Yohannon, Tim. "Maximizing Rock and Roll: An Interview with Tim Yohannon." *Sounding Off! Music as Subversion/Resistance/Revolution.* Ed. Ron Sakolsky and Fred Wei-Han Ho. Brooklyn: Autonomedia, 1995. 180–94.

"You Can." *Harbinger: A Ransom Note Regarding Your Life.* 4th Communiqué.

Youth of Today. *Break Down the Walls.* Revelations Records, 1986.

Žižek, Slavoj. *The Sublime Object of Ideology.* New York: Verso, 1989.

———. *The Ticklish Subject.* New York: Verso, 1999.

Index